A Hidden History of the Tower of London

A Hidden History of the Tower of London

England's Most Notorious Prisoners

John Paul Davis

PEN & SWORD
HISTORY

First published in Great Britain in 2020 by
Pen & Sword History
An imprint of
Pen & Sword Books Ltd
Yorkshire – Philadelphia

ISBN 978 1 52676 176 7

A CIP catalogue record for this book is
available from the British Library.

Printed and bound in the UK by TJ International Ltd,
Padstow, Cornwall.

Pen & Sword Books Limited incorporates the imprints of Atlas,
Archaeology, Aviation, Discovery, Family History, Fiction, History,
Maritime, Military, Military Classics, Politics, Select, Transport,
True Crime, Air World, Frontline Publishing, Leo Cooper, Remember
When, Seaforth Publishing, The Praetorian Press, Wharncliffe
Local History, Wharncliffe Transport, Wharncliffe True Crime
and White Owl.

For a complete list of Pen & Sword titles please contact

PEN & SWORD BOOKS LIMITED
47 Church Street, Barnsley, South Yorkshire, S70 2AS, England
E-mail: enquiries@pen-and-sword.co.uk
Website: www.pen-and-sword.co.uk

Or

PEN AND SWORD BOOKS
1950 Lawrence Rd, Havertown, PA 19083, USA
E-mail: Uspen-and-sword@casematepublishers.com
Website: www.penandswordbooks.com

Contents

Introduction

When William the Conqueror first laid eyes on the City of London in the late autumn of 1066, he did so sound in the knowledge that only one obstacle stood in the way of his being crowned undisputed king of England. On leaving his newly-assembled garrison at Dover and beginning the long march west through the Saxon-dominated Home Counties, representatives of the surrounding cities and boroughs wasted little time in coming forth to pledge allegiance to their new Norman overlord, choosing fragile peace as the preferred alternative to ongoing war.

Not so, the citizens of London. Whether the victor of Hastings was initially aware of the rushed election of the young Edgar Ætheling as Harold Godwinson's successor – nephew of the late Edward the Confessor and, as his closest living relative, possessed of a better claim to the throne than Harold himself – on William's arrival the realities of the situation became instantly clear. Behind the imposing Roman city walls where the survivors of Hastings and their uninjured relatives had further enlarged the local population, hatred for the invaders was high. Eyewitness accounts indicated that on reaching the walls of the city, the advance guard that William dispatched had been met with levels of antagonism not experienced since his victory at Hastings. When the fighting was finally over, London's citizens mourned a heavy loss, and with it Edgar's hopes of kingship. As the conqueror moved swiftly onward, nullifying all further threats while, at the same time, preparing for his coronation, the advance guard was assigned a new task: to construct a fortress 'as a defence against the inconstancy of the numerous and hostile inhabitants'.

Like other fortifications William erected in London that year, this one would only be temporary. Chosen for its strategic importance, located towards the city's south-east corner where Alfred the Great's rebuilt wall continued to stand tall and where the ancient fort Arx Palatina had been established in the fourth century, the setting was practically perfect. Assisted by the engineering genius of England's earlier rulers and the natural defences of the north bank of the Thames, as well as being enclosed by a deep ditch and a timber palisade, William's defence against the 'hostile inhabitants' was achieved on all sides. In doing so, it marked the beginning of the 'Tower of London's' 1,000-year dominance over England's history.

Unlikely though it is that England's new king could have envisioned that such an unremarkable timber assembly would one day lead to the formation of a building around which the nation's destiny would always revolve, even in its early days the Tower was clearly conceived with defence in mind. Within twelve years of the Norman invasion, work was already in place on constructing a massive stone keep behind the wooden palisade, which by the next century had become famed as the city's undisputed focal point. Rising 27 metres into the air and with walls over 15 feet thick, William's typically Norman keep was malevolent yet awe-inspiring, dominating not only the London skyline but also the thoughts of those who bore witness. Nothing of the type had ever been seen in England, nor did construction stop there. Many of England's monarchs destined to follow in the Conqueror's footsteps would add to the structure, culminating in an incredible twenty-one additional towers being placed around the original, all in their own way contributing to what by the fourteenth century had become a unique architectural masterpiece of seemingly unlimited uses. In more recent times, the Royal Commission on Historical Monuments maintained this view, describing the Tower as 'the most valuable monument of medieval military architecture' in England.

Looking back now, exactly what the Tower's primary purpose was is difficult to summarize. Writing in the late-sixteenth century, the antiquarian John Stow paid testament to the castle's adaptability, recording:

> this Tower is a citadel to defend or command the city; a royal palace for assemblies or treaties; a prison of state for the most dangerous offenders; the only place of coinage for all England at this time; the armoury for warlike provision; the treasury of the ornaments and

jewels of the crown; and general conserver of the most records of the king's courts of justice at Westminster.

Had Stow been writing in the modern day, he might well have added how it had played host to diverse royal functions as well as serving as an observatory, menagerie, place of capital punishment, and a popular museum. The Royal Mint that existed in the outer walls between the thirteenth and nineteenth centuries may have long since been remodelled as homes for the Tower's loyal guards, the amazing Yeoman Warders, yet for over 600 years it was the chief economic centre of the entire nation. The buildings that made up the heart of the Tower menagerie and royal apartments no longer stand, but as late as the reign of Charles II the setting was deserving of similar prestige as London Zoo or Windsor Castle. The modern bank vault in the Waterloo Block has been dubbed the most secure in all of Europe and was even used to house the Olympic medals in 2012. To this day, the Crown Jewels still reside at this, the cornerstone of the United Kingdom.

Yet, despite its direct or indirect involvement in almost every aspect of English political life and developing itself a reputation as a building fit for many purposes, even at a casual glance, one disturbing trend clearly repeats itself. Although never designed specifically to include dungeons or torture chambers, the graffiti that marks the walls of its dimly lit chambers bear testament to the darker aspects of its history. The countless suits of medieval armour that line the interior of the White Tower, like the instruments of torture that do the same in the Wakefield, serve as clinical reminders of the Tower's affiliation with war in the same way each ruggedly engraved name of a former prisoner acts as a morbid complement to the memorials on Tower Green and Tower Hill that forever remind us that an Englishman's castle was not necessarily one to be enjoyed. 'No sadder spot on earth' were the words used by the esteemed nineteenth-century historian Lord Macaulay to describe the royal Chapel of St Peter ad Vincula: an opinion not particularly surprising since of the sixty-three former Tower inhabitants interred there, only nine lie entombed with their heads intact. Perhaps equally disturbing is the castle's reputation for extraordinary levels of paranormal activity. If the tales are to be believed, no less than thirty spectres are recorded to have appeared in nightly vigil, the majority striking apparently uncanny similarities to its known victims of cruel, if not always unjust, punishment.

Though the days of brutal incarceration and execution – with the exception of both world wars – have long been a thing of the past, even today the Tower's reputation continues to precede itself. In contrast to the incredible work that led to its construction, the outstanding collection of historical artefacts and glorious variation of decoration, to be sent to the Tower remains a saying synonymous with pain – in many cases, a prelude to the ultimate disaster. How is it, one may wonder, that a building famed as being among the most depressing and cruellest in human history can also be beloved in the modern day as one of special enjoyment, especially when similar buildings worldwide have acquired no such reputation? A site like the Bastille in Paris, for example, was one of the few whose infamy led to similar acclaim, yet its sinister image in the minds of the people led to its demolition rather than to serve as a reminder of important times. In contrast, the Tower's importance shows no sign of diminishing. What was once a place of refuge or incarceration is now a destination for the curious. A place where history lives and is enjoyed.

Separate from previous investigations on the Tower, the purpose of this book is not so much concerned with every aspect of its importance or to catalogue the key events that led to the physical constructions. Nor is it an investigation into the existence of the paranormal. True it may be that the legends and the ghost stories have a tendency to be among the most thrilling, it is to the actions of those who once lived that such stories persist rather than the appearance of ghostly mists or apparitions with their heads tucked underneath their arms. This book has not been written as an attempt to fuel its theme park-like status that sceptics – including this author – have long felt grew out of Victorian melodrama as opposed to any accurate representation of what really took place.

Just as the Tower of London has meant many things to many people it stands to reason, at least partially, that the conclusions of past commentators about what the castle represents can be associated with what they looked for in the first place. In the case of this author, what provokes the greatest intrigue is perhaps the Tower's ability to provoke intrigue itself – a rarity even for an English castle. Of equal fascination is how something apparently designed as a typical Norman citadel could come to operate as a site of so many purposes – an even greater rarity.

Despite the advances in technology, some things have never changed. As late as World War II, whoever the ruling faction in England may have been, the Tower has always served as the kingdom's stronghold: the place where its rulers fled in times of crisis; the place where they sent their nearest and dearest for protection, yet also where they imprisoned their most dangerous enemies. If there is any truth in the old saying that friends be kept close and enemies closer, the Tower's history would seem to be representative of all of this. Who knows? Perhaps the concept even began here.

At the start of this book, the question of how one building can mean so many things to so many people remains something of an enigma to me, but one I hope to understand better in due course. Likewise, it has been necessary to acknowledge certain limitations. Including a list of every prisoner, though largely achieved by the magnificent efforts of former Yeoman Warder Brian Harrison, in a book of this type was simply impossible, especially as it is estimated that during the English Civil War at least a third of the peerage endured time in the Tower. My quest is therefore not to answer every question, nor to confirm whether the Tower deserves its time-honoured reputation, but merely to understand how it came about. Whether a building can be considered a legacy of those who constructed it, those who lived there, were imprisoned there or even died there I have always believed to be a question far too broad to answer succinctly. If a building like the Tower deserves one undisputed place in history, it must surely be that it represents history itself. Most notably, England's history. In which case, we should all be in for a treat.

Chapter 1

1066–1216: A Fortress Fit For a Conqueror

T he precise dates when work began and ended on the original Tower of London are sadly now impossible to determine. Tradition has it the first stones of what would later be known as the White Tower were laid sometime in 1078 and, to a degree, this can be backed up by scientific dating. A fire in 1087 that wiped out much of the wooden city may have breached the timber palisade and the temporary castle – almost certainly some form of motte and bailey – that was established after William the Conqueror brought the city to submission, though this cannot be proven undisputedly. Nevertheless, it seems likely the threat of the flame was at least partly responsible for inspiring the great work that would soon follow.

There are many tales about the building's origins. Legend has it the site was once known as the White Mount, and that the head of the mythical king Brân the Blessed was buried there to ensure the land was never conquered. A similar tradition has it that on capturing the city, William placed his standard there, declaring that as long as it remained standing the land would remain undefeated. It is quite possible both stories are in some way responsible for the Tower's most enduring legend. Since at least the 1500s, conspiracies of ravens are known to have descended on the fortress; even to this day, a minimum of six continue to be held there with one of the yeoman warders designated Ravenmaster in order to ensure their wellbeing. Tradition maintains that as long as the ravens remain, the Tower will stand and England shall remain unconquered. So seriously are the tales taken that another story relates that around 1675 when the royal astronomer, John Flamsteed, complained to Charles II of their interference with his stargazing, Charles decided rather than remove the ravens he would instead relocate the observatory. Regardless of the exact conversations that may or may not have taken place, it is certainly true that the observatory was moved from the White Tower to Greenwich at that time, further immortalizing the ravens and their importance to the Tower. Interestingly, Brân in Welsh translates as raven, which almost certainly offers a point of origin.

It was recorded in the *Textus Roffensis* – the *Annals of Rochester* – that William the Conqueror entrusted oversight of the Tower's construction to a French cleric named Gundulf. Originally of Caen, Gundulf was a pupil of Lanfranc, William's first archbishop of Canterbury, who journeyed to England some four years after the Norman Conquest. Revered for his godliness, spiritual devotion and, at times, erratic disposition – earning him the unflattering nickname, the 'Wailing Monk' – Gundulf was equally famed as a skilled builder and architect who had overseen similar projects in Normandy. During his eight years in England, he had also been charged with the task of rebuilding the Viking-ravaged priory church in Rochester before setting to work on constructing a stone castle in the reign of William II. In recognition for his work there and eventual agreeing to mastermind work on the Tower, the city of Rochester would become his home and into whose bishopric he was installed.

Further to early evidence that work on the keep began in 1078, scientific dating of the time indicates that a brief lull in construction occurred in the 1080s – possibly partly as a result of the fire – and again around 1093, most likely due to labour shortages or the absence of the key players. One possible reason for the delays could be that Gundulf's own busy schedule prevented him from being present in London for long periods. In addition to his chief responsibilities in Rochester, Gundulf was also charged with the task of building Colchester Castle and the enigmatic St Leonard's Tower in West Malling, which later formed part of Malling Abbey. There is a far more recent legend that the novelist and Anglo-Saxon expert J.R.R. Tolkien took a keen interest in Gundulf and his role in constructing the White Tower and Colchester Castle, thus providing the inspiration for the wizard Gandalf and Middle Earth's Two Towers.

Regardless of the exact reasons for the delays, William was never destined to see his fortress completed. Likely though it is that he lived long enough to witness the imposing square tower take shape, work almost certainly continued into the reign of his second son and successor William II (Rufus) and quite possibly into the early years of his youngest son, Henry I. By the time Gundulf passed away in 1108 – some sources suggest at the impressive age of 84 – indications are that phase one of the White Tower had been completed. Ironically considering its enormous height, the original roof was approximately a third lower than the outer walls, which seems to confirm the theory that a large part of the building's mystique was to look outwardly impenetrable, thus satisfying the Norman principle that a keep was deemed a symbol of the lord's power.

Whether England's three earliest Norman kings ever used the lodgings personally is unclear, yet from 1100 there is evidence to suggest that the Tower was being used on a regular basis. Despite the absence of specifically built dungeons, it is little surprise that walls intended to keep enemies out proved equally good at keeping them in. It is surely one of the Tower's great ironies that its first prisoner should himself have been renowned as a great builder. Bigger still one could argue is the thought that the history of a building now famed for incarceration began with a prisoner who defied its walls. The year was 1100AD. The prisoner's name, Ranulf Flambard.

At the time of his arrest, Flambard could undoubtedly have laid claim to being England's key administrator. Son of a Norman cleric and born prior to the Conquest, he followed his father into the church and rose steadily through the ranks in early Norman England. Sources from the time confirm he was influential in establishing the Domesday Book and, after the death of William the Conqueror, became the chief supporter of his successor, the tyrannical William Rufus, and held land in several counties.

When William the Conqueror died over in France in somewhat ignominious circumstances in September 1087, Flambard was chaplain to Maurice, Bishop of London, and, at the same time, keeper of the royal seal: a role more or less akin to the later one of lord chancellor. After acquiring a prebend in the wealthy diocese of Salisbury where its new cathedral at Old Sarum was fast becoming a local centre point, he successfully obtained similar titles while developing a dubious reputation for failing to replace deceased canons, choosing instead to draw their earnings for himself. By the 1090s, his questionable, albeit effective, practices saw him move from Maurice's side to become chaplain of William II's own court, in addition to being appointed chief treasurer and possibly England's first justiciar: a role that has often been compared to the modern-day prime minister.

True to his earlier form, Flambard's activities in those roles was highly questionable. Acting in a position of authority, perhaps confident in the knowledge he reported to no one but himself, he frequently benefited from attempts to raise money. When charged with the task of raising the fyrd – the English militia – for Rufus's battles with his brother in Normandy, he profited personally by obtaining funds from the warriors' home villages, as well as levying 'reliefs' against the sixteen abbeys and bishoprics under his administration. The chronicler William of Malmesbury, writing at the time, lamented, 'he skinned the rich, ground down the poor, and swept other men's inheritances into his net.'

In 1099, Flambard secured his greatest promotion to that date, to the See of Durham. While his first year in the bishopric was blighted by further accusations, including the words of another chronicler that 'justice slept' and 'money was the Lord,' construction of its cathedral, arguably the largest in northern Europe to date, began on his watch – even today it remains revered as one of the finest in the north of England. Clearly sharing many of Gundulf's building talents, Flambard was also responsible for the creation of the first stone London Bridge, Westminster Hall – the largest secular building in northern Europe at the time – and, perhaps most ironically, a curtain wall that surrounded Gundulf's Tower of London.

Within a year of inheriting the bishopric of Durham, William Rufus died, most likely murdered, while out riding in the New Forest. After mourning his king at the new cathedral at Winchester, Flambard's luck ran out on the accession of William's younger brother, crowned Henry I. Well aware of the bishop's sinful reputation and keen to appease his new subjects, the crafty cleric was removed from all offices of state and charged on crimes of embezzlement. With this, he became the first official prisoner of the Tower of London.

For six months, the disgraced bishop wiled his time away peacefully within the walls of the Conqueror's great fortress. As a man of wealth, and due to his exalted position in the Church, he was allowed to maintain his servants, who brought his meals in from outside the Tower. A charismatic man and renowned for his qualities as an entertainer and compère, he frequently hosted banquets for his gaolers, slowly earning their trust and repairing a reputation that had been severely tarnished on the outside world. Having bided his time for the remainder of the year, come 2 February 1101 Flambard put his talents to further use. After organising a banquet for his gaolers, on this occasion taking note to ensure extra quantities of wine – other sources suggest alternative liquids of additional alcoholic volume – it was not long before his captors became inebriated. Using a rope that had been smuggled into his cell inside a 'gallon of wine' – other sources tell of a barrel of oysters – he attempted to abseil down the White Tower. About 20 feet from the ground, however, his rope ran out and he was forced to jump, landing awkwardly. Fit enough to keep moving, he was able to scale the curtain wall to where a horse had been left for him by his allies. Originally gaoled for slippery business practices, the smooth bishop successfully slipped the net and made his way down river. There, a ship took him to Normandy and to the safety of sanctuary with Henry's elder brother, the duke of Normandy, Robert Curthose.

Exactly how Ranulf achieved such a remarkable feat has been the subject of much debate. Though suggestion the constable of the Tower, William de Mandeville, was aware of Flambard's intentions cannot be ruled out, under the circumstances it seems likely lax security measures, the inferior size of the Tower compared to that of the modern day and the shrewdness of the man himself were all contributing factors. Intriguingly, within six months of making his way to Normandy, the ever-busy Flambard was already making plans with Robert to invade England. He was later forgiven by Henry and restored to the See of Durham when the warring brothers signed an uneasy truce at Alton, Hampshire.

Following in Flambard's footsteps in making the Tower his temporary home was Henry I's cousin, William, Count of Mortain. The son of William the Conqueror's half-brother, Robert – himself previously Count of Mortain – William had harboured an intense dislike of Henry I since childhood and wasted little time on Henry's ascension in demanding his father's earldoms in Mortain and Cornwall, as well as his uncle's in Kent. Described as possessing something of an arrogant, juvenile temperament, Henry procrastinated in signing over William's inheritance, eventually removing some of his lands in Cornwall on the basis he had misappropriated their use. Joining forces with Robert

Curthose and attacking many of Henry's holdings in Normandy, Henry stripped William of his English titles and subsequently captured him at the Battle of Tinchebrai in 1106. In retribution, he suffered many years in the Tower before retiring to Bermondsey Abbey as a Cluniac monk.

Within two years of William's capture, the face of the Tower was already showing clear signs of development. According to the Anglo-Saxon chronicle, William Rufus ordered a wall to be built around the White Tower in 1097, most likely replacing William the Conqueror's temporary timber palisade and almost certainly in place to hinder Flambard's escape. Work on the Wardrobe Tower and the royal palace south of the White Tower probably began prior to 1108, and would have been completed by the time of Henry I's death in 1135.

Replacing Henry I on the throne was his controversial cousin Stephen of Blois. By no means first in line, Stephen reputedly only pressed his claim on learning of a sudden change of heart by the dying king regarding the political problems that would arise if he was succeeded by his daughter. Although the majority of the barons had earlier agreed to support Matilda's claim – she being the most obvious choice as Henry's eldest child – Stephen was accepted by both the citizens of London and the Church, news of which Matilda unsurprisingly refused to take lying down. Aided by her young husband, Geoffrey of Anjou, the pair declared war on Normandy and after three relatively peaceful years as king of England, Stephen's tendency to make enemies among the prelates plunged England into its first post-Norman civil war.

The constable of the Tower during this so-called Nineteen-Year Winter was another Geoffrey de Mandeville, grandson of the first constable and son of the man who had been at the helm at the time of Flambard's escape. Possible, if not highly probably, it may be that the previous three kings had all stayed occasionally at the Tower, Stephen was the first monarch to reside there regularly, staying in the newly built royal palace south of the White Tower. Such visits by the monarch being relatively rare, however, being appointed to the position of constable involved taking on all the problems and privileges that went with it, something Mandeville clearly used to his advantage. As constable, he was given custody of Constance, daughter of Louis VI of France, who was betrothed to Stephen's eldest son and heir, and kept her under close confinement in the White Tower.

Thanks in part to the failings of his father, most notably a large fine imposed on him for his failure to hold Flambard, Henry I had been slow to hand over the lands of Geoffrey's grandfather which were lawfully his birthright. He finally inherited some of this around 1140 when Stephen was king.

For reasons such as these, Geoffrey had initially been firm in his support for Stephen. Things would change, however, following Stephen's capture at Lincoln in 1141, after which Mandeville switched his loyalties and joined Matilda's side. On taking the throne, Matilda finally granted him his grandfather's lands in Normandy, as well as confirming his position as constable, which included permission to reinforce the Tower's outer defences. When Stephen was released, violence flared in London and the defensive improvements proved indispensable in quelling the rising. As Stephen's power grew, the tactical Geoffrey defected a second time, only to be arrested and disinherited in 1143 after Stephen became aware that Mandeville had entered negotiations with Matilda about changing sides a third time. In response, Mandeville, quite possibly now the wealthiest magnate in England, launched an ill-fated rebellion from the fen-country in the east of England. He died a year later at Burwell, Cambridgeshire after being besieged by the king.

By the end of Stephen's reign, the face of the Tower had developed beyond recognition from the simple fortress overseen by Gundulf. Subsequent to work on the royal palace, further construction was carried out by Henry II's chancellor, Thomas Becket, who took over as constable in 1161. Despite accepting the role there is evidence that Becket never approved of the Tower, viewing it as a stain on the skyline and an imposing psychological torment on the citizens of London. Further developments would nevertheless follow and continue to do so throughout the reign of Henry II's successors. While Richard the Lionheart was on crusade, his regent, Bishop of Ely, William de Longchamp doubled the Tower's size, digging a moat that proved almost impossible to fill, as well as constructing the Bell Tower south-west of the White Tower. In spite of the new developments, in 1191 the Tower failed to withstand its first attempted siege and Longchamp surrendered to Prince John after three days. Tradition has it the largely hated regent escaped the Tower in the guise of a woman.

Over the centuries, popular revolts have tended to achieve something of revered status in England; however, by the ascension of Richard I there had been no such occurrences. This changed in 1196 following an uprising in London in response to the heavy taxes levied on the poor, notably those for the liberation of Richard the Lionheart who had earlier been held hostage by Duke Leopold of Austria on his return from the Holy Land. Ironically, the hero of this story was himself a charismatic crusader. Born within the city walls, William Fitz Osbert was university-educated and famed for his quick wit and long beard, as well as an ability to hold a sword. On taking up his own cross as champion of the poor, Fitz Osbert became targeted by the archbishop of Canterbury, Hubert Walter, and forced to seek refuge in St Mary-le-Bow after fleeing a mêleé. On re-emerging from Bow Bells, which Hubert had ordered to be burned to the ground – or at least smoked out – Fitz Osbert was captured and imprisoned in the Tower for his role in the uprising. A few days later he was put to death, 'first drawn asunder by horses' before being hanged on a gibbet in the company of nine loyal comrades. Intriguingly, in the aftermath of his execution a number of his followers were noted as having carried away sods of earth soaked with the martyr's blood, thus beginning a minor blood cult around the dead freedom fighter.

Five years into the next century, a far more dangerous rebel would endure the confines of the Tower in the form of John de Courcy. Created earl of Ulster in 1181, King John had ordered the influential Baron Hugh de Lacy to conquer Ulster again in 1199 on learning of de Courcy's 'separatist tendencies'. After a four-year endeavour, complicated by de Courcy's reluctance to expose himself to his enemies, de Lacy finally captured the nobleman, henceforth replacing him as earl while de Courcy languished on the Isle of Man. In 1205, backed by a hundred-strong force consisting primarily of Norse soldiers provided by his brother-in-law, the king of Mann, de Courcy attempted to recapture Dundrum Castle, a mission ironically doomed to failure due to the impressive protections he had erected years earlier. On losing the battle, John brought the defeated de Courcy to the Tower. Eventually being granted his freedom on the promise he would take up the cross, the former earl remained destined to end his life in obscurity.

It is perhaps unsurprising considering the Tower's long history that a number of the early stories lack a clear point of origin. Sadly this often makes it difficult to separate fact from legend. A prime example of this concerns another alleged prisoner dating from the reign of King John. Lying between two pillars of the priory church of Little Dunmow in Essex are said to be the remains of an unfortunate court beauty, the first of many ladies of status to grace the Tower's dark cells. Daughter of the powerful baron, Robert Fitzwalter, a figure who would one day become deeply entwined in the legends of Robin Hood, Maud Fitzwalter was herself one who apparently suffered at the hands of King John. If the story is true, she can perhaps be considered the most appropriate contender for a historical Maid Marian.

Like the legendary Marian, Maud's story is shrouded in obscurity. If the *Dunmow Chronicle* is to be believed, her journey to ruin began with her attending a banquet hosted by King John, during which the king became enamoured with the 18-year-old and endeavoured to make her his mistress. Rebuffed in his initial advances by the chaste woman, John sought to abduct her by force. Removed to the Tower, Fitzwalter sought grievances against the king for his role in abducting his beloved daughter, culminating in a feud that would see Fitzwalter exiled to France. Left alone and isolated from her family, Maud continued to maintain her virtue by scorning John's advances. Infuriated by her constant rejections, the vengeful king eventually moved her into a cage, located in the circular of the four of the White Tower's turrets. Famished and stricken by cold, her end came on eating an egg into which John had injected poison.

Despite its inclusion in the chronicle of Dunmow and the manner of her death being generally in keeping with John's supposed character, it is highly questionable that these events ever really occurred. The story strikes more than a passing resemblance with that of Anthony Munday's heroine in the plays, *The Downfall and The Death of Robert, Earl of Huntingdon*, and one could well be the inspiration for the other. Whether or not the white lady, whose ghost has allegedly been seen in that turret and even seen waving to some passing schoolchildren, could be the apparition of the tormented Maud is another matter that seems destined to remain part of Tower lore.

Much more credible are accounts of Fitzwalter's subsequent initiatives. As John's hold over his kingdom began to weaken, the furious rebel barons, led by Fitzwalter, laid siege to the Tower on taking London as John retreated to Windsor. While the Tower, then under the guardianship of lieutenant William of Huntingdon, stood firm, the constant barrage and eventual surrender proved the long beginning of John's journey to Runnymede and the implementation of a plan put forward from Archbishop of Canterbury, Stephen Langton; this was to demand certain freedoms in keeping with the charter of liberties first proposed by Henry I on his ascension a century earlier. Signing the Magna Carta, a political move to placate the rebels, John's acceptance was almost instantly followed by attempts to evoke the pope's authority to annul it, thus plunging England into what history would remember as the First Barons' War.

Throughout the conflict, the Tower's garrison had sided unanimously with the royals, who protected it nobly from Fitzwalter's charges. This would change, however, following John's signing, and subsequent renouncement, of the new charters. With the barons' cause now championed by the Dauphine of France, Prince Louis, the foreign pretender took up residency there after arriving in May 1216 and was proclaimed king shortly after during a ceremony inside St Paul's Cathedral. Whereas Fitzwalter steadfastly remained true to his cause, on John's death popular opinion gradually swung away from the rebels and towards John's young son who was crowned Henry III at Gloucester. Supported by the loyal royalists, the young man's stock would rise consistently throughout the coming months from a combination of being innocent of his father's crimes and, of perhaps greater importance, acting under the wise counsel of regent William Marshal, 1st Earl of Pembroke. As fate would have it, Louis's surrender after defeat at Lincoln in 1217 would put an end to any chance England would ever be ruled by the French and, in doing so, ensured the rise of the king destined to have the greatest effect on the Tower's destiny.

Chapter 2

1216–1307: Charters, Barters and Hammering Scots

Henry III was just 9 years old when he ascended to the throne of England. A gentle, intelligent boy thrown mercilessly into the rigours of English politics on the death of his father at the height of England's third civil war, Henry's early reign was defined less by the stamping of his own authority and more by the wise counsel of his regents who successfully oversaw the revised implementation of Magna Carta and an overdue end to the two–year conflict. For both England and the Tower, peace was a welcome relief.

An overspill of emotion in 1222 would culminate in a bizarre riot in fields close to the Tower. A series of wrestling matches between citizens of London and nearby Westminster had ended peacefully the first time before the rematch a week later saw several experienced wrestlers brought in for Westminster, infuriating the locals. As things threatened to boil over, former London sheriff Constantine Fitz-Athulf escalated matters with actions that resulted in several houses being burned and people assaulted as they marched on Westminster. When the storm passed, the key parties were all dragged before justiciar Hubert de Burgh at the Tower. Unsatisfied with their explanations, the former sheriff, along with his nephew and at least one other, were taken west to Tyburn and hanged the following day. Incidentally, it is from the reference to being taken from the Tower to Tyburn that the term 'Gone West' has entered the English language.

Fortunately for the young king, such instances were rare and short-lived. During his relatively long life of sixty-five years, fifty-six of which were spent on the throne, Henry III's character developed as that of a pious patron of the arts, not dissimilar to the mould of Edward the Confessor, but also as a magnificent builder. Famed for his achievements in the flourishing gothic architecture that still to this day defines many of England's grand cathedrals, most notably his pet project Westminster Abbey revamped in honour of the Confessor, it was also during his time that development of the Tower was taken to a new level. The great hall of the royal palace and luxury apartments, now demolished, were erected and frescoed in the first half of his reign, along with the inner wall – at that time the outer wall – whose constructions included the Salt, Lanthorn, Garden, Wakefield – then known as the Blundeville – Flint, Devereux – then known as Robyn the Devil's – Bowyer, Brick, Martin, Constable and Broad Arrow Towers, as well as a water gate between the Wakefield Tower and the Lanthorn. Longchamp's ditch from the 1190s was finally submerged, providing an additional form of defence, while the royal chapels of St Peter ad Vincula and St John were both radiantly refurbished, including painting of the former's royal stalls and enhancement of the decorations, placing a statue of the Virgin Mary, timber panels before the altars and the creation of a marble font that would be used for many a Tower baptism. Perhaps most ironically, around that time the Caen stones William the Conqueror had brought across the channel for the creation of the original keep were given a fresh coat of paint. Incidentally, it is from this seemingly minor act that Gundulf's masterpiece gained its legendary name, the White Tower.

A first of his kind, throughout his long reign Henry made frequent use of the Tower. In 1238 he was recorded as having sought refuge there when his sister Eleanor was married in secret to the influential baron, Simon de Montfort, and further visits would also occur during the regular Welsh conflicts that would prove a consistent distraction throughout the following decade. As his reign progressed, many other key events would go on to be of great significance to the Tower's history. From around 1230 onwards, the Crown Jewels were moved there for the first time, a tradition that has remained almost unbroken ever since. Similar was true concerning the Tower's famed collection of animals. Whether or not the records dated around 1210 regarding payments from the constable to the lion keepers indicate a permanent dwelling – quite possibly established to house the plethora of creatures John brought back to England in 1204 – come 1235, Henry followed in the footsteps of his namesake and grandfather, Henry II, by founding the royal menagerie after receiving three leopards as a present from the Holy Roman Emperor, Frederick II.

A royal lion was added in 1240, around which time the gathering collection of animals had been joined by everything in the menagerie at Woodstock, including more lions and leopards, as well as lynxes and a camel. Perhaps most intriguing was the subsequent arrival of a polar bear in 1252, courtesy of Haakon IV of Norway, and an African elephant – believed to have been the first to grace Europe since the days of Hannibal – as recorded by the famed chronicler, Matthew Paris, in 1255.

A key administrative figure during the first half of Henry's reign was the sometime constable of the Tower, Hubert de Burgh. Promoted to the role of justiciar during the latter days of King John and serving loyally as Henry's chief supporter on the death of regent William Marshal, Hubert incurred Henry's wrath in 1232 and was dismissed after being accused of a variety of offences. Preparing to journey from Merton to East Anglia, Hubert sought refuge in a chapel at Brentwood in Essex before being hauled to the Tower, despite the fact he had entered the chapel under the ancient right of sanctuary. Under intense pressure from his prelates, Henry reluctantly approved Hubert's return to the chapel, following which he endeavoured to cut off all food supplies to the beleaguered advisor in an attempt to starve him out. Left with no choice but to surrender, Hubert was soon back in the Tower, with no guarantees of future release. News of Henry's actions would prove far from unanimously popular, highlighted by the story that during his incarceration, a blacksmith refused to chain him. After several months, the archbishop of Canterbury, the future canonised Edmund Rich, negotiated a truce and Hubert was reinstated to some lesser degree of office.

One of the most notable prisoners to be kept at the Tower during this time was the fiery Welsh prince, Gruffydd ap Llywelyn, the eldest son of the powerful Welsh lord Llywelyn ap Iorwerth. After being disinherited by his father in favour of his younger brother, Dafydd, Gruffydd revolted many times against Henry and was captured by Dafydd on his father's death. When Henry mounted a successful invasion of the Welsh marches, Dafydd had little option but to hand over Gruffydd, after which he was brought to the Tower. After three long years in the White Tower, Gruffydd attempted to follow in the footsteps of Flambard by escaping the Tower after knotting together a home-made rope out of bed sheets. Unfortunately for the disinherited prince, on attempting to liberate himself on 1 March 1244, his rope became partially unknotted and he 'plunged to his instant death.' Discovered by one of the Tower guards, his 'head and neck' were reported as being 'crushed between his shoulders' in what was considered 'a horrid spectacle'. As a result of this unfortunate occurrence, Gruffydd now owns the sad infamy of being the first individual of status to die attempting to escape.

Throughout the last fifteen years of his reign, just as in the early periods, Henry made regular use of his expanding citadel. Fresh from conceding new rights and freedoms under pressure from rebellious barons in 1258 that led to the promulgation of the Provisions of Oxford and Westminster – more or less successors to Magna Carta – the king sought refuge at the Tower in 1261 after seeking to follow in his father's example by flouting the new agreements. Though the storm soon passed, the wind of change refused to stop blowing altogether. As English xenophobia towards Henry's foreign favourites – notably his half-siblings from his mother's second marriage to Hugh de Lusignan, as well as relatives of his queen, Eleanor of Provence – led to increased displeasure, two years later, Eleanor herself incurred the wrath of Londoners when the royal barge was pelted from London Bridge as it attempted to sail away from the Tower, forcing her to return.

Yet the greatest challenge faced by the Tower during Henry's reign came two years after the Battle of Evesham (1265). With the Second Barons' War all but over, a final rebellion broke out under the flag of the powerful marcher lord, Gilbert de Clare, who laid siege to its walls in 1267. At the time of Gilbert's arrival, Henry had led his charges to success at Cambridge, whereas Prince Edward – the future Edward I – moved south from Northumberland. Holding the Tower at the time was the papal legate, Ottoboni, who on becoming severely isolated was eventually sprung, as Henry and Edward rode swiftly for the capital. Gathered in such numbers they would have almost certainly recovered the Tower by force, Henry's brother, Richard, Earl of Cornwall, successfully conducted a truce, ensuring the disinherited barons would be granted permission to reclaim their estates and return to their lands.

Henry's death in 1272 led to the ascension of his talented and ambitious son, crowned Edward I. Inspired by his father's love of building, Edward would enjoy his own special affinity with the Tower and was responsible for adding the outer curtain wall in addition to several other key defences. Although the magnificent barbican sadly no longer stands, Edward's first line of outer defence, which also housed the permanent menagerie at the aptly named Lion Tower, was arguably the most sophisticated of its type ever built. Indeed, thanks to Edward's architectural genius, never again would the Tower be successfully sieged.

Maintaining the policy of his father, Edward kept the Crown Jewels at the Tower, albeit with mixed fortunes. After some of the jewels were stolen from Westminster Abbey, he ordered the abbot and forty-eight monks be brought to the Tower as punishment for their failure to keep the valuables safe. It was also during Edward's reign that the Mint really came into its own. Established around 1245 on the orders of his father, replacing the previous system of several regional mints and thus creating a royal monopoly, by 1300 a 400-foot-long building was established within the outer west curtain wall, later spreading along the whole of the outer curtain. Rare visual evidence of the Mint's eventful past has miraculously survived in the form of a mural discovered during the last century in the Byward Tower. Though religious in nature, the picture points an accusing finger at the Tower moneymen, whose lodgings had once been found adjacent to the room in question.

Among the early beneficiaries of the Mint were England's Jewish population. Despite enjoying special status during Henry III's reign, throughout the first six years of Edward I's tenure a number of their unique privileges were repelled. So great was the change that within nine days of Henry III's death, a London Jew, Ben' fil Cok' is described as having taken refuge in the Tower as a result of the king's passing. Already the site of mass imprisonments from 1240 when harsh taxes were imposed, the years 1275 to 1278 would see many members of the Jewish community imprisoned in the Tower, as Edward I's hardening policy towards them included the prohibition of taking interest or granting mortgages. Hostilities reached a peak in 1279 on allegations of mutilation of the silver coins, leading to as many as 280 Jews being executed on charges of coin clipping with a further 300 plus held as hostages. One particularly unfortunate victim was the principled judge, Henry de Bray, who was imprisoned for speaking up in their defence. After failing with a bid to kill himself by jumping with bound hands into the Tower moat, de

Bray later, sadly, became the Tower's first recorded suicide after banging his head repeatedly against the thick walls of his cell. In 1290 Edward brought matters to a permanent conclusion by expelling most of the Jews to the Continent.

Like that of his father, the reign of Edward was destined to be a colourful one for the Tower. Pacification of the Princes of Gwynedd in 1282, thus successfully uniting England and Wales for the first time, brought a long-awaited end to several decades of campaigns against the Welsh. The result was achieved with a typically ruthless Edwardian onslaught culminating with the head of Llywelyn ap Gruffydd being brought to London where it was 'greeted gleefully by the inhabitants playing tambourines, flutes, fifes and other instruments' before being crowned with a wreath of ivy and used to decorate the battlements of the White Tower. A year later the head of younger brother Dafydd would join him. Further to all but ending the Welsh resistance, Dafydd's death was significant for being the first recorded execution of a royal by hanging, drawing and quartering. Exactly when this method began as a way of execution is an interesting subject. According to the chronicler Matthew Paris, the method was devised in 1238 as punishment for a man who endeavoured to assassinate Henry III at Woodstock. Four years later, known outlaw William Marisco, the man behind the assassination attempt, was also captured and dragged from Westminster to the Tower to suffer a similar fate.

Further to the Welsh conflicts, Edward's reign would also witness consistent war with England's neighbours to the north, occurrences that would see him become immortalised with the epithet, 'Hammer of the Scots'. After experiencing defeat to the English in 1296 at Dunbar, the Scottish King John Balliol was left no choice but to abdicate, the result of which saw him journey with his son to London and face incarceration in the Tower. Joining him on the road south were the Scottish Crown Jewels and the Stone of Scone, the latter of which would remain on display in Westminster Abbey for over 700 years. Initially, Balliol was lodged in comfort in the White Tower; however, when his allowance of 17 schillings a day to maintain his staff was slashed, he was moved to the Salt Tower – which for a time was renamed the Balliol Tower in his honour. After two years of petitioning the pope to grant him liberty, he was finally released.

Another prominent Scot forced to endure the inside of the Tower was the lord of Douglas, William the Hardy. Buoyed by the rise of William Wallace a year after Balliol's abdication, Douglas was summoned by Edward I to attend council in London on 7 July 1297, along with some fifty other barons in preparation for an expedition to Flanders to combat Philip IV of France. Flouting Edward's command, the patriotic Douglas instead joined forces with Wallace, at the time a practically unthinkable move, as never before had a noble entered league with someone of lowly status. Famed for his portrayal in the film, *Braveheart*, Wallace's success was heightened when the pair successfully took possession of the English treasury at Scone Abbey, following which Wallace backed it up with an impressive victory at Stirling Bridge on 11 September that year.

Unfortunately for Douglas, news of the rebellion inevitably came to the attention of the king. After failing to have him arrested by Robert the Bruce – who himself took up arms with his countrymen – Douglas was later caught and imprisoned in Berwick Castle. As Wallace led his charges to victory at Stirling Bridge, the English forces moved south from Berwick, taking their prisoner with them. Committed to the Tower in October, Douglas died just a few months later in January of the following year. History remains unclear as to whether he was murdered or died of accidental mistreatment. Either way, his demise has been deemed the responsibility of his gaolers.

Following in Douglas's footsteps was Wallace himself, who, unlike the noble Balliol, was treated as a common criminal. On being captured by the English near Glasgow, he was delivered south to the English capital and lodged in the home of one William de Leyrer before facing trial at Flambard's Westminster Hall. Tried on charges ranging from treason to monstrosities against civilians – apparently relating to the sparing of neither 'age nor sex, monk nor nun' – the captured outlaw, in a scene reminiscent of Christ's crown of thorns, was crowned with a garland of oak. On answering the charge of treason, he responded resolutely he could never be a traitor against Edward 'for I was never his subject.'

His guilty verdict on 23 August followed Wallace's own brief stay inside the Tower. Taken there from Westminster, he was stripped naked and dragged by horse through the city streets, his life ending with a violent hanging, drawing and quartering at Smithfield. Before the year was out, several other Scots suffered similar fates. Arguably the most prominent was the 9th Earl of Atholl, John of Strathbogie. Already a former prisoner of the Tower on being captured at Dunbar in 1296, Atholl's release had only been ensured on his agreement to serve Edward I in Flanders. By joining Robert the Bruce's stand and once again taking up arms against Edward, defeat at the Battle of Methven in 1306 ensured he would follow Wallace to the grave. His execution was unique for his being hung from a gallows some 30 feet higher than usual. In doing so, he became the first nobleman to die for treason since the Norman Conquest.

Chapter 3

1307–1330: Dispensable Despensers and Malicious Marchers

Replacing Edward I on the throne was his son of the same name, henceforth Edward II. Of a far gentler nature than his father, Edward's reign was plagued by regular disputes with his barons, most notably for his empowering of personal favourites as opposed to making appointments on merit. Whereas Edward I had been a stickler for rules and famed for his hard, hands-on approach, evidence of his son's laxity can be found in the case of the Tower's constable, John de Cromwell, who was tried in 1321 and dismissed for wanton abuse of his power. Among the many accusations levelled against him was a consistent lack of attention to detail, most notably for allowing the Tower to fall into an unacceptable state of repair. So bad were the conditions, Edward's queen, Isabella, was reported to have been rained on as she gave birth to daughter Joan in the White Tower.

Throughout her time as queen, Isabella spent significant time at the Tower. Renowned as an avid reader, especially of the contemporary romances which filled the shelves and chests of the Tower library, it was there fate would place her on the path to both success and ruin on becoming acquainted with the powerful Earl of March, Roger Mortimer. Born at his family seat at Wigmore Castle in 1287, Mortimer was another of those figures who would go down in the Tower's history for mostly the wrong reasons. Famed for his emergence on the baronial scene, catching the eye of the headstrong Edward I for his prowess in battle, Mortimer became a firm friend of the Prince of Wales and future Edward II.

How often has it been in the history of England that one who was once a firm friend and favourite should later become the overseer of the other's downfall? Having initially served Edward II loyally, frustrations with the king's military ineptitude and tendency to promote undeserving favourites would lead to Mortimer's disillusionment. Edward's cardinal sin in Mortimer's eyes was the rise of Hugh Despenser, who had long been the great nemesis of the Mortimers, following a feud that began with Mortimer's grandfather slewing Hugh's at the Battle of Evesham. On returning from fighting the king's cause in Ireland, Mortimer was appalled to learn how strong Despenser's grasp over the king had become: not least his being awarded the earldom of Gloucester and for being given the king's blessing to seize the de Clare holdings in Gower and Usk. Concerned no doubt by threats to their own birthright, in league with the other marcher lords, rebellion began in earnest.

Not for the only time in Edward's reign, the wind of change blew steadily against him. Left with no choice but to exile Despenser, he initially agreed to the rebels' terms; however, a series of squabbles among the victorious barons opened up an opportunity for Edward to make a U-turn. Recalling Despenser and meting out justice on those behind the earlier revolt – numbers that totalled no less than twelve peers and over 100 of their followers – Edward and Despenser well and truly regained control. Victorious only months earlier, Mortimer's fortunes had reached an unexpected low. Surrendering to the king at Shrewsbury in 1322, he was stripped of his lands and taken to the Tower.

In the context of England's history, Mortimer's downfall would serve as something of a watershed moment. Though spared death on the king's insistence, Mortimer was ferried back to the Tower after his trial at Westminster and sentenced to remain there for the rest of his life. While the disgraced earl's absence left a hole in council, Despenser swiftly added to his dubiously gotten gains and even demanded of the king that Mortimer's initial death sentence be carried out. Blinded by ambition, Despenser seems to have been naïvely oblivious to the enemies he was making. Not only had he alienated almost all of the barons, he was fast driving an irreparable wedge between Edward and an even more important person: Edward's queen.

Born in Paris around 1295, daughter of Philip IV of France, the precise role Isabella played in the events that followed has been argued at length by many past commentators. Lampooned by the chroniclers of the day, the worst of which branded her the 'she-wolf' of France – a reputation exaggerated further by popular culture – by 1322 any genuine love the queen once had for her husband seems to have totally evaporated. Being the mother of their four children, coupled with a lack of accusation by close rivals or associates, there is little evidence that Edward was gay, yet it is likely that his bisexual tendencies, highlighted by his close relationships with Despenser and, previously, Piers Gaveston contributed greatly to the queen's frustrations. Initially satisfied by Despenser's banishment, around which time she gave birth to Joan in the Tower, whatever hopes she had of a new beginning were dispelled on Despenser's return. Though initially successful in quashing the rebellion, the hapless failings of her husband north of the border, leading to an awkward truce with Robert the Bruce, was further worsened when Isabella was left stranded at Tynemouth Abbey, losing two ladies-in-waiting on being forced to escape by sea. For Isabella, the close encounter would prove the final breaking point. Safely back in the capital, her claws ever sharpening, it is widely speculated that it was to Mortimer that she turned, visiting him regularly in his cell. In February 1323, she protested to the king that Mortimer's loyal wife and mother were being subjected to unfair harassment; it is less clear whether Lady Mortimer knew of their recent affair. Either way, her words fell on deaf ears.

For Mortimer himself, conditions in the Tower had proved intolerable. Despite being of esteemed baronial stock, as a non-noble his time would pass deprived of access to the impressive facilities enjoyed by the royals, instead enduring the same damp and dirty surroundings of the typical prisoner in which his will was severely tested. Using what access he still had with the outside world and what influence he still had to persuade others – including his gaolers – to do his bidding, he successfully sent and received a plethora of messages to coordinate future rebellion as well as conspiring the downfall of the king's favourites. England may still have been more than two centuries away from the days when Sir Francis Walsingham's spies conducted a tight watch on all suspicious activity, but even back in 1322 Mortimer was not without watchers. Further to certain letters falling into unwanted hands, the apprehension and subsequent torture of Mortimer's key ally, Lord Berkeley, led to news of his scheming becoming known to the king and Despenser. Armed with the damning evidence, Mortimer's death sentence was reissued for August 1323.

News of his forthcoming execution was made personally known to Mortimer by Isabella. On a further visit to the Tower, it is likely plans for his escape were discussed in detail. With August now upon them, the first day of which marked the feast day of St Peter ad Vincula, Mortimer seized the opportunity. He used the celebrations as his distraction, and was aided by the help of the constable's deputy – or lieutenant – Gerard d'Alspaye. As the constable, Stephen de Segrave, and the gaolers joined the masses in the great hall, Mortimer prepared to slip out amidst the scenes of heavy drinking. Assisted by d'Alspaye's adding of sleeping drugs to the refreshments, the result of which soon saw the constable and many of his men unconscious, the lieutenant then brought a concealed crowbar to Mortimer's cell, along with a pair of rope ladders. It seems at this point the deputy was either not in possession of the correct keys or else unwilling to make the escape appear too obvious, and went to work loosening a block of stone. As the inside man worked away, on the other side, Mortimer and his cellmate, Richard de Monmouth, worked hard to remove the stones. Eventually, a gap was created of sufficient size to allow Mortimer and his cellmate to creep out and down into the adjoining kitchens. Aided by the cook, they then made their way up an unused chimney. On reaching the roof, ladders were placed over the side of the inner ward, allowing them to descend to the outer. By now, only one obstacle remained. Using the second ladder, they escaped the outer wall and sped away into the night where a boat was waiting to take them to Greenwich. Perhaps following in the footsteps of Flambard, a gathering of horses and men had been assembled in preparation.

Even being in league with several supporters, Mortimer's escape was nothing short of miraculous. Whereas the industrious Flambard had been blessed with great skill and intellect, he had also been dealing with a far smaller area. Having designed the original castle to include two outer walls, Henry III and Edward I had put together a fortress that would have been almost impossible to escape without insider help. Be it a sign of Mortimer's influence, Edward's failings, the corruption of man or quite possibly a combination of several, Mortimer was able to breach the net and finally launch his long awaited rebellion.

For Edward II, Mortimer's escape was effectively the issue of his own death warrant. Having made it from Greenwich to France, Mortimer immediately set to work on plotting military action, and, aided by his new lover, force Edward from the throne. While failure to incarcerate his prisoners inevitably led to Segrave's sacking as Constable of the Tower, Edward's gathering suspicions of his wife would see her being deprived of her children and household staff as well as the imprisonment of Mortimer's own children; no less than three of Mortimer's sons joined their great-uncle, Roger Mortimer de Chirk, in taking their father's place in the Tower. Bewilderingly, come March 1325, concerned of the consequences of Mortimer's escape and the possibility of a French invasion, Edward sent his wife, also sister of the new king of France, back to her homeland to consolidate his intended peace treaty. Although terms were indeed agreed, what followed was even more baffling. In honour of the clause established by Isabella that Edward must pay homage to the king of France for England's lands in France, rather than making the trip himself, Edward instead sent his son, Prince Edward.

Even without the benefit of hindsight, the decision on Edward's part here seems ludicrous. Such a move appears even worse considering that letting the heir to the throne travel to France was a nightmare he had long sought to avoid. Not only does the pattern of events reflect terribly on his own judgment, but also seems tinged with a sense of inevitability. Further humiliated by the new constable of the Tower, Bishop of Exeter, Walter de Stapledon, who had joined Prince Edward on his journey to the French court, Isabella defiantly responded she would not return until the 'Pharisee' Despenser was removed. In truth, she did not have long to wait. Aided by troops from both France and the Netherlands, by September 1326, Mortimer's invasion force had landed on the east coast. Leaving London and the Tower, Edward faced little choice but to flee west. The tide turning, he was deserted by his remaining subjects and as he attempted to bide his time in Wales, was finally captured. Imprisoned in a dark cell, he agreed to abdicate.

One of the more bizarre aspects of the Tower's history at this point comes with the death of the man who succeeded in humiliating Isabella before the French court. Fearing being overpowered, de Stapledon was found in sanctuary at St Paul's where, in scenes reminiscent of what would come to pass later that century, he was beheaded by use of a bread knife. As 1327 neared its end, worse still was to befall the major players. Captured and tried by Mortimer, Despenser was brutally hanged, drawn and quartered at Hereford after which Edward was apparently found dead in the dungeons of Berkeley Castle. Subsequent conjecture has it his death occurred with a red-hot poker placed into his anus as a sign of his believed homosexuality, yet this is unlikely to be historical.

Mortimer's coup, at least in some quarters, was warmly received. Though overthrowing the monarch who had been anointed by God was far from universally sought, few mourned the passing of his tyrannical favourite who had brought England to the brink of anarchy. Not for the first time, however, the beginning of the new reign was one that could have implemented sound logistical planning, yet Mortimer's own failure to learn the lessons of Despenser's errors soon saw him fall into the same trap that had ensured the 'Pharisee's' doom. Effectively ruling England as though he were the rightful king and showing little respect to the young Edward III, Mortimer's own downfall was almost anticlimactically swift. Aided by loyal followers one dark night in 1330, the almost 18-year-old Edward III stole into Nottingham Castle and had the regent surrounded. Sent once more to the Tower, this time there was no escape. To ensure previous measures would not be repeated, Mortimer, along with his son Geoffrey and key ally Simon Bereford, were placed in a cell in which every gap had been filled with mortar, including the window. Motivated no doubt to keep a sharp eye on his father's killer, Edward personally relocated to the Tower, taking quarters in the room next door. During their final month, the prisoners left the Tower only for trial at Westminster before being finally hanged at Tyburn. With it passed one of the most controversial characters in the Tower's history. Described by one as the 'greatest traitor', in the voice of his own son, Geoffrey, he had turned from honourable knight to 'king of folly'.

Chapter 4

1330–1399: Revolting Peasants and Ambitious Appellants

One of the by-products of Mortimer's rebellion had been the military assistance offered them by the Dutch. As part of the deal, it was agreed that Edward would be given away in marriage to Philippa of Hainault, which duly occurred on 24 January 1328. The happy pair honeymooned at the Tower that year and began the coronation march from there in 1330. In similar circumstances to Joan twenty years earlier, Edward III's daughter Blanche was born at the Tower in 1342, though sadly she perished within a year.

Less in keeping with the work of his father but rather that of his grandfather and great-grandfather – Edward I and Henry III, respectively – Edward's own mark on the Tower would be noteworthy. Having arrived there from the Thames one evening in 1340 and sailed through the water gate unopposed, the appalled king swiftly endeavoured to strengthen the Tower's security, constructing the Cradle Tower in the south wall as an alternative entrance via the river. Edward's anger may well have been further increased by the knowledge that very year Sir John de Molines, captured during the Scottish wars, was recorded as having escaped; he would be pardoned six years later. Further to his key additions to the Tower's defences, Edward added lions, leopards and a bear to the menagerie, and reconstructed the Garden Tower as part of his private residence.

The product of the Tower's first royal birth – Edward's young sister, Joan – was given away in marriage in 1330 to David II of Scotland, son of the late Robert the Bruce. Despite being officially crowned King of Scotland, David was soon defeated by the pretender Edward Balliol only to retake the throne shortly after and invade England in 1346 on reactivation of the Auld Alliance between the Scots and the French. Among the many ironies that would colour the Tower's history, David was imprisoned there in 1347 and joined by several other Scottish lords, including the earl of Mentieth, as well as the burghers of Calais who had been imprisoned by Edward III on the capture of the town during the Hundred Years' War.

Three years after King David's release in 1356, the Tower would pay host to another foreign royal following the capture of John II of France in battle by the king's son, Edward the Black Prince. Released in recognition that contact with the outside world would be necessary to collect his ransom, the total sum was never paid, following which the honest John returned voluntarily after his son, Louis – taken hostage in his father's place – successfully mounted an escape. Never so much a prisoner but an honoured guest, John II died at the Tower in 1364, the first king to do so. Somewhat inevitably, he would not be the last.

The imprisonment of commoner Cecilia de Rygeway in 1357 is one of a collection of sorry tales concerning female prisoners at the Tower. Subjected to the appalling ritual of *prison forte et dure* – a process of slow starvation through days alternating between water and no bread or bad bread and no water – the woman, imprisoned on suspicion of murdering her husband, survived with admiral fortitude for more than forty days. So impressed was the king with her spirit, he pardoned her. Examples of this horrid method, often known as 'persuasion', can be dated back to 1275.

The death of Edward the Black Prince in 1376 proved to be yet another watershed in England's history. Deprived of the ascension of arguably the greatest prince Europe had ever seen, a combination of Edward III's longevity and virility would soon lead to a court of meddlers and an unforeseen vacuum of power. With the heir to the throne dead and the king following him to the afterlife the following year, next in line was not one of Edward's middle-aged sons, but the Black Prince's 10-year-old boy, who took his grandfather's place as Richard II.

Perhaps as a sign of things to come, the reign of Richard II started ignominiously for the Tower. Within a year of the new king's coronation, a further two prisoners achieved the impossible and escaped. Accompanied by fellow squire John Shakell, with whom he had served in the Black Prince's campaign in the north of Spain, Robert Hauley experienced the Tower's loathsome interior as a consequence of his decision to capture the Aragonese noble, the Count of Denia. In keeping with the common rules of war, Hauley had apprehended the count during the Battle of Nájera in 1367 in the hope of receiving a fine ransom. Accepting Denia's explanation that he needed to return to Spain in order to raise funds, the pair agreed on the usual terms a hostage be left in place of the count. With Denia meeting his end, apparently of natural causes, on his return home, Hauley and Shakell found themselves encumbered with a prisoner. Hearing of the predicament, a furious John of Gaunt took up the hostage's argument and Hauley and Shakell were sent to the Tower.

What happened next remains something of a mystery. How exactly the pair escaped is unknown, only that it was achieved by violent means. With the alarm raised, constable of the Tower, Sir Alan de Buxhall, assisted by Sir Ralph de Ferrers and some fifty men of the garrison chased the absconding pair up Tower Hill before watching them take sanctuary inside Westminster Abbey. As the frantic escapees interrupted a mass in honour of the festival of St Taurinus, the constable and his men followed them into the abbey, recapturing Shakell and hacking to death the hot-headed Hauley as he attempted to circle the choir. In honour of his apparent martyrdom, Hauley was interred in the abbey's south transept with a long brass effigy marking his place of rest. In the aftermath, the constable and Ferrers were excommunicated as punishment for desecrating the holy site, whereas Shakell reached a compromise with Denia's son before being eventually laid to rest in close proximity to Hauley.

Two years later, Richard had far greater things on his mind than considerations of escaping prisoners. The Black Death – the origin of which has been conclusively dated to 1348 and the arrival of fleas from rats on a ship that docked in Dorset – unleashed its fury on the cesspits of London, which had inevitably become a breeding ground for pestilence. What had long been assumed a pauper's disease was swiftly proven otherwise as the late king's widow, Queen Philippa, and three of Edward's daughters all fell victim to it.

A combination of Black Death and the wars in France had created a labour shortage in England. In consequence of this, the statute of labourers had taken the ridiculous step of freezing wages despite increased levels of inflation. As the bankrupt nation struggled to raise cash, a series of levies or poll taxes were placed on the citizens. After two attempts had bled many of England's poorer citizens dry, a third in four years was largely resisted. Dissatisfied with the results, the collectors were sent back to try again. Almost inevitably, it would be a costly mistake.

A tax strike in Essex was soon recorded as having spread to Kent where a revolt led by Wat Tyler began in earnest. After marching his rebels on Maidstone and Canterbury, mob justice saw the untimely deaths of several wealthy citizens, their successes inspiring the rebels to loot Rochester before marching on the capital.

By June 1381, at the time the revolt was gathering pace, most of England's leaders were absent. Learning that this unruly group was approaching the capital, the council sent for Richard and his mother at Windsor who immediately set up headquarters in the Tower. Hearing of the king's arrival, Tyler sent a messenger, Sir John Newton, to speak with Richard at the Tower at which point the king apparently agreed to listen to their complaints. As night fell, the rebels had already moved to within sight of the city walls, the lights of their camps creating an ominous glow in the distance. Understanding that contempt for the king among the rebels was writhe, greater hatred was aimed upon the man deemed by many to be behind the taxes: Archbishop of Canterbury and Keeper of the Royal Seal, Simon Sudbury.

Sudbury is one of those characters that history has always struggled to present in clear-cut fashion. Hated by the rebels for his apparent underhand tactics, accounts of many contemporary Londoners present Sudbury as a good, honest man who did his best for the people. Aware of the impending doom, the beleaguered archbishop surrendered the royal seal to Richard on hearing of the damage inflicted on Canterbury, choosing to remain at the Tower, a move remarked by his sympathisers as that of a cat's paw in an attempt to save his king. While Simon occupied himself in prayer inside the walls of the Norman Chapel of St John, Richard and his counsellors sailed from the Tower and located the mob on the banks of the Thames. After attempting, without success, to address them calmly, the captain of the barge ordered it be turned around and returned to the Tower to avoid a catastrophe. On bearing witness to this sight of an apparent U-turn, the mob's anger swelled, convinced their demands had not been answered. Either aided by sympathisers or perhaps brute strength, the army entered the city via London Bridge as another peasant army came through Aldgate. The chaos that followed was unprecedented in England, at least since the Norman Conquest. Buildings were destroyed, most notably John of Gaunt's Savoy Palace on the Strand, gaols emptied and foreigners purged. Over 150 are known to have died in the anarchy which saw many of London's wealthy citizens flee to the Tower as their homes and businesses were ransacked.

Richard himself had the perfect view of the latest uprising. Conducting proceedings from the roof of the White Tower – at the time the highest secular building in London – he watched as chaos rained down around him. As night fell, the council met in anxious session. Despite the reservations of his allies, Richard decided he would try to negotiate a second time and the next day rode out to meet the dissenters. When his mother Joan attempted to return, a clutch of peasants somehow successfully swarmed the fortress.

Still occupying the Chapel of St John was the archbishop. After spending the previous night in prayer, Sudbury was found by the intruding mob and dragged out to Tower Hill along with the treasurer Robert Hales; John Legge – a royal sergeant and tax commissioner; William Appleton – the physician to John of Gaunt; and an unnamed monk. By luck or fate, Richard's cousin, Henry Bolingbroke, avoided detection thanks to the help of a loyal helper, destined to return another day. Whereas the future Henry IV slipped away to safety, the key players were all violently despatched by the rebel forces. After suffering an estimated eight blows of the axe, the decapitated Sudbury's mitre was nailed to his head and spiked on London Bridge.

Inside the Tower, the mayhem continued to unfold. The royal palace, including the king's bedchamber, was severely vandalised, with one of Joan's chambermaids violently raped. Narrowly escaping with her life and virtue, along with her other chambermaids, Joan successfully fled to Baynard's Castle in the clothing of a commoner.

Out in the fields that surrounded his city, Richard was oblivious to the breaching of the Tower's defences. Rather than attempt to quash the rebellion with military strength and dish out punishments, he instead spent the day attempting to negotiate with the rebel leaders. Successfully convincing a large number of them to return home, Richard was informed by a loyal herald that the Tower was unsafe to return to, forcing him to relocate to the royal wardrobe office at Blackfriars. After learning of his mother's narrow escape, the king reacted furiously and, neglecting recent promises, the idea of compromise gave way to a resolve to mete out justice.

The chosen destination was Smithfield, a place fast achieving a reputation associated with death and execution. Agreeing to Tyler's request to negotiate further, the king arrived with his council and around 200 knights and other men at arms after paying homage to Edward the Confessor at Westminster Abbey. Tyler, in contrast, led a motley crew that had swelled to an estimated 20,000. On greeting Richard, he referred to him as brother-king, holding aloft a dagger as he read aloud his list of demands. Unperturbed by the unprecedented uncouthness of Tyler's stance, Richard agreed to acquiesce to all reasonable demands provided the peasants returned home. After foolishly taking a sip of beer and spitting it before the king, Tyler then requested the king's ceremonial sword from his page, informing those present he would be wielding it in future. On reacting impulsively to the page's refusal, accompanied by accusation that Tyler was a 'mere villein', the rebel leader stood up in the stirrups attached to his horse and held his dagger aloft, declaring he would not eat again until the page's head was on a platter. Seeing Tyler's anger as the opportunity he had long awaited, the lord mayor of London, William Walworth, shot forward on his own steed and maintained an appearance of being unguarded as Tyler thrust his dagger at his chest, clearly unaware an iron breastplate had been placed beneath Walworth's clothes. Struck to the neck by the lord mayor's counter strike, the ailing Tyler was caught off guard by a second attack, this time to his gut courtesy of courtier Sir Ralph Standish. Wounded, Tyler fell awkwardly to the ground, collapsing in a puddle of his own blood.

At this point, emotions fast threatened to spill over. Watching the rebels approach, Richard stood resolute, declaring himself their 'captain and king'. Riding forth, he led the mob into the fields of Clerkenwell to the north and promised to address their grievances. Initially placated, the rebels began to scatter. Leaving the carnage behind him, the king made his way back to the capital and joined the Lord Mayor Walworth back at the, now, relatively quiet Tower. On returning to Smithfield, Walworth learned Tyler had somehow survived the earlier assault and was expected to make a full recovery. Locating him at the priory of St Bartholomew, Walworth took him back out to Smithfield and executed him personally.

The first spontaneous uprising by English commoners against their noble overlords would finally pass. Later claims in Whig philosophy that the outbreak of violence had represented a long dormant Saxon nostalgia against the Norman yoke probably stretch a point, yet any chance of the creation of Merry England might just have died with this defeat. With Plantagenet authority largely restored, Tyler's head replaced Sudbury's on London Bridge and the other leaders were in turn hunted down. The young king had survived the first great challenge of his reign. Order, for now at least, had been restored.

For Richard, the damage caused by the peasants to both the city and the Tower remained of paramount concern. Rectifying the mess began with the lavish restoration of the Tower's royal apartments with several panes of glass emblazoned with the royal coat of arms and floor tiles depicting leopards and his personal emblem, the white hart. Improvements were also made to the entrance areas, close to which the menagerie continued to thrive. By 1392 the latter was expanded with the gift of a camel from the citizens of London. Another first saw Richard's queen, Anne of Bohemia, presented with a pelican in honour of her renowned piety.

Six years on from the scenes of havoc, however, Richard faced a far different type of revolt. In keeping with the thought process almost certainly experienced by the maturing Henry III in the late 1220s, the king had become disillusioned with the actions of the regents he had been forced to call upon during his minority and set about establishing a younger faction, comprised solely of personal favourites. Among his changes in policy was peace with France, which required surrendering Calais in exchange for the restoration of the Duchy of Aquitaine. Opposition to this sudden development was led by five lords, known collectively as the Lords Appellant that included his uncle, Thomas of Woodstock, Duke of Gloucester – the youngest surviving son of Edward III; Richard FitzAlan, Earl of Arundel; Thomas de Beauchamp, Earl of Warwick; as well as Henry Bolingbroke, Earl of Derby – himself a son of John of Gaunt – and Thomas de Mowbray, Earl of Nottingham.

In August 1387, Richard made his move to overthrow the newly acquired authority of the Lords Appellant. Bringing the matter before seven senior judges, Richard had his way and charged the five with treason. Things came to a head in November that year when the appellants in turn accused five of the king's new favourites of similar crimes. While four of the accused fled, Robert de Vere, Earl of Oxford, gathered an army in his own county and rode for London. Trapped at Oxford, de Vere was lucky to escape, leaving Richard isolated in the Tower over Christmas. Just two days later, the appellants' own forces had him surrounded.

By January 1388, there were signs that things were at last beginning to change. At Richard's request, the appellants were welcomed to the new throne room in the Wakefield Tower where they were received cordially by the king. Forced to comply with his rebels' demands, the purge that followed in the subsequent parliament was unlike anything previously witnessed in England, forever blackening its name, the 'merciless' parliament. Of the many loyalists brought to the Tower, two of Richard's favourites paid the ultimate price and were executed, as did many others including the original seven judges. Of greater concern to the king was the sacrifice of his beloved tutor, Sir Simon Burley, the first prisoner recorded as having been executed on Tower Hill. Also of Richard's retinue who were condemned were Sir John Beauchamp, Sir John Berners and Sir John Salisbury all of whom were executed on 12 May 1388 on Tower Hill precisely one week after Burley (some sources suggest Salisbury may have been hanged at Tyburn).

The tyranny of the appellants would continue throughout the following year, ceasing somewhat on the return of John of Gaunt from Spain. With public opinion for the appellants fading, Richard's control of the kingdom was gradually restored. Embarrassed by those who had opposed him, below the surface his frustrations intensified. On appearing publicly for the first time since losing his wife in 1394, he unleashed them by striking the earl of Arundel in the face with a wooden staff. Richard's ultimate revenge when it came would have all the makings of a scene from *Hamlet*. Having accomplished what he did best and bided his time, he invited three of his enemies to dine with him at a feast. Of the three, Thomas Beauchamp turned up, whereas Gloucester and Arundel, perhaps sensing a trap, made themselves unavoidably absent. With dinner over, Beauchamp was pounced upon and taken to the Tower. Like Balliol before him, his incarceration was noteworthy, leading to the building being renamed, the Beauchamp Tower. Faced with the new pressure, Beauchamp's mind slowly cracked. Tall tales in the centuries since his incarceration have included references to echoing wails in the dead of night throughout the place he despised.

As for his accomplices, different fates awaited. Arundel, despite surrendering, was also imprisoned and executed on 21 September 1397 having made himself a martyr by distributing alms to the poor on his way to Tower Hill. Gloucester, in a scene that would one day directly inspire Shakespeare, was arrested in person by Richard at his estate and escorted to the Tower. Rather than face the axe, he was smuggled to Calais on Richard's orders. Reminiscent of the infamous princes a century later, he was reportedly smothered in his bed, the man responsible none other than Thomas de Mowbray, one of Gloucester's original appellant conspirators. Along with Bolingbroke, the surviving pair were banished. Incidentally, two years later a certain John Hall would be hanged, drawn and quartered at Tyburn after suffering imprisonment in the Tower on being found guilty of being complicit in Gloucester's murder.

Richard's decision to exile Bolingbroke would soon become key in the context of England's future. On making it permanent on John of Gaunt's death in February 1399, Henry landed at Ravenspurn in North Yorkshire at the end of June with a large army, chancing on Richard's sojourn in Ireland. Aided by the Percy family, themselves powerful magnates in the north of England, Henry moved south and intercepted Richard in North Wales. The king's resources stretched, he was taken prisoner and, under force, followed the path of great-grandfather Edward II to abdication. In doing so, Richard II became the first English monarch to be imprisoned in the Tower.

Chapter 5

1400–1455: The Happy Few, Liberal Lollards and Fatal Falstaffs

As was so often the case in England's history, the dethroning of an established king by a new pretender would be far from the end of the story. Revolt by Ricardian loyalists against Bolingbroke duly followed, plunging the nation to the verge of civil war. Just as Roger Mortimer had understood – only to subsequently forget – with Edward II three-quarters of a century earlier, so long as the deposed king remained alive, future insurrection was always possible. As Bolingbroke's hold on the kingdom tightened, Richard was moved to Pontefract Castle and soon after disappeared entirely from history. Whether or not the popular accounts that would inspire Shakespeare were true, that the Christ-like monarch was murdered or starved to death, we shall probably never know. Unlike his father or grandfather, both of whom were widely mourned and passed in a manner befitting a monarch, Richard's death appears to have been cold and alone, almost certainly choked by the hands that now held the royal orb and sceptre that had once graced his own fingers.

Taking his cousin's place on the throne of their grandfather, Henry IV was of a far different mould to his insecure, yet deeply pious, predecessor. Inspired by Edward III's creation of the Order of the Garter, one of Henry IV's first acts as king was the foundation of the Knights of the Bath, the opening ceremony of which was held in the White Tower in the build up to his coronation. Within days of the event, a plot to surprise him at a tournament hosted at Windsor was foiled and Henry opted to return to the Tower as a precaution. After raising an army, the next day a military uprising that reportedly numbered many hundreds was also thwarted. In doing so, the usurper had passed his first major test.

In direct consequence of the failed plot came a story worthy of note. Famed for his devotion to the deposed Richard II, Sir Thomas Blount, described by the chroniclers as a wise and noble knight, had been one of the ringleaders of the Windsor Plot and, despite managing to flee to Oxford, was eventually captured and sentenced to death. On being taken to the scaffold, Blount rebuked the hostilities of the king's chamberlain, who had sniggered the words 'Go seek a master that can cure you' as he watched Blount's insides being removed, with the reply 'blessed be the day on which I was born, and blessed be this day, for I shall die in the service of my sovereign lord, the noble King Richard.' Completing the incredible story, Blount on being asked if he wanted a drink after being decapitated, delivered the witty response 'no, you have taken away wherein to put it.' Twenty-six men in total were put to death as a result of these early conspiracies. One person Henry is noted for having spared, however, was one John Ferrour: the very man who had helped save him from the Tower during the Peasants' Revolt. It was this moment of destiny that had allowed him to hide in a cupboard and escape the carnage.

Throughout the first two decades of the fifteenth century, the Tower once again became acquainted with Scottish nobility following the capture of Prince James Stewart, soon to be James I of Scotland. Having been forced to flee his homeland due to conflict with his uncle, the duke of Albany, James's France-bound ship was seized in an act of English piracy, after which James was brought before the king. James's father, Robert III, on hearing of his son's incarceration took the news badly. Already well into his sixties, the king declined rapidly and died around two weeks later. As for the 12-year-old James, on his father's death the new prisoner automatically became the uncrowned king of Scotland. With Albany taking centre stage as governor, James had little alternative but to begin what would turn out to be an eighteen-year wait for his coronation. The first two of these would be spent in the Tower's sumptuous royal apartments before being relocated to Nottingham.

Although officially Henry's prisoner, the two kings are noted for having struck up a close relationship. Enjoying the luxuries and relative freedoms that came with being of royal stock, James received an excellent education at the English court, much of which mirrored that of his captor. On Henry IV's death in 1413, however, those privileges were initially taken away, culminating in him being incarcerated in the Tower on the orders of Henry IV's son, now Henry V. Awaiting his arrival were several other prisoners of Scottish birth, including Albany's son –

James's cousin – Murdoch Stewart who had been captured back in 1402. As Henry V's reign progressed, relations between the two kings became increasingly cordial, so much so that in 1415 the now skilled poet and warrior voluntarily lined up alongside Henry at Agincourt. After being part of the escort to return the king's body to London on his death in 1422, James was granted his freedom by the regents of Henry V's young son, Henry VI.

On 21 May 1424, James was, at last, crowned King of Scotland.

Others that spent time in the Tower during the reigns of Henry IV and V had been the family of Welshman Owain Glyndŵr, the same fiery rebel renowned for his role in the Welsh wars of independence, as well as being the last native to bear the title Prince of Wales. After Owain's disappearance in 1409, his wife and two daughters were all brought to London for imprisonment, succumbing to death no later than 1415. Most notable of the prisoners was Owain's son, Gruffydd, who was captured following the Battle of Pwll Melyn around 1405. Though he successfully managed to avoid the noose, he would endure the far more drawn out agony of the Black Death around 1412.

The Ricardian John Whitelock, a former yeoman in Richard II's household, would earn a rare distinction the following year in becoming one of what was still a small and esteemed group of individuals to successfully escape from the Tower. Found guilty of involvement towards the end of Henry IV's life in the circulation of literature claiming the late Richard was still alive and preparing to overthrow the king with the aid of a large force from Scotland – rumour of which had hastened the transfer of James and Murdoch Stewart to the Tower – the newly crowned Henry V issued warrants for the arrest of the ringleaders. These included Whitelock and the Scottish knight Sir Andrew Hake, who had himself previously been party to one of the plots against Henry IV the year Richard was dethroned.

The irony of the matter becomes irresistibly clear when learning that Whitelock and two other conspirators – Sir Ellis Lynet and Thomas Clerk – had taken sanctuary inside Westminster Abbey and remained present throughout the time of Henry V's coronation. By June 1413, however, just days after a second set of Whitelock's bills had been nailed to the doors of several London churches, both men found themselves inside the

Tower. Of what remains uncertain means, Whitelock absconded, either before or during his trial, never to be seen again. Hake – sources vary as to whether he was also presently in sanctuary or arrested independently – and Lynet were freed after seemingly having agreed to turn informer. The only death concerning the Whitelock affair was his warder, who was hanged, drawn and quartered on being found complicit in Whitelock's escape.

One of the most bizarre stories relating to the Tower at this time commenced around the year 1409. Famed in later times as the man who inspired William Shakespeare's comical creation, Falstaff, the historical Sir John Oldcastle in truth had little in common with the character. A mild-mannered, hardworking and courageous knight, Oldcastle's life and death was destined not for comedy but tragedy.

Born sometime after 1360 in Herefordshire, John was the son of Richard Oldcastle, and served Henry IV loyally during the campaigns against the Scots and the Welsh before moving up the social scale with his marriage to Baroness Cobham. Originally on the path to great things, in 1408 things took a surprising turn for him when he fell under the influence of the new wave of religious enlightenment that history would later recall as the precursor to the Protestant Reformation.

Exactly what the preachers of the 'new light' hoped to achieve is now difficult to determine. Given the name 'lollards', relating to an insulting Dutch term for mumbling that later became viewed as a term of endearment, this pioneering group had become obsessed with the teachings of English reformer John Wycliffe, who sympathised with the plight of the poor and castigated the rising corruption of the Church. In doing so, Wycliffe was denounced as a heretic.

The entwining of Oldcastle's path with that of the reformers, almost inevitably, led to his subsequent downfall. Beginning in the Kentish estates he had gained after his marriage, Oldcastle's property was placed under interdict by the papacy in 1410 after churches on his land had welcomed the non-clerical preachers. In keeping with his personal sympathy with Lollardy, Oldcastle even went as far as to put them up in his castle. On learning of recent developments from the archbishop of Canterbury, the king raised the matter personally with Oldcastle at

Windsor, to which the knight replied that while he would always be loyal to the king, the undertakings of his soul were a private matter.

Sadly for Oldcastle, his views, though arguably somewhat enlightened for the time, were effectively a death warrant. Branded a heretic, Oldcastle proceeded to complain that the common form of execution during the Inquisition – namely that of burning at the stake – should be prohibited on English soil. In the eyes of his accusers, the final straw came with accusations a heretical book Oldcastle had once owned appeared for sale among the booksellers of St Paul's Churchyard. Charged on crimes of heresy, Oldcastle was brought to the Tower. Lodged in the same set of cells that had driven the poor Thomas Beauchamp to the brink of madness, the lieutenant, Sir Robert Morley, treated the new prisoner with great respect, as was expected of a once esteemed soldier. During his stay, attempts by those of the religious life to steer him from his beliefs failed; interestingly there is no evidence he was violent in his rejections. In September 1413, Oldcastle was ferried along the Thames to Ludgate Hill where he awaited trial in a church court before various prelates and religious officials. Expressing views which would one day inspire protestant reformers, he declared his belief in the sacraments, but not religious images or the real presence of Christ in Holy Communion. When sentenced to be burned at the stake, Oldcastle replied that while physical harm could be done to his body, the same could never be true of his soul.

The king, on learning of recent developments, was devastated. A friend of Oldcastle in their youth, Henry initially awarded Oldcastle a stay of execution in the hope he would recant. Countering claims among the church that Oldcastle had done so, the plot thickened when a rebuttal of this was smuggled out of the Tower on Oldcastle's behalf and copies circulated around the city. Then, in an episode worthy of Mortimer himself, aided by his Lollard supporters, Oldcastle escaped from the Tower.

The scene was now set for open rebellion, yet what followed was baffling, even when compared to Mortimer's actions. In league with the same assistors who had plotted his escape, Oldcastle devised a plan to seize the king and his brothers during an epiphany play and replace the current governorship with some form of commonwealth, with himself to act as regent. On hearing this, Henry closed the gates of the city and announced a mini crusade against the Lollards. The resulting bloodlust was noteworthy, leading to scenes not seen since the Peasants' Revolt. Almost miraculously, Oldcastle, for the second time, managed to evade the king's clutches. Four years of evading recapture would follow with the former court favourite constantly in danger of falling into captivity. Then, one fateful night in November 1417 while hiding out in the Welsh backwater, a meeting with a local noble brought about his downfall. He was returned to the Tower and, being charged as both a heretic and traitor, condemned to death. In a scene unique in its cruelty, Oldcastle died by the noose over a burning pyre at St Giles' Fields, the same ironic setting of his failed uprising.

Oldcastle, as it turns out, was by no means alone in his views. Despite avoiding any personal implication in the rebellion of 1414, fellow Lollard Richard Wyche was questioned about Oldcastle's finances and subsequently imprisoned in the Fleet in 1419. Released a year later, by 1423 he held the first of a series of church positions, which he retained until stripped of his offices in 1440. Found guilty of heresy, Wyche followed Oldcastle to his death, being burnt at the stake at Tower Hill on 16 June 1440.

Away from the fires of heresy, another destined to both escape the Tower but also lose his life around this time was the enigmatic Sir John Mortimer. Seemingly no clear relation of the famous clan from the Welsh Marches – although it cannot be ruled out he was an illegitimate one, which would make sense of his lack of land – Mortimer had endured time in the Tower from around late 1418 onwards after being transferred there from Kenilworth Castle. The exact reasons for his imprisonment have never been fully established, despite being some form of treason. There is evidence that earlier that year while staying in St Albans he had made some questionable remarks about joining with the king of France and driving Henry V out of Normandy; however, there is no clear proof this was used against him at his trial. Interrupting Mortimer's stint in the Tower was a successful gaol break on 18 April 1422 that included fellow prisoners Thomas Payne, John Cobham, Sir John Brakemond, Thomas Seggiswyk and one Marcellinus who hailed from Genoa, all of whom were imprisoned on varied charges including being enemies of the state and heretics, notably for connections to Oldcastle. It has been suggested the breakout was spontaneous, which would certainly account for the high number of escapees; however, the facts behind have never been confirmed. Incidentally Seggiswyk managed to evade capture, the only one to do so. In keeping with normal practice, rewards were given to the informers and lieutenant of the Tower, William Yerd, was gaoled for a year as punishment for his failings.

Returned to the Tower, proceedings against Mortimer were intensified for his second trial. Amongst the charges levelled against him was that of being a known associate of Thomas Payne – himself a clerk and counsellor of Oldcastle – and together imagining the king's death. Further complicating the situation was his escape, along with Payne, other allies of Oldcastle and two French prisoners of war, and allegedly conspiring either to take the dauphin's side against Henry or infiltrating English-held castles in France. The case of Sir John Mortimer was further complicated by the knowledge that his trial delivered a rare verdict of not guilty. Deciding, however, Mortimer had been detained by special order of the king, he was returned to the Tower and five days later, on 20 May 1422, an indictment taken two years earlier before the court of the steward and marshal of the king's household was provided to the King's Bench; strangely this similarly was not acted on. Escaping a second time, Mortimer was again recaptured and taken before a joint session of both the Commons and the Lords on 26 February 1424, during which it was confirmed that three days earlier, while held in the Tower, he had succeeded in mounting an escape with the assistance of one William King, servant of the then keeper Robert Scot, before being re-apprehended and subsequently brought before parliament. Based on an account given in the *London Chronicle*, this was merely a subterfuge by Scot who had used King as a tool to incriminate Mortimer.

Whatever the truth, the endeavour was clearly successful, with Mortimer even going as far as to suggest that on his escape he would join the earl of March in raising an insurrection of some 40,000 men after which the main lords would be executed and the Yorkist Edmund Mortimer take the throne. Found guilty by the MPs and peers, the indictment was made official by the lord protector, Humphrey, Duke of Gloucester, and Mortimer was taken from the Tower to the gallows at

Tyburn to be hanged, drawn and quartered before his head was used to decorate a pike on London Bridge. Incidentally, it was that very same parliament, begun the previous October, that had passed an updating of the Statute of Treasons, issued in 1352, that anyone suspected of treason only to escape prison prior to their trial be automatically, or *ipso facto*, found to be guilty. Repelled at the next parliament, this law would only apply to Mortimer. The uniqueness of this was tackled in an essay by Edward Powell and used in the book, *Rulers and Ruled in Late Medieval England: Essays Presented to Gerald Harriss* which credibly concluded that the strange tale of this mysterious Sir John Mortimer was a clear trap against the Mortimers, themselves possible pretenders to the Crown.

Historical records recall that around this time a particular 'lady' was brought to the Tower, destined to go down in its history for all the wrong reasons. Lovingly nicknamed the 'Duke of Exeter's Daughter' in honour of the constable of the Tower, John Holland, Duke of Exeter, who oversaw 'her' return from the Continent in 1420, the very uttering of 'her' real name has epitomised the Tower's darkening reputation ever since. In reality, being not of human origin but metallic, this seemingly innocuous device – visually described as an open rectangular frame of oak measuring some 6 feet in length and raised approximately 3 feet on four legs with axles fixed to ropes – had the potential to rip prisoners limb from limb. In what must be considered an ultimate mark of gallows humour, a wedding to the Duke of Exeter's Daughter was no ordinary token of marital bliss. Throughout the next three centuries, even death itself often failed to rival the pain of being placed on the rack.

Away from the onset of new torture techniques and religious upheaval, the Tower had also been the setting for the planning of the Battle of Agincourt by secret council. With the most famous victory on French soil achieved, joining the victorious English on their return were a number of their French counterparts destined to follow in the footsteps of the courteous John II. Prisoners of war included Charles, Duke of Orléans; injured, and even briefly buried after the battle, he was restored to health in the White Tower. Like the Scottish prince, James, he would become an accomplished poet and was largely liked by his captors. Despite suffering homesickness, he was never tortured and lived in relative comfort until his eventual release in 1440.

The duke of Orléans' release was in part the work of Cardinal Henry Beaufort, who, in the inevitable vacuum of power following Henry V's premature death, quickly rose through the ranks to become England's chief magnate. Knowing his life was nearing an end, Henry V took the crucial step of appointing regents to guide his infant son, the most influential of which were his brothers John, Duke of Bedford and Humphrey, Duke of Gloucester. With Henry VI, at least in theory, not only inheriting the crown of England but also that of France following the death of Charles VI, Bedford was empowered with control of France with Gloucester as lord protector of England.

There is little doubt that the equal granting of powers was viewed as a prudent step by the successful Henry V to ensure that the power struggle during the reign of Richard II would never be repeated. Indeed, despite being the saplings of two separate Lancastrian branches – one descended of John of Gaunt and his first wife, Blanche of Lancaster; the other Gaunt's second wife, Constance of Castile – there is evidence the two worked together well. Besides the inevitable displeasure of the French towards their potential foreign overlord, question marks concerning Henry VI's strength of character soon became a mounting problem for the future of both realms, even without the added complication of the king's unpopularity among supporters of the dauphin, Charles VII. On Bedford's death in 1435, Humphrey's position as protector was also thrown into question. Still the most able candidate, problems at home ensued with the rise of the Beaufort family – descendants of Gaunt from his third marriage to Katherine Swynford, previously his mistress – whose leader was Cardinal Henry, at the time in possession of the See of Winchester. He was also chancellor of England.

Unlike the cordial relations between the first two lines of Gaunt's lineage, the rise of the questionable third line would be of profound importance to the events that would eventually follow. Loyal to the memory of his late brother, Henry V, Humphrey had become the more loveable in the eyes of England's people, most notably for his wishes to aid English wool producers and continue the war with France. As friction continued to mount, a skirmish was narrowly avoided when Beaufort armed the Tower against Humphrey and his local mob. When the duke of Orléans was finally released, Humphrey's disdain increased and relations further worsened with Humphrey's second marriage to commoner, Eleanor of Cobham. After having her horoscope cast and then proceeding to melt a wax figure of the young king in the fire, Humphrey's new wife found herself imprisoned in the Tower on charges of witchcraft before being banished, the upheaval losing Gloucester most of his influence. Soon afterwards, both himself and Beaufort were dead, leading to something of a vacuum in the power surrounding the throne.

Beaufort's successor was one William de la Pole, 1st Duke of Suffolk, the very man who would take responsibility for negotiating Henry VI's marriage to Margaret of Anjou in 1445. With the Tower menagerie once again echoing to the roars of a lion, a wedding gift to the king perhaps partially given with the intention of replacing those that had died in the reign of Henry V, Suffolk's meddling in political affairs soon culminated in further marriage, this time his son to his ward, the young Margaret Beaufort: the same girl who would one day contribute to the founding of the Tudor dynasty.

At around this time, another who would one day play a decisive role in the establishing of the Tudors was also forced to endure a brief period of imprisonment in the Tower. Renowned for his good looks and charm, Owen Tudor had been appointed clerk of the queen's wardrobe in the reign of Henry V either before or after first gracing the royal court of Katherine of Valois, daughter of the late French king, Charles VI and widow of Henry V. Despite possessing no great connection to royalty, it seems the French princess and queen dowager took something of a shine to the young man, not least when his bungled attempt at a pirouette during an evening of entertainment ended with his head resting on her lap. In a strange twist of fate, the accidental encounter would spark an ongoing love affair that would include at least three children and a possible clandestine wedding. Within a year of Gloucester's threat that any marriage without the permission of the council would have severe consequences, Katherine retired to Bermondsey Abbey before passing away in 1437. Now without the support of his royal lover, Tudor was imprisoned in Newgate after voluntarily withdrawing himself from the sanctuary of Westminster Abbey before spending much of 1438 in the Tower. Exactly what he had done to deserve this punishment remains unclear. Most likely it was an attempt by Gloucester to ensure control of the realm.

The king's marriage settled, England's fortunes on the Continent declined. While any complete conquest of France, even with the heroic Henry V on the throne, had always been somewhat unlikely, peace as the defeated party in war rarely came easily. Angered by England's losses in France, the bulk of the abuse was suffered by Suffolk who was sent to the Tower following a January parliament in 1450. Though the now 28-year-old Henry VI, with Margaret by his side, managed to spare his minister in exchange for a five-year banishment, Suffolk's luck soon ran out. After surviving a witch-hunt by an angry mob, his ship to Calais failed to reach its destination. According to the *Paston Letters* – a collection of correspondence written by the East Anglian family of the same name and often considered among the most important primary sources on the period – the unfortunate duke was executed at sea.

Popular rebellion against the monarchy would come back to haunt the royals in 1450 with the rising of Sussex rebel Jack Cade. Little is known of Cade's background. Most likely a soldier of the Hundred Years War, and, like Wat Tyler before him, of common stock, Cade took up the title Captain of Kent, as well as the Yorkist-pleasing alias, John Mortimer. By May 1450, Cade's preparations had extended to the local counties and the following month a force of at least 5,000 was preparing to march on the capital. So concerned were the powers that be on hearing of Cade's rising, especially the possibility of them being in league with the Yorkists, that steps were immediately put in place to neutralise the threat. When Cade's rebellion arrived in London, a dispatch led by brothers Sir Humphrey and William Stafford was ambushed. Donning one of the knight's clothing as his own, Cade attempted to press home his advantage that had been increased by the murder of the bishop of Salisbury, the king's personal confessor.

With Henry VI settled at Kenilworth and his treasurer and others standing poised behind the thick walls of the Tower, Cade took up residence in the White Hart Inn in Southwark before crossing the bridge north of the Thames, cutting the ropes to ensure no counter measures. After striking the London Stone and declaring himself lord mayor, he attempted to begin legal proceedings, a notable shift from the way matters had been conducted during the Peasants' Revolt. The hated lord high treasurer, James Fiennes, 1st Baron Saye and Sele was handed over by the Tower's governor and subsequently subjected to a shambolic trial and beheading along with his son-in-law. Proceedings that had begun with a clear aim, within the established legalities, gradually gave way to mob violence and drunkenness. With his failure to ensure the sympathy of the locals, whose city they were now destroying, Cade's lack of control effectively cemented his own fall. After suffering defeat in their amateurish battle on London Bridge, Cade initially agreed to retreat with the promise of pardons, which were later voided by the king on the grounds they had not been approved by parliament. On fleeing for Lewes, Cade saw conflict with the man who would later marry the murdered treasurer's son-in-law's widow after being located in a garden in Heathfield. He perished on the way back to London, escaping the need for trial. His cadaver, nevertheless, was quartered and beheaded, his remains displayed prominently to serve as a warning against future insurgency.

By 1453, the king's state of mind had deteriorated significantly. With the House of Lancaster becoming a laughing stock, the increasingly dominant parliament began to turn its eye to their rivals, the House of York. Leader of the Yorkists, Richard, 3rd Duke of York, was himself of royal stock, descended of Edward III's line through his fourth son, Edmund of Langley. Cementing York's position further was his excellent marriage, his wife being also a descendant of Edward III through his second son, Lionel of Antwerp. In the House of Commons the MP for Bristol suggested the increasingly powerful duke of York be made heir to the throne, a recommendation that resulted in the MP's imprisonment in the Tower. By October things had become more difficult when the queen's baby was born.

With the king's mental health showing little sign of improving, a regency council was created. Partially inspired by rumours he was in fact the new baby's father, the new head of the Beaufort clan, Edmund, 2nd Duke of Somerset was impeached. While Margaret managed to spare him, renewed threats of mob violence saw him flee to the Tower. With Somerset temporarily gone, Henry's deteriorating mindset allowed York the long-awaited opportunity to assume the full reins of government. The rise of York threatened to be disastrous for Margaret and worse fortune awaited her when in March 1454, York was made protector of the realm. Almost immediately, Somerset found himself back in the Tower; curiously, when arrested he was found inside the queen's own quarters. York's return to power might have gone on to have a dramatic effect on England's history had it not been for Henry VI's almost miraculous return to sanity on Christmas Day. With York's sudden reversal of fortune, coupled with the queen's efforts to free Somerset, the maligned duke returned in February 1455.

Unfortunately for Somerset, he might soon have wished it had never happened. Driven by either reckless planning or the voice of the queen, a rash summons by the duke and the queen in Henry's name resulted in a major skirmish near St Albans between the Lancastrian forces and those of the House of York. While Henry survived, Somerset and other key personnel were slain. As the annals of history would later record, the Wars of the Roses had officially begun.

Chapter 6

1455–1478: Yearning Yorkists, Conniving Cousins and Despicable Dukes

The previous skirmish, as we now know, would be of profound importance to the intrigue that would follow. Following in the footsteps of Somerset and the defeated Lancastrians, the next generation of ambitious and hot-headed lords, inspired chiefly by the queen, Margaret of Anjou, began to develop plans to oust the Yorkist faction who had regained the ascendancy upon York being officially made constable of England. While the king succeeded for a time in keeping the peace, highlighted in a feast in March 1458 that ended with a joust at the Tower, the Lancastrian-dominated royal council soon made moves to drive home their advantage.

Along with key allies the earls of Salisbury and Warwick, York was denounced as a traitor in parliament, leading to the trio's estates being confiscated. In retaliation, the Yorkists marched into Kent before advancing with a large force on London. The northerners arrived in the capital on 2 July, and were well received by the predominantly Yorkist citizens. So great was their support that, at the time, only the Tower remained in Lancastrian hands. Inspired perhaps by stories of Roger Mortimer's Marcher lords over a century earlier, Salisbury attempted to siege the Tower's outer walls with 2,000 men, leading to its governor Lord Scales firing back from the battlements with artillery that included Greek fire. The event would be of profound significance in the Tower's history, as it marked the first occasion its artillery was ever used on its own citizens. Scales' actions, undoubtedly inspired by the desire to preserve the safety of the several Lancastrian magnates taking refuge there, nonetheless aroused the Londoners' fury.

While the incendiary bombardment rained down, Salisbury set about battering the south curtain walls. Their best attempts to breach Edward I's defensive masterpiece, for now at least, proved fruitless, but unfortunately for the Lancastrians, up in Northamptonshire King Henry had fallen into enemy hands. Dismayed by the news, Scales surrendered on 19 July as Henry was brought to London. In retribution for the bombings, many members of the garrison were executed and Scales butchered as he attempted to flee the resulting carnage.

The ensuing stalemate culminated in something of a truce. York, as heir apparent, resumed centre stage with the king's young son, Prince Edward, apparently disinherited, much to the despair of the queen. While her husband rotted in captivity, Margaret and her key supporters busily gathered troops before mounting their escapes in order to take command of proceedings in the north. Hearing of the latest threat, York left London and marched north in early December 1460, attempting to raise more troops en route. On leaving Sandal Castle on 30 December, led either by rashness or taken in by deception, York's forces clashed with the royalists close to the city of Wakefield. A brutal skirmish saw York and his son Edmund decapitated, the duke's head, in scenes reminiscent of Simon Sudbury, set with a paper crown and spiked on the gates of York. Completing the humiliating defeat, Salisbury was also killed the next day; the Lancastrian lords avenged.

The two years that followed proved decisive, not only in terms of England's history but also that of the Tower. With three of the key Yorkists meeting their bloody ends, the political knife edge would see many other figures come to the fore to fill the voids left by those slain in Yorkshire. Though all the while the realm's wealthiest magnate, Richard Neville, 16th Earl of Warwick, maintained the Tower, the Yorkists' new head, Prince Edward caused havoc in the Welsh Marches. Now a surprise heir to the throne following the premature deaths of his father and elder brother, recent progress was consolidated with a victory over the army of Jasper Tudor at Mortimer's Cross in February 1461. As Margaret and a large army moved south, Warwick made use of the Tower artillery and engaged the enemy at St Albans. Despite the impressive weaponry at their disposal, the Yorkists were once again caught off guard. On the back of a surprise Lancastrian victory, Henry VI, who contemporary sources suggest was present in a tent – or under a tree – and apparently singing away merrily, was reunited with Margaret and his son.

If any realistic opportunity had existed for Margaret to drive home her advantage, the desertion of many of her allies from north of the border made things increasingly difficult. At the same time, the defeated Warwick joined with Edward and marched on the capital, securing the Tower in late February. On 4 March Edward formally claimed the Crown with the backing of the majority of Londoners, after which he defeated the Lancastrians at Towton, with Henry VI and Margaret fleeing beyond Hadrian's Wall. On his return to the refurbished royal apartments of the Tower in late June, Edward created thirty-two new Knights of the Bath. He was crowned king on 28 June and attempted to bring peace to the kingdom with the pardoning of the latest Somerset, Henry 3rd duke and freeing the duke's younger brother, Edmund, from the Tower.

There has been some suggestion that Edward and Somerset regularly shared a bed at the Tower. Whether true or not, this probably offers more to the phrase concerning the choosing of one's bedfellows as opposed to anything homosexual. Besides a certain degree of uncertainty about the strength of their surprising newfound friendship, there is no evidence to suggest notorious womaniser Edward possessed any such tendencies. He was, however, seemingly oblivious that all the while Somerset persisted with plans to restore the Lancastrians to the throne. Inevitably, this would be something Somerset would soon come to regret. Learning of the deceit, Edward marched from London in numbers, bringing the north to submission and forcing Somerset to flee to Scotland. While the castles of Alnwick and Dunstanburgh surrendered, Bamburgh fought on, only to be subdued by the end of 1464 with the help of the mighty guns brought north from the Tower's arsenal.

Among the newcomers at the Tower around this time was the northern rebel, Sir Humphrey Neville. A member of the Lancastrian branch of the prominent Neville family, prior to the Battle of Towton the Lancastrians had rarely swayed in their allegiance beyond the legitimate monarch. With their cause dented by Edward's rise, Humphrey went into exile in Scotland before returning in June 1461 in Durham where he was captured and brought to the Tower. Avoiding death, he was sentenced to life in prison, only to escape two years later. Exactly how he did so is unclear. Once free, he returned to Northumberland, eventually losing his head in York.

Worse fortune befell Lord Aubrey de Vere. Son of John de Vere, 12th Earl of Oxford, Aubrey was the first of five executed on Tower Hill after being found guilty of high treason. Beheaded on 20 February 1462, he was followed by John Montgomery, Sir William Tyrell and Sir Thomas Tuddenham three days later for their roles in a Lancastrian conspiracy to murder the new king. Completing the sequence, three days after that, John de Vere was hanged, drawn and quartered.

After three years of keeping a low profile, 1465 finally saw the dethroned Henry VI return to London. Being received first by Warwick at Islington, the former king was taken to the Tower, marking the start of a reacquaintance with the building that would last five long years. While the old king floundered in the Wakefield Tower, inside the adjacent building, his replacement, Edward IV, enjoyed the perks of kingship by using the Tower as a place to feast and fornicate. During this period the royal apartments were further improved and divided into three great chambers in which he would take care of public and private business, as well as his personal quarters.

Although the people of England had enjoyed the respite from civil war, behind the scenes, discontent spread following Edward's shock marriage to the widowed commoner, Elizabeth Wydville. Not for the first time in the history of England, the destiny of the nation was about to change once more. After staying at the Tower prior to her coronation for which Edward created a further fifty Knights of the Bath – including no less than two of his new queen's brothers – the perceived arrogance of Elizabeth and her ambitious relatives exhausted the patience of England's wealthiest magnate Warwick, a move that would have more than a passing influence on his being dubbed 'the Kingmaker'.

In June 1468, such seeds of dissent offered signs of growth when a cobbler named John Cornelius was arrested as he sought to catch a ship to France. In his possession were a series of letters between Margaret of Anjou and some of her key Lancastrian sympathisers, discovery of which saw Cornelius acquainted with the White Tower's torture chamber. As an ironic punishment, the soles of his feet were toasted with flaming torches, quite possibly by use of hot boots. On revealing the identities of the men in question, including one John Hawkins – a servant of Edward IV's trusted diplomat, but former Lancastrian, Lord Wenlock – they in turn were brought to the Tower. While Cornelius died in the White Tower under extreme torture, Hawkins survived after revealing more names. Among them, another of the questioned parties, Sir Thomas Cook, saw his belongings pillaged by the Wydvilles, news of which succeeded only in further dampening the family's popularity. In what can perhaps be seen as a stark insight into the present corruption, Cook would never enjoy the return of his belongings, despite his later release and would later die in poverty.

Two important figures, as previously mentioned, to have fallen earlier in the war had been the previous earl of Oxford and his eldest son, both of whom had ended their lives in the Tower prior to their grisly executions. Still seething from their demise was the earl's younger son and successor, John de Vere, now 13th earl of Oxford. Despite openly accepting Edward's right to rule – if for no other reason than to legally inherit his father's estates and ensure the release of his mother – privately he remained unequivocally Lancastrian. In 1468, joined by a new wave of Henrician sympathisers, the Tower again echoed with the groans of tortured prisoners. Included in their number were John Poynings and Richard Alford, both of whom endured Edward IV's wrath for allegedly contacting the new duke of Somerset, Edmund Beaufort, himself a former prisoner, whose loyalty lay strictly with Margaret of Anjou. Like many before them, Poynings and Alford were both confined in the White Tower's darkest spots and forced to endure the agonies of its instruments of torture before meeting their deaths on Tower Hill. Joining them there was one Richard Steeres, one of the Tower's most unique prisoners in the sense he would be remembered by history not just for mirroring the actions of Cornelius in attempting to smuggle letters to the queen's exiled court, but also for his contributions to the game of tennis. Soon after their executions, the earl of Oxford himself took their place in the Tower.

Unlike his fellow Lancastrians, Oxford's incarceration lasted only a few weeks – weeks that must have felt like years shackled in heavy chains inside his dark cell. Exactly what transpired during that time remains unclear, other than a short time after two Lancastrian heavyweights, Sir Thomas Hungerford – son of Robert, Lord Hungerford – and Henry Courtenay, were both imprisoned as a result of their apparent involvement in the Cornelius Plot and executed on charges of treason. Though Oxford was pardoned, less than three months later he was once again engaged in conspiracy against the king. Better fortune would befall renowned novelist Sir Thomas Malory, who got off with a pardon.

Still angered by the king's marrying Elizabeth Wydville, Warwick's new distaste for Edward set the scene for one of the most bizarre events to occur in England's long history. Having played such a prominent role in Edward's ascension, Warwick's frustrations with the Wydvilles soon reached breaking point, inspiring him to enter secret communication with Margaret of Anjou. Warwick's defection would prove costly for Edward. Not only was he suddenly deprived of the richest man in the kingdom's funds and military backing, but when a marriage was agreed for Henry VI's son to marry Warwick's daughter, a new dynasty was close to being founded.

Worse news was to come when Warwick enticed Edward's own brother, George, Duke of Clarence, to join him in France. Following a brief period of imprisonment at Middleham Castle at Warwick's hands, Edward denounced Warwick and Clarence traitors, leading to them absconding to France to seek refuge at the court of Louis XI. While Edward left the Tower to put down further rebellion in the north, Warwick and a large force arrived in Devon. With Warwick closing in on the Tower and Warwick's brother, John Neville, Marquess of Montagu, abandoning Edward to defect to the Lancastrians' side in the north, Edward found himself unexpectedly outnumbered. Hunted down, and aided only by his younger brother Richard, Duke of Gloucester, the pair fled to Norfolk and subsequently Flanders.

After a ten-year absence, Henry VI, still a prisoner in the Wakefield Tower, was once again king of England.

One of the first to suffer as a result of the recent changes was the Lord High Treasurer and Lord High Constable, John Tiptoft, 1st Earl of Worcester. Famed by his epithet, 'The Butcher of England', Edward IV had previously honoured Tiptoft's loyalty with a number of appointments, including being made a Knight of the Garter, deputy of Ireland and constable of the Tower for life. Ironically it was such titles that would lead to his downfall. Unable to join Edward and Gloucester in escaping to the Low Countries, Tiptoft was captured by the Lancastrians and left little option but to hand the Tower over peacefully to Warwick. In retribution for his alleged cruel treatment of Lancastrian prisoners of war, the earl of Oxford oversaw the constable's execution on 18 October 1470. His beheading was noteworthy for his request of the axe man to strike his head three times: one each for the Father, Son and Holy Spirit.

Elizabeth Wydville had remained all this time in the Tower, patiently awaiting the birth of her third child – her first with Edward. With news of Edward's departure coming just a short time after learning of Warwick's arrival, the heavily pregnant queen fell into despair and fled to the sanctuary of Westminster Abbey. Had Warwick arrived a day earlier, it is possible their paths may well have crossed. With the Tower once again in Lancastrian hands, Henry VI, though choosing to remain in the same building, was officially liberated. On learning of the improvement in his fortunes, the meek king was rehoused in the apartments recently vacated by Elizabeth before taking up residence in the palace of the bishop of London where he reigned more or less as Warwick's puppet.

Inevitably, such a coup was never destined to pass smoothly. Disillusioned with the realities of his lack of potential for personal progression, Clarence made peace with his exiled brothers and defected back to his native Yorkists. After spending over a year in the Low Countries amassing an invasion force and plotting his eventual return, the exiled king sailed with thirty-six ships bearing some 1,000 Yorkists to be joined by Clarence's own substantial force in the Midlands. Seeing Henry VI's state of mind was showing no signs of improving and learning of Edward's return, Warwick's brother, the archbishop, defected in April and the Tower once again returned to Yorkist hands. Within days, Henry, again a deposed king, returned to the Wakefield Tower as a prisoner. Joining him in the nearby royal apartments would be the third-time mother, Elizabeth.

An inauspicious end it would be for the man dubbed 'the Kingmaker'. With Henry's reign crumbling a second time, Warwick's end was nigh. As Edward headed north, the two foes engaged in conflict at Barnet in heavy fog. While Warwick was despatched by the sword, unseasonal winds had forced Margaret of Anjou to delay her journey from France. Hearing of her later arrival, Edward acted fast and when their armies met at Tewkesbury, all remaining business was settled. Key casualties included

Edward of Westminster, heir to the throne, as well as Edmund Beaufort, 4th Duke of Somerset, and many other prominent Lancastrians. Grief-stricken by the loss of her son, Margaret of Anjou was taken south to join her husband at the Tower.

Despite being in the same castle as Henry, the pair were never destined to meet again. Attempts by Warwick's nephew, Thomas Neville, to batter the Tower's sturdy walls may have proved unavailing, thanks in part to the actions of Lord Rivers in his command of the defences. Yet, for Edward it served as the same timely reminder experienced by Henry II, Richard I, Roger Mortimer and Henry IV that so long as an alternative king lived, the threat of insurrection would always be upon him.

Uncertainty about how Henry VI met his end is another of those sorry tales that has contributed in no small part to the Tower's ever-darkening reputation. Be it the work of evil deeds or natural causes, the chroniclers, though relatively consistent in their belief that Henry was murdered, are unsure of how and when. If the darker accounts are true, Henry's end was the brainchild of the returning king, and carried out by a man who would soon leave his own ignominious mark on the Tower's history. As Edward returned from Tewkesbury, his youngest brother, Richard, Duke of Gloucester, was ordered to proceed to London and secure the Tower. Taking control from Rivers and Elizabeth, preparations were made for the return of the king himself in time for the Feast of the Ascension on 21 May. In the solitude of his lodgings in the Wakefield Tower that included a niche his namesake Henry III had once used as a royal chapel, the pious Henry VI, tradition has long had it, was put to death by Gloucester sometime around midnight. If the Monk of Croyland was somewhat ambiguous in his assertion, 'the king was found lifeless at the Tower,' his later declaration that he was 'strykked with a dagger in the hands of the Duke of Gloucester' leaves far less room for doubt. For others the manner was less clear. The historian David Hume on addressing the matter admitted his ignorance. Or as was put by the anonymously written contemporary chronicle *Historie of the Arrival of Edward IV* – a copy of which was still present in the library of the recorder of London William Fleetwood a century later – Henry met his end at the hands of 'pure displeasure and melancholy'.

Unsurprisingly, the fate of the king caused quite a stir. And in certain cases – profit. As late as the Reformation, the warden of Caversham is noted as having shown interested visitors the bloody dagger Gloucester had used, a stark contradiction to the assertion by Polydore Vergil that Richard had used a sword. Traditional reports of the time may well have started with the chronicle of Dr Warksworth, whose writings recorded that it had happened 'on a Tuesday night between 11 and 12'. Intriguingly on taking the throne twelve years later, Richard had the late king's remains transferred to the royal chapel at Windsor. Be it a common courtesy for a fellow royal or an act of guilt, the truth may never be known.

Gentle in kingship and in life, one way or another the former king's life ended. Later tests have confirmed Henry's skull was crushed: confirmation, it seems, that foul play was afoot. Evidence available suggests it was likely his death was intended to have been relatively clean, save the accusations that would follow. Eyewitness reports claimed when on display the dead king's head would bleed anew, a sign of either Henry's saintly goodness or Richard's guilt. Irrespective of the exact truth, in the late king's honour the Ceremony of Lilies and Roses continues to be held in the Oratory of the Wakefield Tower on 21 May every year, represented by figures from Eton and Kings College, Cambridge – both of which he founded – as well as key dignitaries, including the resident governor and chaplain of the Tower. Of special importance to the ceremony is the reading of a prayer that Henry wrote and the laying of flowers where his body was apparently discovered.

For Margaret, news of her husband's death caused fresh despair. In the weeks to come, Edward ordered her release; eventually she returned to France, never to again trouble the history books. Thomas Neville, whose attempts to take the Tower had seen him imprisoned there, was later executed, as well as the mayor of Canterbury, Nicholas Faunt. Edward IV's brother-in-law, Henry Holland, 3rd Duke of Exeter, fared only slightly better. After recovering at Westminster Abbey from wounds suffered at Barnet, he was relocated to the Tower and placed under close confinement.

While Henry VI's exact cause of death may never be known, an even stranger story concerns one of his pretenders. Despite finding himself back in temporary favour after assisting his brother in retaking the throne, living in a nation where rebellion was never far away, the duke of Clarence became the chief focus of Edward's many enemies. Never one to enjoy solid relations with his siblings, Clarence had become increasingly frustrated by the relatively high number of honours bestowed on younger brother Richard, including winning the hand of Westminster's widow, Anne, the youngest daughter of Warwick. Following the victory at Tewkesbury, Anne joined her mother at the Tower before marrying Richard – a move Clarence feared would affect his own inheritance. After a string of accusations against a number of people on interrupting a council meeting, including the allegation that Edward was a warlock, he was summoned to Westminster in June 1477 where he was charged with treachery and conspiracy and taken to the Tower.

What happened next would prove a decisive moment in England's history – not least that of the House of York. After more than six months in the Bowyer Tower, an unforgiving parliament found Clarence guilty of a rare, extreme form of treason, and sentenced him to death by act of attainder. Due to his status, and perhaps a surviving element of brotherly love, he was permitted to choose his own form of death. Exactly what happened next remains unknown. Only that the duke was found slumped against 'a pipe of malmsey wine'. Whether the common perception that, perhaps an indication of his bravado or deteriorating state of mind, he was drowned in it is true or he simply succumbed to dysentery, or alcohol poisoning from the natural fumes of the butt is unclear. Others have suggested the ruse was a clever cover for his murder, which may fit well with later discoveries that the Bowyer Tower can be entered by narrow passages – including the presence of a hidden stairway beneath the floor that has long been sealed – yet it can also be argued as unnecessary bearing in mind parliament had sentenced him to death. His enemies at court inevitably blamed Richard. Unlike the late Henry VI and the princes in years to come, there is no evidence to connect him here.

Whatever the truth, parliament accepted Clarence's death as a completion of his execution. With it ended the life of one of England's most unique characters and undoubtedly the strangest execution to have ever taken place in the Tower's history.

Chapter 7

1475–1485: Imprisoned Princes, Evil Uncles and Persistent Plotters

John Goose became the third lollard connected to the Tower to be put to death for his faith. Following in the footsteps of Oldcastle and Wyche, Goose was first arrested around 1463 and released on recanting his Lollardism before subsequently recanting his recantation. Thereafter, arrested for the final time, a London sheriff, Robert Billesdon, took the condemned man to his home in an attempt to sway him back to Catholicism. Failing to convince Goose to convert, the visitor requested some food, saying, 'I eat now a good and competent dinner, for I shall pass a little sharp shower or I go to supper,' a reference to his imminent death. On being well fed by the charitable sheriff, Goose confirmed he was ready to meet his maker. He was put to death at the stake on Tower Hill – sources vary 1473–75. Five years would pass until the area would see another execution, with four church robbers recorded as having endured the noose in 1480.

The end of the House of Lancaster in such explosive, yet mysterious circumstances, though clearly intended by Edward IV as a means to secure long-term stability for the House of York, actually proved not only the first step towards their impending destruction, but also a cautionary tale that would be heeded in no uncertain terms by the monarchs destined to follow in their footsteps. Clarence's death, whether an official execution or not, contributed in no small part to the chaos that followed. The duchess of York, Cicely, widow of the late Richard, 3rd Duke of York but also mother of the king and Clarence had pleaded in vain with Edward for her son's life. The duke of Gloucester, the future Richard III, was also rumoured to have been unimpressed with Edward's obstinate stance. Nevertheless, Richard, for the time being, remained ever loyal.

Like many kings who had thrived in conflict, Edward's later years on the throne saw him descend into the shadow of the man he had once been.

Famed at his prime for his valour and resilience, his end was surprisingly sudden. After a day's boating on the Thames, he became bedridden and proceeded to dictate his last will. The man who had led the Yorkists to victory on two separate occasions, in doing so joining William the Conqueror in the select group of England's rulers who never once lost a battle, decreed that the throne would pass to his 12-year-old son and heir, henceforth Edward V. By choosing a replacement that honoured royal protocol, England would once again fall into the hands of a minor.

The boy's destiny, like his brother's, would be shrouded in mystery. Being far too young to rule of his own accord, the newly ascended Edward V needed a protector. And who better than a man who had shown his father such loyalty and devotion? The man earmarked was Gloucester, the only suitable candidate. A staunch supporter of Edward and an accomplished military leader and administrator, Richard had benefited greatly from the fallout of the Rose wars, marrying the widow of Margaret of Anjou's son – Anne, the youngest daughter of Warwick – thus uniting the marcher estates of Gloucester with the Neville properties of the Midlands and North. Partly because of this, for the previous twelve years Richard had been Edward's lieutenant of the north, effectively king of the north.

Taking away the benefit of hindsight, there seems little evidence the late king's actions were in any way reckless at this point. Gloucester's role to this time, with the possible exception of the deaths of Henry VI and Clarence – which were unlikely to have been his decisions – had been largely exemplary and many records of history are equivocal on many of the matters that follow. While Shakespeare and Tudor propaganda invariably depict the man as evil, the Ricardian apologists have long argued something far different. In such ways, we now face a decision. Which side is to be believed?

As usual, the answer is far from straightforward and probably lies somewhere between the two. Following the king's death, Edward's former boon companion – and now Gloucester's key ally – Lord William Hastings wrote to inform him of the tragic news while also persuading the Wydvilles to limit the retinue earmarked to escort the new Edward V to London. On hearing of his brother's death, Richard hastened south with at least 300 men and on reaching Northampton was joined by his key ally Henry Stafford, 2nd Duke of Buckingham, who arrived with a similar number. Liaising with Buckingham, it was decided their first objective would be to intercept the recently proclaimed king. Exactly why Gloucester considered this necessary is subject to debate and depends on his motives at that point. Even if he had no clear desire to take the throne, it would arguably have been an expected move from the regent to ensure the young man avoided capture.

Prior to that time, the young king had been at Ludlow with a strong Wydville faction, most notably his uncle Anthony Wydville, 2nd Earl Rivers. Back in the capital, meanwhile, the Wydvilles had wasted little time in preparing the young king's coronation for 4 May. In the Tower, Rivers had been replaced as constable by his nephew Thomas Grey, a largely irrelevant switch in the grander scheme of things besides freeing up Rivers for more important tasks and ensuring the Tower's guardianship was kept in the family. With the new king lodged at Stony Stratford, Thomas Grey's brother Richard returned to Northampton to meet Gloucester. Joined by Buckingham and Rivers, the evening passed merrily with eating and drinking till the late hours. By dawn, however, the mood had changed, with Rivers and Grey arrested by Gloucester on charges of political scheming. At the same time, in what Richard's critics have argued was a demonstration of precise planning, the young king was collected from Stony Stratford.

The king's mother, Elizabeth Wydville, on hearing of the developments was understandably horrified. Fearing a Richard-led insurrection was imminent she put her trust in historical precedent and took sanctuary in the cloisters of Westminster Abbey that had served her so well some thirteen years earlier. Joining her was her second royal son, Richard of Shrewsbury, now elevated to duke of York following his father's death. Gloucester, meanwhile, wasted little time ousting the remaining Wydville advisors from government, beginning with the transfer of Richard Grey and Rivers to his Yorkist castles. While Edward V contested the charges against his kinsmen and begged his uncle to reconsider, Richard's progress south continued. Securing the Tower from Grey's brother, his own charges marched on London, arriving on the projected day of Edward V's, now aborted, coronation. On 10 May, a council meeting at the palace of the bishop of London confirmed the new king would take up residence in the Tower's royal lodgings, following which bills were soon issued in his name.

With things in the capital progressing well, Richard set up his HQ at Bishopsgate, where his party included John Howard, later duke of Norfolk; Stafford, Duke of Buckingham; Sir William Catesby, Sir Richard Ratcliffe and Francis, 1st Viscount Lovell. Fellow loyal ally, Lord Hastings, now master of the Royal Mint and lord chamberlain, had continued with the assistance of the council to firm up plans for Edward V's coronation, which had been officially delayed until 24 June. On 10 June Richard wrote personally to the civic council of York, primarily to warn them against the manipulations of the Wydvilles, and set up a meeting at the Tower three days later. What started off well, after a brief adjournment, then became far more aggressive. Hastings, rather strangely considering his recent loyalty, was charged with treason against the protector. Accompanying the claim was the even more surprising suggestion that Elizabeth Wydville and Elizabeth Shore-related sorcery had caused the withering of his arm. Richard's soldiers quickly surrounded the defenceless Hastings. While charges were also brought against Lord Stanley, Bishop Morton and Archbishop Rotherham of York, all of whom were placed in separate cells throughout the Tower, Hastings was dragged out of the White Tower and on to Tower Green where workmen had left a long beam. In an almost unprecedented move, Richard had him beheaded on the spot. With this, Hastings became the first person to be beheaded within the walls of the Tower.

Whatever change had come over Richard during the course of that meeting, it is clear that in the weeks since his brother's death his character had become far detached from the loyal ally seen in the previous wars. Sources from the time, notably a fragment discovered at the College of Arms in 1980, Polydore Vergil and accusations by Richard himself, imply a counter-coup against Richard; however, Croyland in particular was quick to distance Hastings from any involvement in that. Whether Hastings was guilty of any secret conspiracy, we may never know. Far more likely is the suggestion that it was Hastings' clear loyalty to Richard's brother and, *de facto*, to the new king that forced Richard to strike.

While Morton was later carried off to Wales, Elizabeth Shore, once mistress of the king and thereafter of Hastings, was incarcerated in the

Tower and forced to do public penance for her adultery. Three days after the fateful council meeting, a further meeting took place in the White Tower, the chief topic of discussion, the second son of Edward IV. As the new king was safely secured in the royal apartments in the south wall of the inner ward, his younger brother remained in nearby Westminster with his mother. Accompanied by an armed body, Suffolk and the archbishop of Canterbury, Thomas Bourchier, arrived at the abbot's house, attempting to convince Elizabeth that the new king needed a playmate. Tearfully, Elizabeth relented, perhaps accepting that she had little option.

Leaving Westminster, Bourchier and Suffolk escorted the duke of York to the Tower by boat, passing through what is now Traitors' Gate. On the same day, Gloucester took up residence within the walls. Setting up his base in the recently vacated royal apartments as the boys moved into the nearby Garden Tower, Richard's next act is difficult to defend. Issuing the only proclamation of his reign, ratified by the act of parliament *Titulus Regius* a year later, on 22 June, the new assertion confirmed the apparent illegitimacy of the boys. Complementing the dubious claim – apparently alluded to by Clarence years earlier – that a marriage agreement between Edward and one Lady Eleanor Butler existed some years before Elizabeth Wydville, thus rendering the marriage null and void, allegations were also made concerning the legitimacy of Edward IV and Clarence, bringing into question the honour of Cicely. With the act passed, Richard now had a clear path to the throne. His assumption was made formal on 25 June. A day later, two days after the second aborted coronation of Edward V, Gloucester was proclaimed Richard III of England.

Things now moved forward with great speed. Whereas the coronation of Edward V had been constantly delayed, Richard's was all set for 6 July. In keeping with the usual tradition, he spent the pre-coronation period at the Tower, ironically within metres of his young nephews whose reputations he had besmirched. Rotherham was released, along with Morton and Stanley, though preparations were put in place to ensure no trouble would arise on the day. The event itself was recorded for its magnificence, albeit one that Richard might have found nerve-wracking. The feared uprising having not come to pass, he rode north, leaving his capital and the boys he had disinherited.

Sometime in the days after Richard's coronation and prior to the end of July, a plot was devised to gain access to the princes by a body of men apparently in league with potential claimant Henry Tudor. According to the historian John Stow, their plan was to start a series of fires in London by way of a diversion and to liberate the two boys. At some point Richard seems to have learned of their scheme, leading to their trial at Westminster. According to Stow, the guilty party included: John Smith, Groom of King Edward's Stirrup; Stephen Ireland, Wardrober of the Tower; Robert Ruffe, sergeant of London and William Davey, pardoner of Hounslow. Found guilty of treason, all of them were executed on Tower Hill on 26 February 1484.

Prior to their deaths an even darker conspiracy is believed to have unfolded, the full details of which have never been unanimously agreed. Helped in no small part by conflicting reports as to what happened, the event has become famed as arguably the darkest in the Tower's history. Besmirched, disinherited, dethroned, the young sons of Edward IV, initially destined for lives of royalty, instead endured a far different journey. While their uncle rode north with his queen, the young boys were confined within the walls that had previously kept their family safe. From mid-June onwards, confirmed sightings of the princes became fewer. Writing in the Great Chronicle, the chronicler affirmed after York's arrival that they were sighted playing with arrows in the constable's garden. Writing his own work around the same time, the visiting Italian monk Dominic Mancini – whose writings were undiscovered until 1934 – confirmed the princes had been deprived of their servants, withdrawn to the inner apartments and seen less and less. This may indicate they had been moved to the White Tower, but there is no way to confirm this. The London Chronicler Robert Fabyan also weighed in on the matter, contesting they may have been subjected to closer confinement, without elaborating where that could have been.

Against the background of such varying accounts, it is not surprising that there is little or no hard evidence about what happened next. The only consistent conclusion among the chroniclers is a shocking one: that the boys were murdered. Mancini, the anonymously written Croyland Chronicle and Polydore Vergil all attest to the boys' fate, but without offering any substantive proof. Mancini is known to have left England within two weeks of Richard's coronation and lends suggestion to the possibility that the princes were already dead at that time, writing that they had already 'ceased to appear altogether.' While there is actually little doubt the princes were still alive at that point, sadly it seems unlikely that they remained so for much longer.

That Richard departed the Tower and the capital after his coronation can be affirmed by various sources from the time. Leaving London on 20 July, authority of the Tower, and the surrounding city, fell on the shoulders of Buckingham, who, one way or another, was destined to be a key player in the events that would soon unfold. With Buckingham installed as lord high constable of England, lieutenantship of the Tower was given to Lord Howard with Sir Robert Brackenbury named as constable – the man ultimately responsible for the princes. Impressive though both Fabyan and the Croyland chronicler are for their commentaries on events taking place at the time, the best source on the matter is almost certainly Sir Thomas More, whose blunt account must rank as the most detailed. Though scathed by future apologists that Richard was a victim of Tudor propaganda, which certainly did occur in the Tudor era, More's attention to detail is striking. Aided by well-placed informants from the Tower, More's overview includes mention that the two boys were both 'shut up, and all others removed from them, only one called Black Will or Will Slaughter except, set to serve them and see them sure … but with that young babe his brother lingered in thought and heaviness and wretchedness.'

That Will Slaughter was indeed gaoler to the princes can be affirmed from other sources. More also contends the princes' attendants soon stood at four, one of whom was named Miles Forrest, apparently a known murderer and almost certainly the same man who had served Richard as keeper of the wardrobe at Barnard Castle. Exactly who was ultimately responsible and when any murder took place is difficult to confirm. The chronicler Philippe de Commines wrote that it was Buckingham who 'caused the death of the two children,' a view echoed by the fragment discovered among the College of Arms that suggests the princes were murdered 'on the vise' of Buckingham. A third manuscript, this kept in the Ashmolean in Oxford, refers to 'the prompting of the Duke of Buckingham,' while Jean Molinet reported Buckingham's presence at the

Tower on the day of the murder in late July. This, however, contradicts the facts reported in Croyland that the princes were still alive in September.

While Buckingham's involvement cannot be ruled out – as constable of England the Tower was under his jurisdiction – the evidence available suggests he was unlikely to have been directly responsible. Interestingly, Richard and Buckingham later fell out, Buckingham rebelling against the king, yet no accusation against the duke in the disappearance is made by Richard. If More is correct, Buckingham even later spoke in confidence to Morton, 'I never agreed or condescended to it.'

There is conjecture here that at some time in August – at which point Richard was in the Midlands – the king sent his servant, John Green, to the Tower, to deliver a message to Brackenbury. On finding him at prayer in the Chapel of St John in the White Tower, the constable was informed of Richard's desire to have the princes dispensed with. There is also suggestion here Brackenbury responded negatively, at which point Green had no choice but to inform Richard. With Brackenbury an unwilling conspirator, Richard's attention turned to Sir James Tyrell. Like many of Richard's closest allies, Tyrell was a devout Yorkist who had earned his master's trust as a result of his valour on the battlefield of Tewkesbury in addition to successfully snaring the dowager, countess of Warwick, Richard's own mother-in-law and widow of Warwick. It cannot be ruled out Tyrell was a descendant of his namesake of centuries earlier, the man suspected of murdering one of the Tower's key contributors William Rufus in 1100, but this is also unproven.

If More's account is to be considered accurate, after conscripting a further two men, Forrest and John Dighton, Tyrell led the trio to London in the guise of buying cloth and picking up robes for the forthcoming investiture of Richard's son as Prince of Wales before descending on the Tower. According to More, Tyrell was much up for the task, a view refuted by Vergil who, nevertheless, confirmed Tyrell as the guilty man. By late August/early September – More suggests as early as mid-August, which contradicts Croyland – inspired by a letter signed by the king in Tyrell's possession, Brackenbury was persuaded to part with the keys to the Tower for at least one night. It has been suggested that the guards, including Black Will, had been either removed or distracted. If More is correct, Dighton and Forrest smothered the princes in their beds.

Whether the young boys were smothered, slaughtered, poisoned, stabbed, drowned Clarence-style in malmsey, walled up in a secret chamber and there left to starve, placed in a wooden chest or their lives ended by other means, as many other accounts suggested, one thing that can be proven is that from September onwards they vanish from history. While much of the accusation has landed at the door of Richard, suggestion concerning Buckingham or even Margaret Beaufort, mother of Henry VII, cannot be ruled out entirely. With Buckingham leading a revolt and Henry Tudor poised across the Channel in Brittany, both had much to gain from the princes' deaths. Whether the 'old manuscript' Ricardian apologist Sir George Buck claimed offered evidence of Beaufort's role in the poisoning of the princes ever existed is another suggestion lost in the sea of rumours. Besides the testimonies of the majority of the chroniclers, further evidence against Richard can perhaps be seen in the knowledge that the very month he took the throne, Lord John Howard was invested duke of Norfolk, while Lord William Berkeley inherited the earldom of Nottingham. As both titles had belonged to the younger prince, Richard of Shrewsbury, the promotion of Richard's close followers confirmed all previous titles concerning the princes were then forfeit. For the rest of the lives of the key players, no proof of their whereabouts came to light.

The mystery would endure until 1674.

Even in the context of the Tower's already bloody history, the slaughter of innocent children was something new. So great was the crime that about a century later the once aptly dubbed Garden Tower had been renamed the Bloody Tower – a legacy that owes its origin to William Shakespeare in honour of the widespread belief that it was within those walls the princes had been smothered. Of arguably greater consequence for Richard himself was perception of the king in the eyes of his subjects. While he may have been successful in disposing of his nearest rivals, the reaction to the deed was unwelcome. Dissent against the 'child murderer' inevitably saw uprising from chief opponents, including, most intriguingly, Buckingham, previously his most important ally and according to some chroniclers far from blameless in the spilling of innocent blood. Plagued by internal strife, the Yorkists' loss would soon become Lancastrian gain; only now concerning a different line. And what in time would breathe life to a new rose. A Tudor one.

Back in 1483, the man who would later be known as Henry VII was still a long way from sitting on William the Conqueror's throne. A distant part of the all but disappeared Lancastrian line, Henry Tudor was the only son of Margaret Beaufort, and thus descended from the dubious line of Edward III through John of Gaunt and Katherine Swynford: the mistress Gaunt would eventually marry. On his father's side, the connection was equally distant as Edmund Tudor, Earl of Richmond, was half-brother of Henry VI on his mother's side as opposed to Henry V's. As a son of Owen Tudor and Catherine de Valois, there was some royal French blood too; however, it is unclear if Owen and Catherine were ever married.

Like many of his family, Henry Tudor had been born within the walls of Pembroke Castle in south-west Wales. Having been too young to remember his uncle, Henry VI's, first reign, his only taste of court life had come in the brief Lancastrian revival of 1470, during which the ever-challenged king apparently foresaw the young Henry's destiny. Following the Lancastrian defeat at Tewkesbury, Jasper fled to Brittany, taking his teenage nephew with him. With Edward of Westminster cut down in battle and Henry VI soon to follow, Henry Tudor was now the Lancastrians' last hope, remote though it may have seemed back then. Exactly what knowledge the future Henry VII had of Buckingham's rebellion is unclear. While Buckingham was doomed to failure and subsequently beheaded in Salisbury, Henry's own path to England had been delayed by storms. After his eventual arrival, he had been lucky to make it back to Brittany safely.

Henry's fortunate escape back to France may have been a significant moment of destiny, yet for another Henry caught up in Buckingham's rash rebellion, the outcome would prove far more complicated. Born in Kent, Henry Wyatt was 23 when he came out in support of Buckingham, adhering to the Lancastrian cause that his family had supported throughout. Captured in the aftermath, indications are he suffered the rack before being placed in a low and narrow cell dressed in clothing insufficient to warm him. There is a fantastic legend here that in Dick Whittington-style, the stubborn prisoner was visited by a cat, of which he became somewhat enamoured. So great was the animal's assistance that it often brought him pigeons that the gaoler would later cook for him. A monument placed in the village church at Boxley records the gratitude of Sir Henry for the helpful feline.

One who would suffer at the Tower for Buckingham's rebellion was the eldest surviving son of Sir Thomas Browne, Sir George. After switching his allegiance and supporting a proposed invasion by Henry Tudor, Browne was captured and brought to the Tower to face trial. He was beheaded on Tower Hill on 4 December.

Richard III's successful quashing of the Buckingham rebellion meant he had passed his first significant test. Yet, as was so often the case in the history of England, one failed attempt was rarely the end of the story. Unable to abduct Henry Tudor in Brittany, and in turn forcing him into neighbouring France, Richard faced a crisis of unrivalled proportions after his only son was stricken down by illness, probably tuberculosis, followed by his queen in March 1485. Rumour at the time and since has abounded that Richard poisoned Anne after she failed to become pregnant a second time; however, there is no proof of this. Stricken by his double grief, Richard moved to protect his failing hold on the kingdom by importing gunsmiths from Flanders, setting them up among the Tower's already mighty arsenal, to begin the assembly of the latest breakthrough in modern warfare – the serpentine cannon. On hearing of Tudor's landing at Milford Haven in August with a band of mercenaries, Richard moved to vanquish his foe, coming face to face at Bosworth Field in Leicestershire. There, despite leading a numerically superior force, the charges led by Sir William Stanley, brother of Margaret Beaufort's husband, Thomas Stanley, 1st Earl of Derby deserted him. So ended the life of Richard III, not bemoaning the lack of a horse, but instead crying out the word 'treason' many times over for the man who had deserted him.

Chapter 8

1485–1507: Neglected Nephews, Counting-House Kings and a Plethora of Phoney Pretenders

Lewis Caerleon was one of many forced to endure imprisonment in the Tower during the final year of Richard III's reign. Physician to the deposed Edward V and, ironically, also to Margaret Beaufort, Caerleon spent much of the year drawing up sophisticated tables concerning lunar and solar eclipses after using his time in prison for scientific purposes. The reason for his incarceration is unclear, though it would appear to have been more concerned with his questionable loyalties than dubious practises. His notebook suggests the tables he was making were largely replacements and successors to those Richard had stolen. He was finally released within a few months of Richard's defeat at Bosworth.

Henry Tudor's victory and swift ascension may have been the answer to many a Lancastrian prayer, but the end of the war came too late for two of his supporters. One who lost his life for championing Henry's cause was the landowner and administrator William Collingbourne. Remembered for his famous lampoon the rhyme of Collingbourne that mocked Richard and his councillors, Sir William Catesby, Sir Richard Ratcliffe and Francis, Viscount Lovell (the cat, the rat and Lovell our dog, ruleth England under a hog), Collingbourne had been arrested around early November 1484 for high treason along with accomplice John Turburvyle. Accusations regarding the exact crimes he may have committed are also fairly vague. Although Collingbourne's defenders have suggested his demise was a direct punishment for the lampoon, others have indicated Collingbourne was indicted more specifically for his encouragement for a Henrician invasion.

Turburvyle got off with life in prison, but like many a condemned man, Collingbourne met his end on Tower Hill. The famous Tudor historian and antiquarian John Stow recounted that after being hanged, he was cut down quickly, castrated, his entrails burned before him and his heart removed. Such was the speed of proceedings, Collingbourne was reported to have uttered the words, 'Oh Lord Jesus, yet more trouble!' Joining Collingbourne on the scaffold around that time was the equally Lancastrian Sir Roger Clifford, who was beheaded on Tower Hill, again for championing Henry Tudor's cause.

To be forced to dwell within the now infamous walls of the Tower even for a day could seem like a long time, especially for a noble. To survive two years in a dark and dingy cell, therefore, one might consider particularly remarkable. Such considerations aside, it is surely one of the Tower's surprisingly warmer stories that fresh from victory at Bosworth, one of Henry VII's early acts was to liberate the brave victim of Yorkist England, Henry Wyatt, whose dirty skin would soon tingle in the warm waters enjoyed by a Knight of the Bath. It is also perhaps the Tower's most ironic story that in sight of the hellish prison that had once been his home, the Tower would become his place of employment. In reward for his loyalty and astute financial mind, Wyatt was promoted to custodian of the Crown Jewels as well as controller of the Royal Mint. In contrast to many of the Tower's prisoners, he lived out his days in comfort before breathing his last at the grand old age of 80.

In ascending to the throne, Henry VII had achieved a feat almost everyone except Henry VI had considered impossible. The Yorkist era may have officially ended with Richard III's death, helped in no small part by the convenient earlier demise of Clarence and the disappearance of the sons of Edward IV, yet the family line had not been wiped out completely. Sister of the late kings and herself a daughter of Richard, 3rd Duke of York, Margaret, Duchess of Burgundy was now the eldest survivor of the family and hence shepherdess of the flock. Normally in such situations, a well-placed pretender emerged almost instantly but with the princes widely assumed to be dead, Margaret had little option but to place her hopes in a different candidate.

So great continues to be the intrigue concerning the sons of Edward IV, it is easy to forget a third prince also called the Tower his home. Much maligned due to the death of his father and his own apparent mental shortcomings, Edward, 17th Earl of Warwick, was the only son of Clarence and his wife, Isabel, daughter of Warwick the Kingmaker. Having spent much of his early years incarcerated in Yorkshire, Henry VII wasted little time before ordering the transfer of this potential claimant to the Tower.

Clearly wary of the threat of insurrection, Henry spent much of his early reign at the Tower. Having created a dozen new Knights of the Bath, following which he spent the traditional night there prior to the procession to Westminster Abbey for his coronation, Henry moved the court to the Tower, where a great banquet was held either in the White Tower or the great hall. At the start of the new year, he consolidated his position by following up his promise to marry Warwick's cousin, Princess Elizabeth, sister of the doomed princes, as well as rescinding Richard's controversial *Titulus Regius*.

While pregnancy with their first child would delay Elizabeth's coronation until November 1487, six months prior to the event Henry was forced to confront his first major test – an event that is often remembered as the final battle of the Wars of the Roses. Fresh from her recent scheming, Margaret, Duchess of Burgundy had aligned herself with the earl of Lincoln, John de la Pole, grandson of the duke of Suffolk whose life had ended so horrifically and discretely at sea in what was arguably the event that began the wars in the first place. De la Pole's father, another John, was himself of the Yorkist line having married Edward IV and Richard III's sister, Elizabeth, the result of which made Lincoln a clear pretender in his own right. So great was his claim that, following the death of Prince Edward, Richard III had recognised Lincoln as his rightful heir.

The best candidate for usurpation, however, was Warwick. Nevertheless, any chance of a rebellion in the young lad's name was unlikely, with or without the prince being held in the Tower. In an act that can either be considered a masterstroke or one of sheer desperation, a Yorkist priest named Richard Symonds concocted a plan to use one of his pupils, a boy named Lambert Simnel, to impersonate the mentally challenged Warwick. So apparently convincing was this façade, on bringing the boy to Dublin, the Yorkist-supporting Fitzgeralds acknowledged him as the real Warwick and sent news of recent developments to Burgundy. Despite managing to drum up a force of some 8,000 troops between them, which included the support of the Percys, the revolt was quashed when the force reached Nottingham.

Lambert Simnel's actions may have led to the executions of John Ashley and two unnamed men around 1488/89 for their involvement, yet intrigue against the Tudor dynasty did not cease there. Within three years of their deaths, Sir Robert Chamberlain would follow them to the scaffold on 12 March 1491 for his own plot against the monarch.

The second pretender to show up in Ireland, however, was of a much more convincing mould. Claiming to be none other than Richard of Shrewsbury, Duke of York and second prince in the Tower, the man known to history as Perkin Warbeck was officially the son of a Flemish boatman, yet this was far from the view of everyone at the time. Despite being ousted as a commoner, a noted facial similarity with Edward IV offers evidence he might well have been an illegitimate son of the late monarch, most likely from his enforced stay on the Continent in 1470–71. Another possibility is that he was a son of Margaret of Burgundy herself, however this is far less likely.

Whatever Warbeck's actual pedigree, the enigmatic foreigner was accepted by Margaret as well as Charles VIII of France and even the Holy Roman Emperor as the missing Shrewsbury. Although his visit to Ireland achieved little, in 1495 a Burgundy-backed invasion force landed on the coast of Kent. When the advance guard of around eighty was swiftly defeated and imprisoned in the Tower, Warbeck was left little choice than to return to Ireland, from where he subsequently travelled to Scotland. Whether or not James IV was really convinced of the pretender's bloodline, he accepted Warbeck as Richard IV of England. Not only did he fund an invasion force in the missing prince's name, but also set him up with a noble wife.

James's best attempts at meddling would initially fail to see the forces make it past Northumberland. After trying to restart things further south, Warbeck was captured seeking sanctuary at Beaulieu Abbey and brought to the Tower. Initially well received by a probing Henry VII, his attempts to escape did him little favour. Imprisoned, ironically in a cell next to the lad who was allegedly his cousin, the two prisoners struck up an unlikely friendship. When whispers of a plot reached the ears of the king, Henry had all the excuse he needed. The hapless Warwick was beheaded on Tower Hill, his only true crime being Clarence's son. In contrast, Warbeck was tried as a commoner, confessing his false pedigree at the last. With it, at least for the time being, ended any attempts of a Yorkist revival.

Henry Tudor's ruthlessness here was evident for all to see. The death of Warwick in particular was remarked upon for its cruelty. Nor was it an isolated moment. Four years earlier, and in a shocking twist every bit as callous as seen by Richard III himself, Tudor turned on the man who had consolidated his victory at Bosworth. Swayed by Sir William Stanley's acceptance that if Warbeck was the real Shrewsbury that he would be obliged to support him, his father-in-law's brother was imprisoned in the White Tower and executed on Tower Hill, thirteen days after one William Daubeny who was beheaded on 3 February 1495. A third, Captain John Belt was also executed there on 7 September.

Soon to join them was Sir James Tyrell, the man believed by many to have been an accessory to the conspiracy to murder the princes. Initially pardoned by Henry, Tyrell was later imprisoned after supporting another Yorkist pretender Edmund de la Pole – a younger brother of Lincoln – in 1501. When facing the torture chambers in the basement of the White Tower, Tyrell reputedly confessed his role in the murder of the princes and joined Sir John Wyndham on Tower Hill on 6 May 1502. That such an admittance may have swayed Henry Tudor's thinking must be considered likely; however, their official crime was assisting Pol and for surrendering Guînes Castle too easily to the French. The following year, the civil servant Sir Thomas Thwaites, who had been knighted on the ascension of Richard III only to be arrested for treason in 1493 for his role in the Warbeck conspiracy, avoided execution after being sentenced to death, but was brought to the Tower where he suffered the rack.

Away from the political intrigue concerning Tyrell and the Pols, a popular rising was recorded as having started in Cornwall in the summer of 1497. The catalyst was an angry response from the impoverished populace to attempts by Henry to raise funds for a military campaign against the Scots by a series of taxes on the county's tin miners – a stark contradiction to the earlier terms given to the county's stannary parliament back in the reign of Edward I. Further to local claims in the parish of St Keverne on the Lizard Peninsula against the local tax collector, rising discontent was voiced by St Keverne blacksmith Michael

An Gof and Bodmin lawyer Thomas Flamank in protest at the king's unreasonable terms.

Inspired by the passion of the two men, a force of 15,000 marched on Devon before spreading out across Dorset and Somerset. On reaching the city of Wells, the uprising acquired its most senior recruit yet, the 7th baron Audley, James Tuchet, henceforth their political voice. Progress continued unopposed as they headed across the south to Winchester, after which much of the momentum was lost when they failed to rally the people of Kent. While the royal family and the archbishop of Canterbury sought refuge inside the Tower, the first clash with the royalist forces occurred near Guildford. Hampered by some desertions, the remaining Cornish forces pitched battle at Deptford Bridge on 17 June 1497. With the benefit of greater experience and larger forces, the royalists won the day, quashing the rebellion. With it, the key trio of An Gof, Flamank and Audley were all captured.

True to Henry's consistent intolerance for law-breaking, retribution against the ringleaders was swift. The county where the revolt began was hit the hardest, with certain areas reduced to pauper status for years to come. As expected, An Gof and Flamank were tried and sentenced to be hanged, drawn and quartered and, after being held for a time in the Tower, put to death at Tyburn on 27 June 1497. A day later, Lord Audley was despatched via the axe on Tower Hill. In stark contrast to An Gof who went to his death confident in his belief that his memory would be celebrated, his head placed on a pikestaff on London Bridge, Audley's end, dressed in a paper suit of armour, would be immortalised as a stout mark of defiance against the king. In an intriguing yet strange final twist that is sadly difficult to prove, it has since been suggested the event would go on to inspire one of history's favourite children's rhymes, of the king in his counting-house counting his money and four and twenty blackbirds baking in a pie.

Chapter 9

1501–1535: Divorced, Beheaded, Died …

enry VII was as proud as any father when the Tower hosted the wedding of his eldest son Arthur to Catherine of Aragon in November 1501. A month earlier, in the company of his wife, Elizabeth, he had moved into its royal apartments whose grand improvements he had personally overseen throughout his reign. In contrast to the grisly atmosphere that had often plagued the Tower, and would continue to do so, the environment at the time was peaceful, the occasion sumptuous. Scenes of beheaded lords and frightened children that had dominated the inner ward some twenty years earlier had been replaced by jousting in the day and magnificent banquets at night in the great hall. Just like the modern-day Windsor Castle, the Tower portrayed every hallmark of an esteemed royal residence.

Revamping of the Tower had not been restricted to the royal apartments. After work modernising the king and queen's quarters was completed, a gallery was added to the Cradle and Lanthorn Towers; the Lanthorn – as its name suggests – had previously contained a lantern before being converted into an annexe of the royal apartments. Other developments of note would also occur. It was around this time the Yeomen of the Guard came into existence, the predecessors of the modern-day yeoman warders. Though the menagerie continued to thrive, Henry personally abhorred the cruelty suffered by the animals and was especially livid on learning that two mastiff dogs had been deliberately set upon a lion. The menagerie had often been a source of bloodlust for previous monarchs and the citizens of London, but for the man history would dub 'the Winter King' it was a largely unwelcome distraction.

It has often been argued that the reign of Henry VII marked a time of transition for the royal palace. Indeed, Henry would be the last king to treat the Tower as a proper home, bringing such scenes of merriment as those that surrounded the wedding of Arthur to something of an end. The decline probably began when Arthur himself perished, most likely another victim of TB. Within a year the same had happened to Queen Elizabeth, ironically after giving birth at the Tower. Sadly for the unfortunate king, the child also died.

For the victor of Bosworth, such cruel twists would be of great consequence. In honour of his late wife, the queen's body was moved from the royal apartments to St John's Chapel in the White Tower, which was lovingly decorated in black and illuminated by 500 candles before her body was laid to rest in the new Lady Chapel of Westminster Abbey. Her husband would join her six years later, leaving behind a country that was, at least administratively, on a far sounder footing than it had been during the Rose wars.

Almost inevitably, the stability of this period was to be short-lived. Taking Henry VII's place on the throne was his eldest surviving son. Like his grandfather on his mother's side, Edward IV, the prince had initially been viewed as the 'spare', something that changed following Arthur's death. Aged just 17, Henry junior was still a long way from becoming the man who would make history, yet even in these early days there were signs that the recently proclaimed Henry VIII possessed an unwavering ruthlessness that would characterise his infamous legacy.

Almost immediately on journeying to the Tower in preparation for his coronation, the proverbial axe had already fallen on two of his father's key ministers, both of whom were imprisoned in the nearby cells. Edmund Dudley and Sir Richard Empson, financial agents and lawyers by trade, had developed something of a loathsome reputation among the populous for their ability to extract large amounts of cash from their subjects to aid the royal coffers. Their exploits not necessarily illegal, Henry instead charged both with the crime of attempting to block his accession if not kill him. On being brought to the Tower, of the two it was Dudley who attempted to put his time to good use. After failing to escape, he wrote a treatise praising the young king while also attempting to exert on him words of wisdom. Sadly for Dudley, his writings proved in vain. He joined Empson at the block on 17 August 1510.

Like his father, Henry was not entirely immune to the charms of the Tower. The refurbishment that began in preparation for his coronation, along with that of Catherine of Aragon's, saw the great hall once again overly lavished and included one of the Tower's more lasting features: a quartet of pepperpot domes on the four surviving turrets of the White Tower. A total of twenty-six new Knights of the Bath were created in the traditional manner before the king made the well-trodden journey to Westminster for the great event.

Though things may have seemed superficially well and good, away from the scenes of grandeur and political progress, the Tower continued to serve its primary purpose. The Wars of the Roses had officially been over for more than twenty years, but of all the unwanted records held by prisoners at the Tower, none were worse than that of the latest member of the de la Pole clan, William. His family were no strangers to the Tower. From the days of the cousins' war, the current descendant of the Yorkist faction spent an astonishing thirty-eight years at the Tower, primarily as a precaution because of his status as the 'Yorkist pretender'. Joining him for about seven years of this had been his brother, Edmund, who had earlier been sheltered by Sir James Tyrell in Calais. While William survived, Edmund was beheaded on Tower Hill. Sources vary as to whether it occurred sometime in April 1513 or as late as 4 May.

With Edmund executed, one of the other few surviving pretenders of Plantagenet ancestry was Edward Stafford, 3rd Duke of Buckingham. Son of the controversial Henry – who was rumoured to have been involved in the disappearance of the princes – and suspected of his own traitorous intent in 1520, the king swiftly launched an investigation into Stafford's dealings, most notably his associations with other nobles. On considering the evidence brought before him, Buckingham was brought to trial in April 1521 and charged with a long list of offences that included listening to prophecies concerning the king's death and intended regicide. Found guilty, Buckingham was executed on 17 May 1521 and posthumously attainted to ensure his children would be unable to inherit their birthright.

Another to incur the wrath of the king around this time was the Welsh rebel, Sir Rhys ap Gruffydd. A powerful landowner, Gruffydd was accused of plotting with James V of Scotland about an alliance against the king, culmination of which would have seen Rhys inherit the ancient title of Prince of Wales. Husband of one Lady Catherine Howard, daughter of the controversial Thomas Howard, 2nd Duke of Norfolk – who himself had spent time in the Tower after lining up on the side of Richard III at Bosworth – and thus himself a Howard by marriage, the rebellious actions of some of Rhys's supporters led to his imprisonment, at which time the true claims came to light. Most strikingly, Rhys had apparently added Fitz-Urien to his coat of arms – the name Urien being of great significance in Welsh mythology. Intriguingly, claims of his union with the Scots itself potentially fulfilled an ancient Welsh prophecy. Imprisoned for a time in the Tower, he was executed on 4 December 1531 at Tower Hill.

The year 1532 was a significant one for the Tower. The arrest and execution of criminals for coin offences was relatively rare in England's history, in its own way serving as a small reminder of the abhorrent scenes endured by the Jews in the reign of Edward I. Brought to Tower Hill, the five guilty parties were condemned to be hanged, drawn and quartered on 15 June.

Another to endure the Tower around that time was the early Protestant priest, John Frith. Stationed in Oxford in 1525 after being made a junior canon at Thomas Wolsey's cardinal college, Frith was imprisoned along with nine others for being in possession of what the university officers deemed 'heretical books'. On being released and making his way across the channel, Frith's next move was to Antwerp where he was reacquainted with the leading reformer, William Tyndale.

Frith's return to England occurred sometime in 1532, at which time Henry VIII's chancellor, Sir Thomas More, issued a warrant for his arrest. In October that year he was finally apprehended, following which he spent some eight months in the Tower. A prominent writer, Frith was another who put this time to good use, most notably penning essays on Communion – a decision he undoubtedly knew could one day result in his death – before ending his time there writing his famous book, *The Bulwark*. Brought to trial on crimes of heresy, during which his writings were presented in evidence against him, Frith answered most crucially to two questions that the Scriptures could prove neither purgatory nor transubstantiation. On 4 July 1533, just a week before Henry VIII faced his own excommunication in consequence of his disagreements with the papacy, Frith was martyred at the stake at Smithfield.

Frith would not be the only heretic to encourage the wrath of Sir Thomas More in 1532. A lawyer by trade, James Bainham experienced all the horrors of his body being bound in irons and the stocks before being taken to More's Chelsea townhouse and tied to a tree in the garden: something More called 'the tree of life'. Surviving a hard whipping and interrogation, Bainham was relocated to the Tower and racked. Despite recanting, he later rediscovered his protestant convictions and was burnt at the stake at Smithfield.

The following year would be noted for the only escapee of Henry's reign. Imprisoned in the enormous, now demolished Coldharbour Gate which at its height split the inner ward in two and whose remains still lie to the west of the White Tower, Alice Tankerville spent time as a prisoner for financial irregularities before successfully charming one of her guards and managing to flee beyond the walls. The story of this, the first and only woman to escape, is unsurprisingly a fascinating one.

When agents of the king and parliament arrived in London docks in October 1531 in expectation of receiving a shipment of 366 gold crowns, they soon discovered the hoard had disappeared, presumably during the course of the voyage. Two years of largely fruitless investigation eventually brought about a much-needed lead, culminating with the finger of blame being pointed at a controversial sailor by the name of John Wolfe. Convinced by a combination of Wolfe's known presence on the voyage and reputation for skulduggery, the prosecutors brought forward their case and Wolfe found himself spending the summer of 1533 inside the Tower.

A frequent visitor to Wolfe's cell was his wife, Alice Tankerville. A common face in the local community, it was here this reputedly charming woman is recorded to have put her many talents to good use, most notably in befriending two of her husband's gaolers, the young William Denys and John Bawd. Noting that they were distracted by her beauty, Tankerville began to visit on an almost daily basis, bringing food and wine, some of which she shared with the gaolers.

The process lasted almost six months before a lack of evidence against Wolfe ensured his release. Choosing to keep a low profile in Ireland, Wolfe engineered a final meeting with Bawd, requesting the friendly gaoler to keep a look out for Alice during his sojourn. Intriguingly, less than a month passed before new evidence came to light, implicating not only Wolfe but Alice herself. Tried in absentia by parliament – there is evidence that Alice had been unaware of recent developments – the pair were found guilty and sentenced to death, culminating in Alice's own imprisonment in the Tower in February 1534. Evidence from the time also indicates that the treatment she was forced to endure was abnormally harsh: the conditions of her bare cell, in which she was shackled and chained, eventually resulting in an intercession on her behalf by the daughter of Sir Edmund Walsingham, the Tower's lieutenant. Successful in having the irons removed, she was, nevertheless, confined to her barred cell with food slid in through a gap beneath the door.

It was while the wife of the now absconded Wolfe wiled away her time in the gloomy surroundings of the Coldharbour Gate that she renewed acquaintances with Will Denys. Concerned by reports of Denys's kindnesses, it was not long before Walsingham fired him, ironically leading to Bawd taking his friend's place. Falling ever deeper in love with his prisoner, Bawd agreed to a collusion with Alice that might result in her escape. Buoyed by earlier claims from Denys that the Coldharbour Gate had a plausible escape route, Bawd proceeded to purchase two lengthy pieces of rope and had a second key cut for the tower's outer door. With the prime ingredients gathered, Bawd waited at least a fortnight until around 10pm on the night of the next new moon in March. With Alice now in possession of the duplicate key, as well as a long stick, she waited until the final guard was gone for the day before using the stick to free the pin of the door. Once the door to her cell was open, she made her way through the darkness down to the main door of the tower, which opened to the turn of Bawd's copied key. Successfully out, she made her way stealthily across the darkened Tower yard and onto the roof of St Thomas's Tower where an anxious Bawd awaited her arrival. In preparation of what might follow, he had already secured the rope to an iron hook located in the stone parapet wall, which soon ensured their freedom. Untying a small boat commonly used to transport prisoners across the moat, they disembarked at the Iron Gate Steps and fled along a nearby road where Bawd had tied a brace of horses.

So close to the end, it was here disaster struck. Posing as young lovers, the guise failed to fool the returning night watch, at least one of whom recognised the pair. Surrounded, Alice was returned to her cell and Bawd taken in for questioning. A short time later, Bawd is recorded as having been removed to the infamous 'little ease', a confined cell frequently mentioned in the 1500s–1600s. Despite its clear importance to the Tower's history, other than being located somewhere in the White Tower, sadly little evidence of its exact location exists.

Ironically, as luck would have it, Wolfe had also been captured attempting to return to England. As Bawd languished in solitary confinement, Wolfe and Tankerville met their end together on 31 March 1534 as retribution for crimes of theft, conspiracy and treason. Out of keeping with the usual form of execution for treason where the guilty party would meet their end at the gallows or at the hands of the axe man, instead the hapless couple were carted to the walls that lined the river's embankment and enchained at low tide. There, a morbid crowd watched as the water level slowly rose, trapping them as they were submerged beneath the filthy waters.

Equal misfortune would befall Bawd. Racked to the point his muscles were torn and his joints ripped from their sockets, he met his end not below the chilly waters, but above the walls, defenceless to the horrors of exposure and dehydration. Deprived of a fitting burial, the charmed gaoler's body was left to gradually succumb to the elements and the birds, as a clear lesson never to betray one's king. Far less clear is what became of the alleged theft.

Guilty or innocent, the gold was never found.

Similar bad luck would follow a second woman associated with the Tower. A woman of the cloth having entered the nunnery of St Sepulchre in Canterbury in 1527 and who would be better remembered to history as the Holy Maid of Kent, Elizabeth Barton was also revered for her apparent 'second sight' that had caught the eye of many a distinguished native of her county, including those of the religious life. According to some contemporary accounts, she was even credited to have inspired Sir Thomas More and Bishop John Fisher with her devotion.

Convinced by her own abilities and ever fervent in her preaching, Barton's downfall followed her gloomy prediction that the king's marriage to Anne Boleyn would see his death within a month. Convicted of high treason for having predicted the king's death, in June 1533 she was arrested along with her supporters among the clergy and held in the Tower. How she and her associates were treated is largely unrecorded, despite clear indications at least some of her allies were tortured. Deemed an imposter, her own excuse being that she had been led astray, on 23 November every member of the original party was taken to St Paul's Cross at St Paul's Cathedral in order to participate in a show of public penance. After being witnessed by a great crowd, they were returned to the Tower to be placed in her cell in the Coldharbour Gate, dubbed in her honour 'Nun's Bower'. Despite being subjected to such public humiliation, the January parliament condemned the entire group to death, undoubtedly fearing insurrection or conspiracy should they fail to act decisively. All, including Barton, were dragged to Tyburn to be hanged, drawn and quartered, with Barton suffering the ignominy of becoming the first and only woman to be beheaded, her head spiked on London Bridge.

It was around the time these two unfortunate women were forced to endure the horrors of the Tower that another 'daughter' would begin 'her' infamous affinity with the castle. Invented by lieutenant of the Tower, Sir Leonard Skeffington, much has been made of the mysterious 'Skeffington's Daughter' or 'Skeffington's Gyves'. An expert on the rack, Sir Leonard endeavoured to create a device capable of achieving the opposite effect, literally compressing the victim as opposed to stretching them.

A horrific account of the capabilities of this strange instrument was penned by the Jesuit historian, Matthew Tanner, stating:

> while the rack drags apart the joints by the feet and hands tied, this one constricts and binds as into a ball. This holds the body in a threefold manner, the lower legs being pressed to the thighs, the thighs to the belly, and thus both are locked with two iron clamps which are pressed by the tormentors face against each other.

As well as describing how the victim's body becomes 'almost broken by this compression,' Tanner added that the device is more complete than the rack, 'by the cruelty of which the whole body is so bent that with some the blood exudes from the tips of the hands and feet; with others the box of the chest being burst, a quantity of blood is expelled from the mouth and nostrils.' Though details from the time suggest the victim was hung beneath the structure, the evidence also implies there may have been many variations of the device.

One who was not destined to suffer such hardships or die within the walls was Cardinal Wolsey. The king's chief advisor since 1515, as well as his one-time chancellor and England's cardinal, Wolsey's stock crumbled following his failed attempts to convince the papacy to annul the king's marriage to Catherine of Aragon. Outshone in his endeavours by the young Cambridge cleric, Thomas Cranmer, Wolsey was arrested and summoned to the Tower. Ironically, he died en route.

Of the many forced to suffer the horrors of the Tower in Henry VIII's reign, there is no sadder story than that which concerns Wolsey's replacement as lord chancellor, the later canonised Sir Thomas More. Appalled by the development of the English reformation led by Wolsey's replacement on spiritual matters, Thomas Cranmer, now Archbishop of Canterbury, not least parliament's levying of fines on a church that remained loyal to Rome, More resigned as lord chancellor in May 1532, passing the mantle of chief minister on to another reformer, the young lawyer, Thomas Cromwell. When Cranmer married Henry to Anne Boleyn, More politely refused the invite. A year later he found himself in the Tower.

Come the time of More's arrest, it is notable just how far the king once dubbed 'defender of the faith' by the Pope had moved in the opposite direction. Even if the order of mass was still essentially Romanist in nature, Henry's insistence that every subject should be required to swear him an oath, acknowledging him as head of the church and thus confirming him unequivocally as the pope's replacement as Holy Father of the English Church, proved too much for many of England's devout Catholics. Running out of patience with More's refusal to take the oath, the king ordered that the former chancellor be taken up river from his Chelsea pad and escorted inside the Tower. On his arrival, the man previously revered as the second most important in England was asked to part with both the heavy gold chain of office and his fur gown as payment to his boatman, both of which he did without fuss.

More's prison was different to most at the Tower. Although sources indicate the room was prone to damp and that he was required to sleep on a thin straw pallet bed on the stone floor, the chamber was far from ghastly.

Located on the ground floor of the Bell Tower, the star-shaped chamber survives to this day, and remains somewhat revered for its connection with him. As a distinguished guest, More was allowed many freedoms, including his servant and visitors, permission to walk the grounds and to attend daily mass in the Chapel of St John.

Despite his ongoing pain and physical challenges, not least sharp leg cramps and chest issues brought about by the damp conditions, More's primary torment was emotional. Satisfied by his decision to resign and strengthened by his unbreakable devotion to his Catholic faith, his writings at the time indicate the hardship of being apart from his wife and children concerned him far more than his personal welfare. In addition to letters to loved ones, his time in captivity was mainly spent writing flowingly of the Passion, as well as a *Dialogue of Comfort Against Tribulation*, the latter offering clear insights into his mindset.

In 1535, More knew death awaited. Having been forced to watch the, apparently happy, ordeal suffered by four Carthusian monks who Henry sent to death at Tyburn, More's reaction was to express regret he had never entered the church himself. A few days later, Cromwell and the Privy Council summoned him, at which point he declined the offer to sit with them. It was there, before his former colleagues, he made what has since been regarded as one of history's great speeches.

Held in close proximity to More was another of the Tower's important religious prisoners, the equally revered Bishop of Rochester, John Fisher. Once confessor of Margaret Beaufort – mother of Henry VII – Fisher, too, had refused to take the Oath of Supremacy, and was subsequently forced to suffer the harsh conditions in the cell above More's. Hearing of his suffering and devotion, the new pope, Paul III, actually rewarded Fisher by making him a cardinal, provoking the impulsive response from the king that he would send his head to Rome for his red headwear.

On 22 June, the then lieutenant of the Tower, Sir Edmund Walsingham, whose lodgings adjoined the Bell Tower – just as the current resident governor's do to this day – entered Fisher's cell to inform him that he was to be put to death. After a period of rest, time Fisher spent in spiritual preparation, he made his way with great difficulty up Tower Hill. On climbing the scaffold, he addressed the crowd heroically, asking for their prayers. Beheaded, stripped naked and impaled on spears before being laid to rest in a pauper's grave, the late bishop was later dug up and reinterred. His headless remains are now one of the many that lie in the crypt of St Peter ad Vincula.

By the time Bishop Fisher met his end, More's own predicament had further worsened. Undoubtedly warmed by the strength shown by Fisher, after another meeting with Cromwell achieved nothing for the new chief minister, Cromwell endeavoured to persuade More with gentle reasoning. Beginning with the confiscation of his cherished possessions, most notably his books and writing apparatus, he was also subjected to further questioning, this time by a former student, Richard Rich, who had somehow risen to the rank of solicitor general. Of all the questions Rich asked, More's alleged assertion that parliament's passing of the Act of Supremacy was not in line with other countries gave Henry evidence to charge More with treason. Despite a denial at his trial, and no witnesses to confirm the original conversation, More was nevertheless condemned to death.

Like Fisher before him, More made the most of his death. Welcoming his martyrdom, he warned the judges that they too stood on a potential knife-edge, both on the human plain and the spiritual. On returning to the Tower, the gaoler's axe pointing menacingly in his direction as indication of the guilty verdict, the constable was apparently moved to tears by the unjustness, a scene matched by his embracing family.

Alone in his cell, More wrote a final letter, in charcoal, to his favourite daughter Margaret, confirming he was ready to meet God. On Thursday 6 July 1535 he was informed by his former friend and privy councillor, Sir Thomas Pope, he would die that day, news he received gladly. Donning the clothes of his servant, understanding anything he wore would become property of his executioner, he made his final journey up Tower Hill, holding a small red cross between his fingers before tipping his executioner with a gold coin. In honour of Henry's demand that More make little in the way of a speech, he simply asserted himself 'the king's good servant, but God's first'. Placing a blindfold over his eyes and lowering himself over the block, his final act was to lift his beard, asking it should not be struck with the axe for the beard had committed no treason.

Joining his fellow martyr in a surprisingly low profile grave somewhere in the royal Chapel of St Peter ad Vincula, More's headless body lies as one of many whose life ended both violently and prematurely. As More's head was given pride of place on London Bridge, replacing that of Fisher whose famous features had acted as both a cautionary tale and sight of inspiration for London's onlookers, within the royal confines the king's anger was now being directed on the woman who had contributed significantly to the split from Rome in the first place. While in all likelihood the Protestant Reformation that was sweeping Europe would have made an impact on England at some stage in any case, the necessary schism in order to ensure his second marriage had proven the straw that broke the camel's back in terms of England's relations with the papacy – not to mention the catalyst for Fisher and More's stout defences of it. Of Henry's feelings, an eyewitness account on learning of More's death speaks volumes. Playing dice at Greenwich, Henry is reported as having scoffed at his queen, stating that because of her the most honest man in the kingdom was dead.

His views far from wrong, Henry's frustrations with Anne had clearly been simmering for some time. Further to his personal guilt at the death of both martyrs, helped in no small part by his newfound lusting after Jane Seymour and disgust for Anne's headstrong ways, of chief importance was his famous inability to father a legitimate male heir. Being well aware that a lack of sons had indirectly brought the ruin of the House of York, siring an heir had been of paramount importance to a man hell-bent on ensuring history did not repeat itself. Having already been pregnant three times, initially giving birth to a girl – the future Elizabeth I – before subsequently miscarrying, Anne's fourth attempt sadly resulted in a stillborn child. For Henry, whatever love he had once felt for Anne had evaporated along with his hopes of an extended male Tudor dynasty.

By 1536, a journey that had started so well for Anne now seemed years away. Gone were the days when the king had kissed her passionately on her arrival at the Tower's wharf in preparation for her coronation. Provoked in no small part by her own early-feminist ways, Anne was not without enemies, especially at court. Stories abounded that the rise of the woman who would enforce a change in England's religion was itself clear indication of the presence of devilry or sorcery. As Henry's attentions turned to Jane Seymour, his soon-to-be third queen and the woman who would be mother to England's next king, the case of disposing of Anne fell on the shoulders of Cromwell. Already armed with accusations of witchcraft and whispers that a flirtatious nature that had once charmed Henry had also worked on many others, Cromwell was not short of ammunition. The fall guy, however, was not a courtier, but a lowly musician named Mark Smeaton.

Whether or not a relationship between Anne and the humble, apparently gentle, musician ever really occurred remains a contentious issue. What is less doubtful is that Smeaton's naivety offered Cromwell the perfect excuse to bring the hammer crashing down. After inviting the unsuspecting musician to dinner at his residence close to the Tower, Smeaton was immediately arrested and subjected to torture. Within hours, he confessed to being not only Anne's lover, but one of many, presenting Cromwell with a list that included Sir Henry Norris, Sir Francis Weston, and Sir William Brereton. Far from naming just prominent courtiers, he also implied Anne's inappropriate relations with her own brother, Sir George Boleyn, now 2nd Viscount Rochford. Within a day, the unfortunate musician found himself locked up in the Tower, along with his fellow accused.

For a time Smeaton remained out of sight, probably in the basement of the White Tower, while his social betters were brought in through Traitors' Gate and incarcerated in the far more comfortable Martin Tower. Though all except Smeaton, still fresh from his recent anguish, denied the charges, on 2 May Anne herself was informed of her deepening predicament. A four-man deputation, including Cromwell and Anne's own uncle, Thomas Howard, 3rd Duke of Norfolk, interrupted her dinner at Greenwich, informing her of the seriousness of her situation. Hearing of the crimes levelled against her, the shocked queen protested her innocence. As usual at such times, it mattered little. Within a short time of their arrival, Anne was escorted on to a barge and taken along the same stretch of river to the Tower as she had travelled in such joyous circumstances only a few years earlier. Ironically, on her arrival the very same constable who had welcomed her did so again, his cheery warmth replaced by a stone cold shoulder.

Entering the Tower, reports tell that Anne fell almost immediately into the pit of despair. Walking beneath the arch of the Garden Tower, heading for the royal palace that had earlier been her lodging in preparation for her coronation, she fell to the ground, weeping, professing God as witness to her innocence. In the absence of her usual ladies, her company came in the form of four other women, including the wife of the constable whose motives were at least partly ulterior.

At some point prior to her trial, Anne appears to have been moved to the lodgings of the lieutenant, where the Queen's House now stands; the country cottage that had been commissioned for her as a wedding present and was probably in place at the time. Within its walls, Anne wrote desperately to her husband, professing both her innocence and eternal love for him. Further to the emotive prose, she begged her husband for justice for herself and those who had been accused with her, and for guarantees for the safety of their daughter, Princess Elizabeth. Despite clear evidence in her favour, all the accused bar Anne and her brother were brought to Westminster on 12 May, to a court, bizarrely, overseen by Anne's father. Smeaton aside, all maintained their innocence, but to no avail. Death would wait on Tower Hill.

Whereas the four condemned 'lovers' underwent trial at Westminster, due to their royal status, Anne and her brother, Rochford, remained in the Tower, making the short journey three days later from the Lieutenant's Lodgings and Martin Tower to Henry III's great hall. In addition to charges of adultery, she was also accused of supplying poison to Norris intended for Catherine of Aragon, as well as Princess Mary and the king's bastard, Henry Fitzroy. In spite of a complete absence of credible eyewitness accounts, the guilty verdict was delivered. Presiding over the case, her uncle read it aloud. She would be burned. Hearing the sentence, Anne responded with admirable composure, stating that her only crimes were her lack of humility and frequent jealousy. Further to Anne, Rochford was also destined not to escape, the key charges being of spreading rumours of the king's lack of virility.

Any final hopes Anne had of a reprieve were quickly dashed. In response to her willingness to enter a nunnery in exchange for her life, her only good fortune was to avoid being roasted at the stake. In a visit by Cranmer the following day, Anne was informed that by accepting the marriage was invalid due to Henry's past relations with her sister, the sentence would be beheading rather than burning. Agreeing, Cranmer dissolved the marriage the following day. With all remaining business settled, it was scheduled that the queen should die three days later.

Inevitable questions, both contemporary and from later commentators, concerning the bias of the trial came with full understanding of the two executions. While George had initially been sentenced to hanging, Henry, perhaps with no desire to delay or encourage a public backlash, changed the sentence to beheading. It is commonly assumed that Anne asked Henry, having such a little neck, that an expert be brought in to decapitate her with a sword rather than an axe; strangely this request seems to have been presented before the trial. As for Anne's alleged lovers, all five were sentenced to be despatched together on Tower Hill on 17 May, two days prior to Anne's own execution. Whether of her own wishes or under calm command, Anne watched from her window in the lieutenant's lodgings as the doomed Norris, Weston, Brereton and Smeaton made their way across the courtyard on leaving the Beauchamp and Martin Towers.

Her brother was the first to be put to death. Careful to avoid further recriminations against his family or having his speech halted, Rochford admitted to a general deserving to die without admitting specific charges while also imploring the watchful crowd to place their faith in God alone. Of those who followed, all but Smeaton denied the queen's guilt while admitting some sins on their own part. Finally the musician was put to death, asking the crowd to pray for him for he deserved to die.

In keeping with the usual protocol, the body of each man was returned to the Tower, no longer to be incarcerated in dark cells but rest for all eternity, initially in the chapel's cemetery. On being informed of recent events, Anne declared her sincere belief that all except for Smeaton, at whose refusal to retract his confession she was furious, were already in heaven. As for herself, heaven, so she hoped, would soon await. After a night of disturbed sleep, the noise of her hastily erected scaffold ruining any chance she had of peaceful slumber, she received a final visit from Cranmer, in whom she had found an unlikely ally in light of their shared devotion to the Protestant faith. Visiting the site, the imperial ambassador, despite a loathing for Henry's 'concubine', wrote of his praise for Anne, noting, 'no person ever showed a greater willingness to die,' while reporting the constable's wife had witnessed her final confession during which she had clung steadfastly to her innocence of the crime for which she had been sentenced.

By 9am the following day, the execution was scheduled to be completed. Much to Anne's annoyance, however, it was delayed due to Cromwell's insistence the inner ward be cleared of those who had no right to be there. On meeting the constable, Anne affirmed her hope that the swordsman would live up to his reputation, she having a very little neck.

In spite of Anne's complaints of the delay, the execution was put back to the next morning. After passing the evening composing a message to Princess Mary, asking forgiveness of her wrongdoings, and perhaps also against her late mother, another restless night, broken with the dawn and a final mass, would be her last. Dressed in a dark gown, her hair purposely done up in a cap to leave her neck exposed, she accompanied the constable to Tower Green, along with John Skip, her almoner, and four ladies. It was reported by Sir Francis Bacon she muttered a final message to her attendant, asking him to thank Henry for advancing her throughout her life and for ending it with the blessing of martyrdom.

As Anne prepared to meet her end, it was noted that at this time another Wyatt was presently enduring his own depressing experience within the Tower. Son and heir of the previously liberated Henry Wyatt, Thomas Wyatt, while not without talent, seems not to have inherited his father's resilience and economic expertise, instead becoming an accomplished poet. Imprisoned in the Bell Tower at that time, he witnessed Anne – according to rumour he was another of her lovers – walking to her end and composed a poem in her honour. There is also a poem, entitled, *O Death! Rock me asleep*, which Anne herself is conjectured to have written during her final days. Despite clear evidence remaining elusive, the tradition is long-standing and the words encapsulating of her plight.

> *O death! Rock me asleep,*
> *Bring me to quiet rest;*
> *Let pass my weary guiltless ghost*
> *Out of my careful breast.*
> *Toll on thy passing bell,*
> *Ring out my doleful knell,*
> *Let thy sound my death tell,*

Death doth draw nigh;
There is no remedy.
For now I die
My pains who can express?
Alas! They are so strong,
My dolour will not suffer strength
My life for to prolong:
Toll on the passing bell.

My pains who can express?
Alas, they are so strong;
My dolour will not suffer strength
My life for to prolong.
Toll on, thou passing bell;
Ring out my doleful knell;
Let thy sound my death tell.
Death doth draw nigh;
There is no remedy.

Alone in prison strong
I wait my destiny.
Woe worth this cruel hap that I
Should taste this misery!
Toll on, thou passing bell;
Ring out my doleful knell;
Let thy sound my death tell.
Death doth draw nigh;
There is no remedy.

Farewell, my pleasures past,
Welcome, my present pain!
I feel my torments so increase
That life cannot remain.
Cease now, thou passing bell;
Rung is my doleful knell;
For the sound my death doth tell.
Death doth draw nigh;
There is no remedy.

Most likely oblivious to the watchful eyes of Wyatt, at last Anne appeared, now the sole attention of a crowd of 1,000 that included her uncle Norfolk and Cromwell, but not the king. After taking several minutes to cross the courtyard, she distributed alms to the crowd. Taking the usual step of forgiving the executioner, she made her speech in a gentle voice, asking again for God's blessing on her former husband. Finally, she removed her headdress and collar, handing them to one of her ladies-in-waiting before finally descending to her knees, her back remaining vertical as death by sword required no block. With her last moments, she muttered quietly in prayer.

According to the accounts of the time, even in death her lips continued to move before stuttering to an inexplicable halt.

Chapter 10

1535–1547: Divorced, Beheaded, Connived

With Anne Boleyn's fears of a prolonged death proving unfounded, the swiftly dispatched second wife of Henry VIII became the first queen of England to be executed at the Tower. What happened next would be notable for its rarity, not least a clear case of disorganisation on the part of the authorities. Having successfully taken care of business, it was subsequently discovered no coffin had been prepared for the queen, following which the quick thinking of a yeoman warder saw an elm-made arrow chest brought in as a suitable alternative.

Her remains blessed, Anne's body was carried inside St Peter ad Vincula and placed close to the altar where it would await burial for several months. Contrary to rumours that the Wyatts smuggled her remains out of the Tower, later to be buried in Norfolk or Suffolk, in 1876 her bones were among those discovered with, in inspiration for the famous English ditty, 'her 'ead tucked underneath her arm.' Along with the many others discovered at that time, Anne's remains were reverently reinterred; most likely the same was true of her alleged lovers who were almost certainly laid to rest in the Tower cemetery adjacent the chapel where the Waterloo Block now stands. Completing the mystery of Anne's end, to this day the Ceremony of Roses marks the anniversary of her death, as it has done since at least the 1960s. Exactly who is responsible remains unclear, only that the ceremony is funded by a private trust.

True to his impatient, impulsive nature, Henry wasted no time in finding a new wife. As the court would soon see, and in typical Henrician form, he had in fact already lined up bride number three well before Anne's trial. Shortly after her execution, Henry finally married his new love, the court beauty Jane Seymour who was in her late twenties.

Unfortunately for the increasingly hot-tempered king, the marriage would be one of mixed blessings. Successful in the sense that within eighteen months of the wedding the king witnessed the birth of his long awaited legitimate male heir, as fate would dictate the 'love of his life' would soon be parted from him. Within a fortnight of the birth of Prince Edward, Jane, still suffering complications from her pregnancy and labour, died a long-drawn-out and likely painful death. In contrast to the death of Anne, Henry mourned.

The task of finding Henry a new queen fell on the shoulders of chief minister Thomas Cromwell. Widely acclaimed as being the legal mastermind of the Dissolution of the Monasteries, the Catholic Jane would be replaced by another Protestant: a Lutheran princess, also named Anne. Hailing from the small German state of Cleves, Henry's fourth match was negotiated almost entirely by Cromwell. Though neither king nor counsellor had met the princess in person, Henry had been enamoured by an enchanting painting of her by the now esteemed artist Hans Holbein the Younger. Sadly, when seen in the flesh she did not meet Henry's expectations.

As Henry's wrath fell on Cromwell for his disastrous engagement to the 'Flanders Mare', the Tower became the home of Lord Thomas Howard and Margaret Douglas. Younger son of the duke of Norfolk and daughter of the queen dowager of Scotland, Margaret Tudor, by her second marriage, respectively, the pair were imprisoned in the Tower in 1536 as punishment for their unlawful engagement. Although the relationship was not destined to last – the break cemented with Howard dying in his cell in October 1537 – Douglas remained confined to the Tower until the king took pity on her, moving her to Syon Abbey when her health showed signs of deteriorating. Three years later, she was incarcerated for a second term, this time as punishment for her affair with Sir Charles Howard, younger brother of Henry's future queen, Catherine.

Other prisoners in the Tower around this time would include those who had found themselves directly on a collision course with the king as a result of the Dissolution of the Monasteries. Unsurprising considering its swift and brutal nature, the Dissolution had incited such widespread opposition that it was recorded 'divers abbottes and monkes were putt in the Tower for treason.' Those caught up in the drama included Lawrence Cooke, Prior of Doncaster and Robert Salisbury, the abbot of Vale Crucis. Joining the duo in the Tower around this time, Thomas Kendall, the vicar of Louth, William Morland, a monk of Louth Abbey, Abbot

Mackrell of Barlings, Nicholas and Robert Leach, Philip Trotter and William Longbottom of Horncastle along with many others were later executed in London after a failed rising in Lincolnshire. Particularly prominent among the religious prisoners to have been confined within the walls of the Salt Tower at this time was John Houghton, the prior of the London Charterhouse, who went to his death on 4 May 1535 at Tyburn for refusing to swear the Oath of Supremacy. Famed as one of the four Carthusian monks Sir Thomas More saw go merrily to their death, unseen by the former lord chancellor was a sadly more laboured end. During a violent demise where he was cut down from his hanging only to regain his breath, his last words to his executioner amidst the removing of his heart was 'Most good Jesu, what will you do with my heart?' at which he mercifully breathed his last. Incredibly, on being quartered, one of his limbs was nailed to the charterhouse's inner gate, only for two monks to attempt to take it abroad, there to serve as a holy relic. When their intention became known, they were also condemned to death.

Around that time another challenge to face the king was the first of many counter-attacks against recent proceedings. Led by the charismatic northerner Robert Aske, the Pilgrimage of Grace broke out in Yorkshire on 13 October 1536 following a failed rising in Lincolnshire a week earlier and steadily spread throughout the north, gaining the passionate support of a number of staunch Catholic heavyweights, including the Nevilles and the Percys. Seeking firm retaliation for Cromwell's 'illegal' dissolution of the monasteries, their aim was clear. To undo what had recently been done, and, when completed, replace the spiked heads of the Catholic martyrs with Cromwell's.

From a military standing, the Pilgrimage of Grace was far and away the most significant domestic challenge to be faced by the monarchs during the entire Tudor era. Of key strategic consequence was the rebels' taking of Pontefract Castle – a vital fortification in the north. To put the rebellion down, in addition to making a host of idle promises and placing the Catholic Norfolk in charge of negotiations, Henry sent ten warships north, fully equipped with cannons from the Tower armoury. Shortly after their departure, the fortress welcomed its first prisoner, the charismatic Marmaduke Neville who had failed in his attempts to bring the rebellion to East Anglia. Joining him in the Tower were Sir Ingram and Sir Thomas Percy, both of whom were outwitted by Henry and Norfolk's pretence of requesting dialogue. Equally deceived was Aske himself.

Aske's writings a month on from his capture display clear evidence of a man whose spirit had been ruthlessly broken. Having been hoodwinked into making the journey south in the first place, like many of the rebels he realised his luck was out. Rather than meet his end on Tower Hill, he was returned to York and hung from the castle walls to serve as a warning to those who had known him.

The leader of the Pilgrimage of Grace as we have already seen was far from alone in being destined to die horribly for his faith. A somewhat reluctant accomplice in the endeavour had been the abbot of Jervaulx, Adam Sedbar. After attempting to flee to Bolton Castle on being targeted by the royal commissioners, Sedbar survived several days on Witton Fell before being captured on 12 May 1537. After enduring the confinements of the Beauchamp Tower – on the walls of which the carving of his name can still be seen – Sedbar was found guilty of attempting to deprive the king of his new title as supreme head of the church and was condemned to death at Tyburn alongside the prior of Bridlington, a few days after the abbot of Fountains Abbey and prior of Guisborough Priory.

Shocking as many of these cases were, few rival the lot of the unfortunate Margaret Cheyne. Wife of one Sir John Bulmer and an illegitimate daughter of Edward Stafford, 3rd Duke of Buckingham, Cheyne was accused of encouraging her husband's involvement in the Pilgrimage of Grace, as well as Sir Francis Bigod's subsequent rebellion the following year. Arrested along with Bulmer for high treason, Cheyne was martyred at the stake on 25 May 1537. There are conflicting reports as to whether or not she was tortured. If she was indeed racked, she was almost certainly the first woman ever to suffer such treatment at the Tower.

A month later, Lord Thomas Darcy of Templehurst would also meet his maker. Fresh from his written diatribe against the ubiquitous Cromwell, he was beheaded on 30 June 1537 for his treasonous correspondence with Aske, his head replacing those of the abbots on a pike on London Bridge.

What happened following the suppression of the rebellions was perhaps both surprising and completely predictable. Having witnessed the hatred spewed against Cromwell from the northern rebels, the Catholic duke of Norfolk, a hero in Henry's eyes but a traitor to his Catholic lords, saw the opportunity to finish off the despised chief minister. Buoyed by Henry's frustrations at the failed marriage to Anne of Cleves, Henry, it appeared, was ready to listen to the criticisms. Cromwell's response here can be deemed either despicable in its dishonesty or a masterstroke in its genius as he framed the recent Pilgrimage of Grace as nothing more than a guarded attempt at restarting the Wars of the Roses that had ended almost half a century earlier.

If any genuine Yorkist pretender still walked the earth, the best candidate was none other than Reginald Pole, grandson of Clarence through his daughter, Margaret the countess of Salisbury. Famed in later history as the final Catholic archbishop of Canterbury – a role he would fill in the reign of Mary I – Pole's life path had been primarily of religious devotion, during which he had steadfastly maintained the ideals of Rome. Having fled England due to fears for his safety around the time of Henry's divorce from Catherine of Aragon, he inadvertently found himself leader of the exiled Catholic faction and, subsequently, made a cardinal by the pope. Despite being out of the country, he had been partly responsible for rousing support for the Pilgrimage of Grace and avoided attempts by Cromwell's agents to assassinate him.

In 1538, apparently in an attempt to draw out the absent cardinal, Henry had Reginald's younger brother arrested. Throwing the unfortunate Geoffrey in the Tower, it has often been held that his sufferings were among the hardest ever endured. Kept in almost perpetual darkness, he failed with an attempt to take his own life before being questioned in the presence of his wife. After holding out for two months, he finally accused members of his family of harbouring a conspiracy against the king.

For Cromwell, the forced confession was quite literally the answer to his Protestant prayers. Almost instantly, Cromwell had Henry Pole, 1st Baron Montagu, another brother, arrested along with Henry Courtenay, the marquess of Exeter, whose blood also flowed with that of the white rose. Joined by their families in the Tower, both were charged with high treason, most notably for colluding with the exiled cardinal, in what would later be called, the Exeter Conspiracy. Armed with little more than vague words akin to those that Rich had extracted – or fabricated – of Sir Thomas More, both men were sentenced to death and beheaded on Tower

Hill on 9 January 1539. Poorly nourished during his imprisonment, Henry Pole's son of the same name perished in his cell. Geoffrey, scarred for life, met with better fortune and was freed as reward for his cooperation. Eventually he would be joined by the 11-year-old Edward Courtenay who for the time being was returned to his bedroom in the Bell Tower, which had served as his home since his parents' arrest.

The execution of a Lady Pargitor's manservant in 1538 for coin clipping was one of many incidents to concern the Tower in what had proven a terrible year of hardship for many a devout Catholic. A month before the death of Henry Pole, his cousin – the equally staunch Catholic Sir Edward Neville – had been executed on 8/9 December 1538, after apparently conspiring with Reginald Pole to topple the king. Shortly after the executions of the Poles, Sir Nicholas Carew joined them on 3 March 1539 for his own alleged role in the Exeter Conspiracy.

Away from the schemes concerning the cardinal, other prominent Catholics also would meet their premature ends. Among them, Sir Thomas Dingley was beheaded on Tower Hill in July after being implicated in the Pilgrimage of Grace. Joining him, Sir Adrian Fortescue was beheaded for sedition, the same day as his servants were hanged at Tyburn.

Before the year was out the unfortunate abbot of Glastonbury, Richard Whiting, would follow them to the afterlife. After refusing to surrender the abbey, at that time the final one standing in Somerset, the ageing Whiting was brought to the Tower on Cromwell's orders and questioned in detail. Prominent evidence cited against Whiting was the presence of a book reportedly found among the abbey's treasures that included arguments in favour of Catherine of Aragon's marriage. After being found guilty of 'robbing' the abbey, Whiting and two of his loyal monks were dragged to the top of Glastonbury Tor on hurdles and subsequently hanged, drawn and quartered. In honour of his bravery and steadfast devotion, the Catholic church beatified him in 1895.

Exactly what Thomas Cromwell had hoped to achieve by targeting such innocents is really anyone's guess. Of the Poles, royals in name only, there is little to suggest Reginald's distant involvement in the Pilgrimage of Grace was anything more than an aftershock of the Dissolution, rather than any genuine attempt to gain the throne his family had lost over fifty years before. Nevertheless, for the man who had brought about such change, there would be no lasting celebrations. Within a year of being made earl of Essex, in part for his targeting of the Yorkists, Norfolk's own scheming finally got the hated minister ousted. And in dramatic fashion.

Similar in some ways to the far more unfortunate Hastings prior to the ascension of Richard III, Cromwell's end was as sudden as it was shocking. Ironically, it also stemmed from a council meeting. Shortly after his arrival at Westminster carrying several important papers, proceedings were interrupted by Norfolk. On entering, he is reputed to have said, 'Cromwell! Do not sit there! That is no place for you! Traitors do not sit among gentlemen!'

Refused the opportunity to bring up recent developments with the king, Cromwell was arrested on the spot – much to the satisfaction of most of the attendees. Evidence that the king immediately ordered repossession of his goods offers weight to the theory the decision had been made with the king's consent well in advance. Quickly taken from the meeting room and hustled into a boat, Cromwell ended the day in the Tower. Probably fearing it would do little good, he quickly penned several letters to the king, receiving no answer. As the disgraced minister waited, his enemies endeavoured to ensure his only way out of the Tower would be via Tower Hill. When the bill of attainder was passed by parliament it confirmed two things: firstly, a minister lining his own pockets was not acceptable and, secondly, heresy is only forgivable when the king is in the right mood to do so.

Though many may point the finger at Cromwell on accusations of corruption and his clear role in masterminding the Dissolution, in the eyes of the king, his failings in relation to the royal marriages were his primary offences. As a last service, Henry extracted from Cromwell the proof he needed to divorce Anne of Cleves, most tellingly that the marriage had not been consummated. For Cromwell, the duty would indeed be a final one. Insufficient in achieving the king's forgiveness, he wrote Henry one last letter. While the body of the text confirmed the situation with Anne and that he was ready to take death, a postscript begged for mercy. It was recorded that the king asked Cromwell's plea to be read out to him three times. Nevertheless, clemency was not forthcoming.

On 28 July, almost three weeks after Henry's divorce from Anne was finalised, energised by his final breakfast, Cromwell left the same residence that had briefly served Anne Boleyn before making his way to the specially erected scaffolding at Tower Hill. As a final insult, the man who had risen through the ranks to become the most important statesman in England, having been deprived of his earldom, would die a commoner. It is a clear testament to his lost status that joining him on the scaffold was the mentally disturbed peer, Lord Hungerford, alleged to have been both a sodomite and an incestuous rapist.

Famed throughout his career for seeing off many challenges, Cromwell is recorded to have met his death courageously. On addressing the crowd, he affirmed he died a Catholic: an astonishing suggestion after having been so active in the Dissolution. After praising the king and asking those present to pray for him, he did his best to ignore the gloating presence of Norfolk and his other nemesis Eustace Chapuys – Charles V's imperial ambassador to England – concentrating instead on his final prayers. His request to the executioner to end his life swiftly did not come to pass. Like so many who met their end on Tower Hill, it took a combination of hacking and sawing amidst the echoing groans of the crowd before body and head were finally separated. His body, like most subjected to the same fate, was laid to rest in the royal Chapel of St Peter ad Vincula, his head raised on a pike on London Bridge.

Henry's treatment of Cromwell, abhorrent though it was, does little to compare to that of his earlier treatment of the Pole clan, notably the young Henry. Had a greater mystery endured about this potential heir to the throne, the reputation of the young man, aged somewhere between 14 and 21, would have been comparable to the poor sons of Edward IV. Alas, the facts being well known, his story perhaps echoes more with that of his great-uncle, Edward, 17th Earl of Warwick.

Equally shocking is the sad story that surrounds the unfortunate boy's grandmother: mother of Reginald, Geoffrey and the elder Henry Pole, sister of Warwick and daughter of the hapless Clarence, Margaret, Countess of Salisbury. Thought to have been 67 years old at the time and revered for her stout loyalty – her love for her father was famously shown by an unusual trinket she wore around her arm of a small silver barrel on a bracelet, apparently indicative of Clarence's strange death – Margaret had offered little enthusiasm for any Yorkist revival. Despite her loyalty to Catherine of Aragon on the queen's divorce and her adherence to the old faith, there is similarly no indication she had any personal issues with any of the Tudors.

Questioned by Thomas Wriothesley, 1st Earl of Southampton – the same man who had interrogated her son – Margaret gave nothing away of Reginald's whereabouts. Despite the inevitable scepticism of the council, it cannot be ruled out that Margaret's decision to maintain her silence may have been because in fact she knew nothing of her son's present location. In the absence of any significant confession during her imprisonment at Cowdray House, Margaret was brought to the Tower in 1539 where even her gaoler protested to Cromwell of the despicable conditions in which the ageing countess was kept. Coming at a time when Henry was once again distracted by whispers from the north about a revived Pilgrimage of Grace, he made the hasty decision of ordering all state prisoners to be killed, including the poor Margaret.

The ruthless command would ultimately lead to another of the Tower's most unfortunate executions. With no time to bring in a professional executioner, the task was assigned to a complete amateur. On being brought from her dark cell into the morning air of Tower Green on 27 May 1541, the innocent Margaret was led to her end. Situated within some 50 metres of where her father had met his equally appalling end, Margaret asked prayers of the witnesses, most notably for the king and the Catholic Princess Mary.

What happened next has ensured the story's lasting legacy. On apparently having her speech cut short, the headstrong woman lost her temper and ran away from the makeshift site. Exactly how she died has become a matter for speculation. Tradition from the time has it she was chased around the parade ground and ultimately hewn to death. Irrespective of the exact facts, the hapless amateur made it far from instantaneous.

Following Cromwell to the block had been the principled Catholic priest, Thomas Abel. Previously chaplain to Catherine of Aragon, Abel had remained fully committed to the queen, even to the point that he wrote a treatise denying the lawfulness of Henry's reasons for divorce. Inevitably, knowledge of the book ensured his downfall. Imprisoned initially in the Beauchamp Tower, but later released, Abel was returned to the Tower on charges of circulating prophecies made by the Catholic nun

Elizabeth Barton that Henry would die if he married Anne Boleyn, while maintaining his view Catherine should maintain her right to the title, Queen of England. Executed at Smithfield on 30 July 1540, his graffiti in the Beauchamp Tower survives to this day. Joining him were Richard Featherstone – another former chaplain to Catherine of Aragon, Edward Powell for charges of denying Henry's supremacy, as well as Protestants Robert Barnes, a doctor of divinity and his fellow Cambridge scholars Thomas Gerrard and William Jerome.

One who would receive a somewhat unexpected pardon around this time was the illegitimate Arthur Plantagenet, otherwise known as Lord Lisle. A known son of Edward IV, Lisle was brought to the Tower in May 1540 in consequence of his apparent conspiring with the governor of Calais – at the time still an English property – to betray the port to the French. After enduring some twenty months in the Tower, Lisle was released and ordered he be restored to his former status. Sadly for Lisle, he apparently died of joy on receiving the news. In his commentary on the matter, the writer Francis Sanford mused ironically that the king's 'mercy was as fatal as his judgments.'

Two days prior to Abel's execution, the 28th had been a significant one in the history of England. While the brains behind the Dissolution was meeting his botched end on a wooden scaffold, a second, far more colourful, event was occurring elsewhere in the city. On that day Henry VIII married for a fifth time. His blushing bride, just like his second, was destined to become more than a mere footnote in the annals of the Tower's history.

Catherine Howard was, in many ways, the most unique of Henry's wives. Lacking the intellect, strength of character, wit, streetwise nature and experience of her predecessors, the 17–year–old beauty still had much to learn and life to live. As daughter of Lord Edmund Howard she was, like Anne Boleyn, a niece of Norfolk and, hence, Anne's cousin.

In contrast to Anne who, evidence suggests, seems to have coveted the throne from an early age, there is no evidence that Catherine possessed such aspirations. Brought to court for the first time to form part of Anne of Cleves's household sometime early in 1540, there is little reason to suggest the ageing king, now suffering severe health issues that included a smelly ulcerated leg from a jousting accident, would have been high on her list of future husbands. Ever cursed by his libido, Henry fell hard for Catherine's charms, almost certainly something her ambitious family had conspired. By the time Cromwell was put to death, she had already made enough of a mark on the king to free the imprisoned Wyatt who wept openly at Cromwell's execution, while accepting a request from the doomed countess of Salisbury to provide her with warm clothes.

As Catherine's kindness made a mark, notably on Henry, not for the first time in Tudor England, sex was to be the undoing. With accusations abounding that she had lost her virginity to her music teacher, Henry Mannox, more concrete reports concerned one Francis Dereham with whom she had been seen prior to her arrival at court. Unfortunately for Catherine, both men were back on the scene by July 1541 as Henry travelled north to finish off an attempt at reviving the Pilgrimage of Grace.

In a move testament to her naivety, Dereham was appointed Catherine's private secretary – a favour, so said the queen, to the lad and his grandmother. News of Catherine's past would soon find its way to the ears of Archbishop Cranmer and, perhaps concerned for the king's reputation – or else to accelerate the downfall of the Howards – Cranmer wrote to Henry, unable to stomach the challenge of voicing his concerns in person. On receiving the letter, Henry had been enjoying a mass of thanksgiving with Catherine on their return to Hampton Court Palace. Reading it, the king is reported to have pulsated with rage, cursing the wife he had recently given thanks for. Avoiding the embarrassment of decapitating Catherine with his own sword, Henry had the queen placed under house arrest. Catherine was reported to have been dancing with her ladies-in-waiting when news came. Failing with a drastic attempt to speak to her husband inside the Chapel Royal, she was dragged kicking and screaming back to where she had come.

Lacking the thirst for power that had consumed Cromwell, Cranmer, nevertheless, now had a job to do. Incriminated by past accusations of premarital sex with Dereham, charges against Catherine soon moved to that of adultery with one Thomas Culpeper. A recent favourite of the king, Culpeper's next destination would be to follow Mannox and Dereham to the Tower. Joining Catherine in being condemned, meanwhile, was her lady of the bedchamber, Lady Jane Rochford, the widow of George Boleyn. Jane's role in proceedings would prove of key significance here, as without her assistance it was deemed the alleged affair with Culpeper could never have happened.

Cranmer apparently succeeded in proving all of this. On 6 November, he informed the Privy Council of the actions of the queen, Mannox and Dereham prior to the wedding as well as with Culpeper after it, news that saw a distraught Henry weep openly before the council. With the meeting over, Cranmer made the short journey to visit Catherine directly. Encouraged by news that a confession might be rewarded with kingly lenience, Catherine confessed to foreplay with Mannox and sex with Dereham, mentioning nothing of Culpeper. As the queen was relocated to Syon Park, Jane Boleyn was brought to the Tower. It was here Cranmer concentrated his efforts. After learning from Mannox that full sex had never occurred despite certain levels of intimacy, incriminating papers were apparently found among Culpeper's belongings. No sooner had Jane confessed to full knowledge of their relations, next to be questioned was Culpeper himself. Admitting to falling in love with the queen, he nevertheless denied adultery. Despite neither Culpeper nor Catherine confessing, for Cranmer, and subsequently Henry, the mounting evidence had reached a tipping point. Catherine was officially stripped of her queenship on 23 November. Just as had been the case with Anne Boleyn, her family, ruthlessly, deserted her.

The axe of revenge, nevertheless, would also be destined to fall on the Howards. Blamed for allowing the early trysts to have occurred in the first place, next to be brought to the Tower was Catherine's grandmother, the dowager duchess of Norfolk – wife of the second duke. Plagued by illness, the ageing duchess was already bedridden when interrogated. Narrowly surviving implication, largely due to her age, in a trial presided over by her stepson, Culpeper and Dereham were sentenced to be hanged at Tyburn.

For Dereham, the ordeal was far from over. Of common blood, and still protesting his innocence – unlike Culpeper who eventually confessed – in early December he was moved to the basement of the White Tower. Also brought in for questioning was his friend, Robert – other sources say William – Damport, another who entered the Tower via Traitors' Gate before suffering the rack and the brakes. Exactly what the brakes were remains unclear; thanks in part to the grand storehouse catching fire in 1841, no working examples of it have survived. Available evidence suggests that the little known device was used to break a victim's teeth; so bad was Damport's experience, he is reported as having at least one tooth violently removed when subjected to it. Needless to say, the varying degrees of torment worked. Succumbing to torture himself, Dereham finally confessed not only to regular sex, but that himself and the queen had secretly been betrothed and engaged in a plot to kill the king. Culpeper, of noble blood, was decapitated quickly. Dereham's end, contrastingly, was far more painful.

As a punishment for guilt by association, the task of notifying the queen was given to Norfolk. Informing his niece she would die inside the Tower, on the same spot as her cousin Anne Boleyn, Catherine was brought from Syon Park to the Tower on 10 February. Arriving by enclosed barge, the coverings separating her from the sight of Dereham and Culpeper's heads on pikes, she was brought in via Traitors' Gate and met by the new constable, Sir John Gage. Once inside the inner ward, walking again in Anne's footsteps, she was taken to the lieutenant's lodgings in which she would pass her final weekend.

The execution was scheduled for 13 February. Recovering from her initial bouts of despair, she found solace spending her time in prayer, making her final confession to the bishop of Lincoln. In preparation for her execution, she made the unique request of the constable that the executioner's block be brought to her room, in order that she could rehearse her final moments.

The Monday morning air was typically cold, a thick mist rising from the Thames. By the time Catherine arrived at the spot where Anne had been executed six years earlier, a number of privy councillors had already arrived. According to a letter written by the confectioner Otwell Johnson, who was one of the former queen's witnesses, Gage had collected Catherine at 7am, finding her well-prepared and dressed in black. On reaching the scaffold with her ladies, she carried out the traditional act of forgiving her executioner and tipping him before making her speech. Of the legend that she claimed to have died a queen and would rather have been the wife of Culpeper, there is not a shred of evidence. Instead, she conceded death was just punishment. She knelt down on the block and was killed with a single stroke. The practice in her room, it seemed, had made perfect.

Chapter 11

1541–1547: Remarriage, Womanly Rackings and Hapless Howards

With Catherine's body packed away by her ladies, her accomplice Lady Jane was brought up not far behind her. In many ways, their deaths were comparable, ending with a single stroke after making a humble speech.

Together, the now headless former royals had met death with dignity and great courage. As a small act of courtesy, the king granted Catherine's final wish for the liberation of her relatives, albeit at the cost of depriving them of much of their vast estates as punishment. Whether there is any truth in the stories that the ageing king later endured his own punishment in witnessing Catherine's ghost regularly haunting the corridors of Hampton Court Palace – similar stories concern a headless Anne Boleyn at the Tower – we shall never know. Intriguingly, such reports are known to continue to this day.

Uprisings and massacres in Ireland had been of regular distraction for the king throughout the 1530s. Among the victims, Lord Leonard Grey, Viscount Grane, was accused of treason for allowing his nephew, the young earl of Kildare, to escape to France. Despite his denials, Grey was imprisoned in the Tower and beheaded for high treason on 28 June/ July 1541.

Another two years would pass before the man who had seen off five queens would marry a sixth. While divorce, beheading and natural death had awaited all of the first five in various ways, the Cumbrian widow Catherine Parr was destined to fare rather better – at least during the king's lifetime. A Protestant by faith, Catherine shared Catherine Howard's tendency for forgiveness and kindness; however, unlike Howard, her thoughtful nature and inquisitive mind made her something of a conversationalist, particularly in the eyes of her ageing husband. In the changing air that had been sweeping the landscape since Cromwell's execution, the languishing of would-be Catholic martyrs in the Tower's cells had been replaced by their Protestant rivals. Sympathetic to their plight, Catherine was rarely shy in her attempts to save them.

It was around this time there appeared on the scene another woman of Protestant leanings who would go down in Tower history for the unfortunate reason of being quite possibly the first woman to suffer torture there. Aged somewhere in her early twenties, Anne Askew was a woman who, in many ways, could be considered ahead of her time. Born in Lincolnshire and related to Robert Aske, the now executed leader of the Pilgrimage of Grace, her committed reformist values, coupled with a willingness to speak her own mind, made her another clear example of pre-suffragette feminism. Evicted from her home by her husband as retribution for her passionate preaching, Anne made her way to London where she soon drew unwanted attention for her fiery brand of sermonising. After initially being returned to her husband, Anne's undeterred spirit eventually saw her confined within the walls of Newgate Prison and by late June 1546, locked up inside the Tower. On being charged with heresy, most specifically her denial of the sacraments, her haughty response of 'God made man, but that man can make God I never yet read' must have raised more than a few eyebrows. Concerned by rumours Anne had friends at court, including those of the new queen if not Catherine Parr herself, the outspoken Anne faced the prospect of being tortured. The task fell on the shoulders of the usual suspects: Lord Chancellor, Sir Thomas Wriothesley, 1st Earl of Southampton; Richard Rich, now chancellor of the court of augmentations – the body created to handle the legal transfer of property in the Dissolution of the Monasteries – and Sir John Baker, the chancellor of the Exchequer.

Brought from her cell, most likely somewhere in the Beauchamp Tower, to the basement of the White Tower on 29 June 1546, Anne was questioned repeatedly about her connections with those at court, notably her friendship with the queen herself. Receiving little in the way of cooperation and denying the opportunity to recant, the lieutenant of the Tower, Sir Anthony Knyvett, was summoned to assist in the inquisition, which would include her being placed on the rack. Initially appalled by what he witnessed, Knyvett was ordered to persist with the racking until she finally name her accomplices. Though reluctantly complying, on being ordered to increase the pressure on Anne's aching limbs, the principled Knyvett stoutly refused. Relinquishing control, Southampton and Rich cast off their cloaks and took personal command of Exeter's Daughter. As the minutes passed, their cruelty became insatiable. So bad were the screams, Knyvett's family apparently heard Anne's shrieking voice as they strolled the Tower gardens.

The torture was eventually stopped, again thanks to the intervention of Knyvett, who had set off for the king's chambers at Westminster – other sources suggest it was the similarly named constable, Sir Anthony Kingston. Arriving ahead of Southampton, he was successful in obtaining royal permission to cease the abhorrence. Returning immediately, he ordered in the Tower surgeon to help revive the ailing Askew, by which time she was reportedly 'fainting and half-crippled.'

Exactly what degree of cruelty Anne was exposed to is contentious. Over the coming days, she is recorded as having been somehow able to write of her experience: an account included in Foxe's *Book of Martyrs* states 'they did put me on the rack because I confessed no ladies or gentlemen to be of my opinion, and therefore kept me a long time on it and because I lay still and did not cry out, my Lord Chancellor and Master Rich took pains to rack me with their own hands, till I was nigh dead.' Confusingly, the bishop of Ossory in Ireland, John Bale, wrote that she had been able to discuss religious matters for over an hour afterwards, seated on the edge of the rack; a similar report concerns how on being returned to Newgate she passed the evening 'talking pleasantly on godly things until very late.' Collectively, these accounts, though by no means verified statements of truth, may lend a certain degree of doubt as to the extent of her injuries. The idea that any prisoner could write or talk at length after being racked stretches credibility. Manacled some fifty years later, the Jesuit Father John Gerard temporarily lost use of his hands; a decade on from Gerard, a racked Guy Fawkes's signature was so shaky it was barely legible. Regardless of what degree of torture Anne was actually submitted to, the questions kept coming for at least another two hours. She would be questioned again before being put to death, martyred at the stake at Smithfield. On being brought to her place of execution it was reported she had to be carried, so weak was her body.

Yet while Anne – irrespective of the exact nature of the torture she underwent – met death head on, the queen was more fortunate. Drawing up an arrest warrant for her prior to Askew's torture, the lord chancellor incredibly dropped it in one of the Palace of Westminster's sprawling corridors, only for it to be recovered by a royal attendant and delivered to the queen personally. Deeply concerned by the lord chancellor's endeavours, Catherine went straight to the ailing king, successfully placating him by the time Wriothesley arrived with a fresh warrant. Ignored, and even chastised by the king, it seems highly likely it was this episode that doomed poor Anne Askew to such excessive torture. Fortunately for the queen, any suffering Southampton and company laid upon Anne would be in vain. Unlike Anne Boleyn and Catherine Howard, Catherine Parr would survive not only the witch-hunt, but also the horrors of martyrdom.

Succeeding Askew in the Tower was the fiery hell-raiser, Henry Howard, the earl of Surrey. He was the son of the humbled duke of Norfolk and one of the select few personally invited to have witnessed the executions of Anne Boleyn and Catherine Howard – both of whom had been his relatives. Surrey had developed something of a chequered reputation, both for his exploits with his family – the influential Howard family, of course, having played a persuasive role in English politics throughout Henry's reign – but also for his own, often misguided, actions that included disturbing the peace in the company of Thomas Wyatt's son of the same name in London's seedy red-light district.

Political intrigue was, of course, rarely off the table in Tudor England, but even for the time, it is difficult to ignore the exploits of this traditionally Catholic group. Surrey's, at times, uncouth ways had contributed in no small part to a developing feud with the Seymours, notably Edward Seymour, the earl of Hertford, who on one occasion he punched in the face in response to accusation the Howards had secretly supported the Pilgrimage of Grace. Surrey's downfall, if not an exact consequence of his recent actions, was at least accelerated by the resulting feud. As Christmas approached in 1546, at which point the ageing king was becoming increasingly weak, the conniving Seymours played heavily on Henry's fears regarding the succession – the prince Edward being a sickly child – informing him of the Howards' private ambitions to rule in his stead. Among the evidence brought forward was how the minor royal Surrey had created a dubious coat of arms whose icons included the insignia of Edward the Confessor quartered with his own. For the king, the coat of arms indeed painted a disturbing story. Ordered to ensure Surrey's arrest, the young noble was lured into an ambush at the Palace of Westminster by Sir Anthony Wingfield – himself the same man ultimately responsible for the arrest of Thomas Cromwell – and taken by boat to the Tower on 12 December. Joining him was his astounded father, Norfolk, who was consequently stripped of his offices.

As was the case with the now deceased Cromwell, the retribution that followed would be swift. With his new prisoners safely confined within the Tower, Henry wasted little time in ensuring anything of value from their estates was transferred over to the royal coffers. Writing from the lodgings of the lieutenant, Norfolk appealed for forgiveness, even offering to change religion if necessary. While he proceeded to remind the king of those close to him who he had cut down in the line of duty, in St Thomas's Tower – the thirteenth-century lodgings that Edward I had constructed to arch over Traitors' Gate – Surrey spent his time composing verse: writing, often ironic, poems concerning his plight and of those who had put him there. In the warm comforts brought about by his trappings of status, he also made translations of the psalms.

At some point, realisation of his plight must have dawned on the downfallen earl, inspiring him to attempt an escape. Aided by one of his servants, who had smuggled in a dagger before arranging for a boat to be present at St Katharine Docks around midnight of the evening in question, the fulcrum of the plan involved a latrine, a recent addition to the chambers that had been added during upgrades in preparation for Anne Boleyn's coronation.

Surrey would almost certainly have got away had it not been for one costly mistake. Taking the necessary steps to ensure he was unlikely to be disturbed by informing the warders he was feeling unwell and wished to turn in early, he attempted to make his way down the water shaft and out into the moat. Unfortunately for the earl, he waited slightly too long. Finding his bed empty, the warders discovered him still in the shaft. Before he could reach the end, he was pulled back up.

While death would most likely have awaited the earl in any case, the attempted escape hastened his demise. On 13 January he was led to the Guildhall for his trial and found guilty of treason. For Surrey the final nail in the coffin was his father's confession concerning the coat of arms. On returning to the Tower, the gaoler's axe pointing in the direction of the guilty man, the earl's recorded outburst was overheard: 'I know the king wants to get rid of the noble blood around him and employ none but low people.'

Despite being sentenced to being hanged, drawn and quartered, Henry offered some leniency, changing the sentence to beheading on Tower Hill. On 19 January 1547, a week after his trial, the doomed earl was executed. Found in his cell was a final poem, lamenting his poor fortune. Historically it would ensure his reputation as a talented wordsmith.

Whether or not Norfolk was himself able to witness anything of his son's end, or at the very least be numbed by the noise of the crowd, his own fate turned out to be slightly different. The passing of the bill of attainder a week later should have sealed his own fate had it not been for one unexpected final twist. Needing only the signature of the king to make the bill act and thus condemn the treacherous duke, Henry breathed his last on 28 January, one day after the bill was passed.

Chapter 12

1547–1553: Reformation, Rebellion and Ridiculous Wills

Henry VIII's death may have been a godsend for Norfolk, but it would not mark the end of his misery. Spared execution on a technicality, the former powerbroker would instead be destined to remain in the Tower throughout the reign of Henry's son.

Though Henry's time on the throne will always be debated for his strengths and weaknesses that at times threatened to turn the Thames red with the blood of 'traitors' and tear the country in two, for the Tower his reign was largely a blessing. Having spruced up the royal apartments for the coronation of Anne Boleyn, the half-timbered Queen's House remains an outstanding example of Tudor sophistication that, like Henry III's and Edward I's inner and outer wards, has survived the ages. From a military perspective, although the Tower saw little in the way of revolt, the reinforcement of Legge's Mount and Brass Mount at either end of the north wall were also significant contributions. Not since the reign of Edward III had the Tower's defences been developed in such ways.

For Henry's sole male heir, the newly installed Edward VI, the Tower had always held particular fascination. His father had ordered the cannons there be fired 2,000 times in celebration of his birth, and as a regular visitor throughout his youth, Edward had taken a keen interest in the refurbishment work and elements of the menagerie. In keeping with past traditions, the new king spent a solid fortnight at the Tower prior to his coronation where plans were also made for Henry's funeral. Creating forty new Knights of the Bath, on 20 February 1547 he set out for Westminster Abbey on a white horse, and in doing so, marked the beginning of a short reign that would prove rich both in intrigue and religious upheaval.

The Edwardian Reformation, although rarely viewed in the common mindset as being particularly noteworthy, was, in reality, far more significant than the changes brought about during the reign of his father. Despite being chiefly responsible for the break with Rome, Henry went to his death a Catholic, a designation that enters Edward into the history books as the first Protestant ruler of England. While such distinctions have provoked many a past commentator to label Henry something of a hypocrite, it is a notable coincidence that whatever purges had taken place against the Roman religion during his reign had been largely subdued since the passing of Cromwell.

That would all change with the ascension of the boy king. A product of Henry's brief union with Jane Seymour – Jane, herself, was ironically a Catholic – it was never likely the product of the third marriage could ever be destined to end the wider reformation, particularly as he had to conduct his entire reign under the guardianship of predominantly Protestant councillors. Under the watch of the loyal Cranmer, Edward was soon placed under the tutorship of John Cheke whose reformist views would play no small part in shaping the young king's mind.

With the face of England subtly changing, so too did that of the Tower. Vacating the royal chapels, just as was the case with churches throughout England, the priests who had hitherto conducted mass in the Catholic rite were now replaced by Protestant equivalents, while the lavish decorations gave way to something far plainer.

Outside God's walls, similar changes were also made. Within metres of the smart lieutenant's lodgings where the fortunate Norfolk languished, the new power behind the throne, Edward Seymour – uncle of Edward VI, and now duke of Somerset – saw his own attempts at consolidating power compromised by the reckless behaviour of his younger brother. Thomas Seymour – now styled first Baron Seymour of Sudeley – himself an uncle of the new king, and, within two months of Henry VIII's death, husband of the widowed queen, Catherine Parr – prior to her becoming queen, Catherine had actually been his mistress – had also found himself guardian of the teenage Princess Elizabeth. While Thomas's behaviour around the princess, which may or may not have developed to being fully sexual, left Catherine little alternative but to send Elizabeth away from their Chelsea townhouse, in August 1548 Catherine herself died within a week of giving birth to a baby girl. Bereaved by the loss of wife and daughter, Sudeley concentrated instead on political matters, poisoning the king's ear with rumours against his Protector brother, while at the same time considering further advancement by marrying Elizabeth or wedding his ward, Lady Jane Grey, to Edward.

Sudeley's best-laid plans aside, access to the king proved a mounting problem. Having originally gained Edward's favour by advancing him regular pocket money as a means to convince him that Somerset was deliberately keeping the king poor, in mid-January, Sudeley ignored his brother's attempts to restrict his access to Edward. On making a rash decision to break into the king's privy garden at Westminster, chaos ensued as the raised alarm culminated in his being bitten by Edward's pet spaniel. On finding the dog shot, Sudeley was swiftly arrested.

Confined to the Tower, Sudeley's world crumbled around him. Rumour of his familiarity with Princess Elizabeth saw Elizabeth's maid, Kat Ashley, brought to the Tower where her answers under interrogation incriminated Seymour for treason. On his refusal to answer the council's charge sheet, parliament proceeded to create an act of attainder that was reluctantly signed by Somerset. For the condemned Sudeley, one last throw of the dice remained. Provided with similar materials to Sir Thomas More, and others before him, he wrote in invisible ink to Mary and Elizabeth, imploring them to overthrow Edward and rescue him. Unfortunately for the desperate prisoner, as was so often the way in Tudor England, the actual recipients of the letter would be the Privy Council.

Seymour's death was scheduled for 20 March on Tower Hill. Of the event itself, little survives, except for an assertion from Bishop Hugh Latimer that he had died, 'dangerously, irksomely, horribly', perhaps indicating that he endured a similar botched job to that experienced by Cromwell and others before him. For Somerset, his brother's death was probably something of a mixed blessing. On the one hand, it rid him of a man whose personal follies had endangered his own position far beyond that of simple embarrassment, but just as similar things had affected the Howards, execution for treason would seldom have a positive effect. Talk in the streets escalated well beyond personal criticism of Somerset for his role as protector, in some instances predicting his downfall. If besmirching the family name was not enough, it was difficult to escape the fact Somerset had himself put his signature on the act of attainder that doomed his own brother.

For Somerset, 1549 was destined to be a year of utmost struggle. Fortunate in the sense that his brother had at least avoided the folly of mounting insurrection, such would soon follow, thanks in no small part to the developing reformation. Further widening the break that Henry VIII had made in the 1530s, the recent changes in the upholstery of the religious buildings, added to full implementation of Cranmer's *English Book of Prayers*, saw widespread objection to the dismantling of ancient traditions. Coupled with landlords raising rents and enclosing common land due to rising inflation, a protest in Devonshire developed into full-scale rebellion. So serious had the rising become, the rebels successfully conquered the city of Exeter and two officials sent to calm things down were brutally murdered in scenes reminiscent of the Peasants' Revolt.

Quashing the rebellion could have been Somerset's finest hour, but, instead, responsibility fell on the shoulders of others in the council. Fresh outbreaks were soon noted in Norfolk with fears growing it could escalate further still. Although initially targeted by the mobs, landowner Robert Kett saw reason to sympathise with the rebels' plight and, in scenes reminiscent of Wat Tyler and Jack Cade, took over leadership of the swelling numbers.

Failure to stop both movements now threatened London from two sides. By the time Somerset finally had his act together, the damage in the eyes of the council had already been done. Quelling the prayer book rebellion had proven costly, just as had been the case with Kett's simultaneous rising. When the untrained peasants were defeated and the minor ringleaders hanged, Kett and his brother saw their journey west end within the Tower's walls. In scenes reminiscent of Robert Aske, they were later returned to Norwich and lynched publicly in chains.

The end of the revolts would also see the inevitable end of Somerset as protector. In contrast to John Dudley – son of the hated Edmund Dudley, councillor of Henry VII, and since Edward's ascension, earl of Warwick – whose hard-line actions had brought an end to things in the east of the country, Somerset's lack of military nous led to his dismissal. Irrespective of whether there is any truth in accusations in recent times that the Kett rebellion was a false flag operation conducted by Dudley with the sole intent of overthrowing Somerset, Somerset's indecision was his undoing. Now leader of the council, Dudley secured the Tower against any possible counter-movement by Somerset who was informally holding the king hostage at Windsor. On being arrested, Somerset was brought to the Tower.

The arrest of Somerset was in many ways a watershed moment in Edward's reign. For the Catholic faction, imprisonment of the main proponent of the reformation had been briefly seen as a tipping point; however, at the king's insistence, Dudley confirmed the recent movement would continue as planned. During his time in the Tower, Somerset received a visit he had probably long expected. On being questioned by Thomas Wriothesley – still styled 1st Earl of Southampton – Somerset replied if indeed he was guilty of treason, Dudley was guilty of the same. Seeing this as a perfect response, Southampton put the wheels in motion to indict Dudley, only to discover one of the two men who had visited Somerset with him, William Paulet, Earl of Wiltshire, had already revealed the threat to Dudley. On attending the next council meeting at Dudley's house, Southampton and fellow accomplice Arundel were themselves arrested.

Still somewhat in the dark of recent proceedings, the king pushed hard for Somerset's release from the Tower. By February 1550, Somerset's liberation was confirmed in exchange for the enormous bail of £10,000. Welcomed back at court, the early indications were that Somerset had learned from his mistakes. So reversible was the rift, Somerset's daughter was even given in marriage to Dudley's son.

Yet almost predictably, the new accord was never destined to last. Visiting the imprisoned Catholic bishop Stephen Gardiner at the Tower and convincing him to agree to Cranmer's *Book of Common Prayer*, Gardiner changed his mind after a second visit from Dudley led to his demand for a full confession. By October 1551, Somerset's neck was once again on the block when word reached Dudley of a potential revolt in his name. Arrested with other 'ringleaders', Somerset was returned to the Tower, along with two of his sons and, a week later, his second wife, Anne Stanhope. Faced with the prospect of being unable to resort to torture on the noble duke, Dudley instead gave orders for the interrogators to concentrate on the 'lesser' prisoners in the hope of extracting the necessary confessions. When they duly came, Dudley paid Somerset a personal visit, accusing him of plotting to seize the Tower and its treasures as well as inciting insurrection. In a rare moment of contemporary legal justice, Somerset's trial delivered a verdict of not guilty, despite condemning him for attending unauthorised meetings.

Publicly promising Somerset his life was not in danger, Dudley continued to visit him at the Tower. Exactly what happened next is curious to say the least. Having once adored his uncle, Edward himself appears to have willingly put his signature to Somerset's death warrant. Whether Dudley, who later showed remorse for what was about to happen, had influenced the king is unclear, but it was Edward himself who ensured that his directive would be carried out.

In the annals of the Tower's history, 21 January 1552 would prove a date of double catastrophe for Somerset. Not only did he learn his end was nigh, but also that his final day would be the very next. At 8am that following day, the fallen duke made his way before a large crowd on Tower Hill. Showing no regret for the religious reforms of recent times, he offered up his prayers and hopes that they would continue. With what must have appeared something of a biblical judgment, a thunderstorm began, prompting many of the crowd to seek refuge in the Tower's cesspit moat. Of all people, it was the condemned man himself who calmed them, asking that they offer up their prayers for the young king. After reading his confession, he shook hands with all concerned and tipped the executioner. Unlike Cromwell, his end was swift and painless.

Edward VI's journal entry is particularly striking here. Once somewhat in awe of his protector uncle, he now displayed a cold, callous streak. A solitary sentence, written in Edward's hand, is every bit as sharp as Somerset's execution, reading simply, 'The Duke of Somerset had his head cut off on Tower Hill between eight and nine o'clock this morning.' Taking this at face value, it appears that the execution of his once beloved uncle was now little more than a footnote in the king's day. After years of pain and struggle, the young successor of Henry VIII had truly unleashed himself on the world.

As for the other key players, Somerset's death seems to have gone on to have a variety of effects. Within a year of his father's death, John Seymour died while still in the Tower, officially of unknown, though probably natural, causes. His success in obtaining the grant of his maternal inheritance, however, was not to be enjoyed. It would eventually pass with his blessing to his younger brother, Lord Edward.

Others of note would also not be spared. On 26 February 1552, Sir Miles Partridge and Sir Ralph Vane were both hanged for their respective plots against Dudley and the council. Sir Thomas Arundel was beheaded on Tower Hill the same day after being implicated in the Seymour treason. Watching from a safe distance as those involved in conspiracy against the monarchy were despatched from this life, Dudley's satisfaction appears to have reached obscene levels of near sadistic pleasure. Elevated to the dukedom of Northumberland, having earlier seen fit to display a more forgiving streak, the new protector's actions displayed all the usual traits of a man corrupted by power. Medieval penalties such as ear cropping, in particular, would become a personal favourite, escalating to extreme heights as the year progressed.

The escape of Irishman Brian O'Connor by unknown means after four years at the Tower would prove an interesting distraction in a year that had been severely troubled by political unrest and a downturn in Dudley's health. Recaptured, he was returned under heavy guard and suffered closer confinement. Another stricken by poor health was the king himself. Now 15, Edward, never of the soundest constitution, had been plagued by a persistent cough, which soon caused him to be bedridden. Diagnosed with the early signs of consumption, if not something far more sinister, the king, now closely haunted by the harrowing spectre of death, turned his thoughts to the matter of royal succession.

In England at this time, the rights of succession were straightforward on paper but a nightmare to put into practice. Leaning on the will of his father, Henry had decreed that should Edward die childless, the throne would pass to the next in line, his Catholic daughter by his first wife, the equally Catholic Princess Mary. Having reconciled with her father prior to Henry's death, and having enjoyed a relatively easy relationship with Edward, Mary was well placed, albeit a clear obstacle with regard to an ongoing reformation.

Almost inevitably the preferred candidate would have at least one opponent. As the only child of the king's first wife, Mary had precedence over Elizabeth – not only was Elizabeth the younger of the two, but also the daughter of a dethroned traitor – yet for Edward's Protestant councillors the latter was rightly viewed as far more lenient when it came to religious tolerance. Be it the product of poor advice or fallacious logic, Edward decided to bypass both parties and take the controversial step of disinheriting both sisters, declaring succession would move laterally along the family line to the branch of the youngest of his father's sisters, Mary, who had briefly become Queen of France, after her wedding to Louis XII, a man over thirty years her senior. During her second marriage, however, to Charles Brandon, 1st Duke of Suffolk, she had produced four children. Intent on avoiding the problems incurred by the successors of Henry I and insisting on his successor being a male, Edward originally wrote that the heir would be the first son from this line. Following Mary, however, had been her daughters Frances and Eleanor – both her sons, both named Henry, had already died – and following Frances were Jane, Catherine and Mary, none of whom were even close to mothering boys.

Undeterred by the inevitable pitfalls, the king's proposal was far from lacking support. Also Somerset's successor at the heart of the Edwardian Reformation, Dudley feared the accession of Mary, realising not only would the results of his recent work be undone, but it would almost certainly cost him his life. As Edward's health continued to deteriorate, the necessity for the accession plans to become more formal became pressing. Inserting two words into the crude, childlike, handwritten will, Edward declared the next in line to be the daughters of Frances 'and their' male successors rather than just the male successors.

With this, succession would fall to a girl whose reign was doomed from the start.

Chapter 13

1553–1558: Nine-Day Queens and Bloody Bonfires

For many, Lady Jane Grey remains an enigma in the context of English history. Famed as the 'nine-day queen', it has become a matter for much debate as to whether the girl destined to die uncrowned should be acknowledged as a queen at all or, indeed, whether her reign lasted exactly nine days.

Of her early life, there is much to praise. The eldest daughter of Henry VIII's niece, Frances – herself daughter of Mary, daughter of Henry VII – Jane had been blessed with both an outstanding mind and formal education. This was typified by the story that she was discovered by the visiting scholar Roger Ascham reading the works of Plato – written in the original Greek – under a tree. Also accomplished in Hebrew and Latin, the young scholar had already garnered herself a reputation as being among the most learned girls of the age.

For Northumberland, Jane was everything England needed in a queen. An intelligent, devoutly Protestant girl still only in her teens, she was unlikely to prove a major obstacle in his continued attempts to wield power. Avoiding the complexity of a Henry VIII descendant, Lady Jane's veins nevertheless flowed with the royal blood of Henry VII, which, according to certain scholars, offered a royal line all the way back to Arthur and Merlin.

Debatable though that may be, a descendant of both the red and white rose while avoiding the complications created in Henry VIII's reign appealed to many key players in the Privy Council. Northumberland's original plan had been to give Jane in marriage to his youngest son; however, as Edward's life began to slip away, it became increasingly clear the possibility of the crown falling to Jane's still-to-be-conceived first son would be impossible. With Edward's death on 6 July, Jane, still unaware of her cousin's aspirations for her, was brought to Syon Park to learn that she had been named Edward's rightful successor in his last will and testament. Jane was understandably shocked on hearing the news, protesting that Princess Mary was the lawful heir. With news of the king's designs emphasised further, Jane's secondary reaction was to burst into tears. Clinging to her steadfast ways that had so far guided her upbringing so well and arguing vehemently to the contrary, on finding herself cajoled by a combination of ambitious parents, a politically relevant new husband and a predominantly anti-Catholic government, Jane reluctantly accepted the role. Within two days, the unwilling queen followed in the footsteps of all would-be monarchs and was sailed downriver to the Tower.

Jane entered the fortress via the Byward Tower, accompanied by her new husband, Guildford Dudley, and a small retinue. Entering the great hall, she experienced the throne for the first time. Although she refused to even remotely entertain any offer to try on the crown, she later made the curious remark that the man she had just married would never rule as king, leading to an evening of petulant sulking as the furious Northumberland clan failed to get their way. In spite of the fraught atmosphere, Jane nevertheless ordered Guildford to remain by her side throughout, as expected of a good consort.

Eyewitness accounts of these events paint a startling picture. Appalled by the initial suggestion she was to be queen, Jane wasted little time asserting her authority. Beyond the Tower walls, however, the intrigue was building. If response to Jane's accession had not already raised eyebrows, Northumberland sought to diffuse any rising tension by sending two of his sons in search of Princess Mary, concerned that news of Jane's ascension would lead to insurrection. Approaching Mary's residence at Hunsdon with 300 horsemen, they found it deserted.

How Mary responded on hearing of Jane's accession is not recorded. Learning, probably from the Catholic earl of Arundel, her brother was dying, Mary immediately fled deep into East Anglia, a county that had earlier proved troublesome for Dudley during the rising of Robert Kett. On her arrival at the village of Kenninghall, renowned as being a Howard stronghold, Mary opened correspondence with the Tower, exerting her better claim, in addition to confessing her surprise that the council had kept her in the dark of the major developments that had taken place throughout her brother's illness. When an unfortunate messenger brought the bad news to the Tower, he was immediately imprisoned.

News of Mary's potential rising was met at the Tower with appropriate severity. After placating his distressed duchess, Northumberland and the council rallied, composing a formal response to Mary that the council had decided to exercise the late king's will and expected her obedience. In a concurrent move, a proclamation was issued by the Privy Council that Mary was no true daughter of Henry VIII due to the annulment of Catherine of Aragon's marriage and the wedding having occurred outside the Protestant church. Though many members of the council doubted their recent work would prove sufficient, after making the decision to put together an armed force to bring Mary to the Tower, Northumberland took the reins, praying that history in East Anglia might repeat itself. Armed with 600 horsemen, 2,000 foot soldiers and a selection of the Tower's best cannons, they reached Cambridge on 14 July, by which time Dudley had been reacquainted with his sons.

A day earlier, Mary, swelled by additions to her own force, had reached Framlingham Castle in Suffolk, the largest fortress in the area. In Northumberland's absence, other members of the Privy Council, perhaps aware of the bigger picture, also came out in support of the princess. Despite remaining inside the Tower, which was now locked, the keys in Jane's possession, the mood had clearly changed. A meeting outside the walls at Baynard's Castle, led by Arundel, confirmed the turning of the tide. On hearing the news, Jane apparently agreed that this was far more sensible than Northumberland's earlier ill-conceived ambitions. Watching as her closest supporters deserted her, Jane was left little choice than to make the short move from the royal palace to the lieutenant's lodgings: the same area once endured by Anne Boleyn and Catherine Howard. With this development, any hope she had of becoming queen had gone.

Dudley's race was also run. Joining Mary and proclaiming her queen in Cambridge, he must have feared retribution would be striking if not swift. On 20 July, Mary, still at Framlingham, received news of her bloodless success from Arundel, who in turn was instructed to arrest Northumberland in Cambridge. Returning to the capital, on the way to the Tower, it required a force of 4,000 to spare him the malice of angry

Londoners. Reaching the Tower, he was taken to the Garden Tower, which at the time still endured something of a darkened reputation for its alleged connection with the vanished princes. Joining him in the inner ward were his five sons, all of whom were placed in the Beauchamp Tower. Among them was Robert Dudley, who would one day make his own mark on England's troubled history.

Her ascension assured, Mary, contrastingly, took her time in completing the journey. Entering London in glorious triumph on 3 August, her destination was also the Tower. One of the first to greet her on her arrival was Thomas Howard, 3rd Duke of Norfolk, spared death by her father's timely demise, along with two key Catholic bishops: Stephen Gardiner of Winchester and the bishop of London, Edmund Bonner. Joining them was the long-imprisoned Edward Courtenay, in theory now the Yorkist heir, and the widowed duchess of Somerset, Anne Seymour (née Stanhope), who had been kept in the Tower since Seymour's execution. After embracing them all warmly, Mary officially liberated them from captivity.

Key state business inevitably awaited the new queen. With her brother still to be laid to rest, the task of overseeing the service was offered to Cranmer, now England's chief Protestant. Shortly after her arrival, Mary received a long apology from Lady Jane, asking her forgiveness while trying to explain how recent events had come to pass. After thoughtfully taking the apology into consideration, along with the counsel of her key advisors, it was decided the threat of insurrection remained too large a risk to allow Jane to walk free. Like many a pretender before her, Jane would be forced to reside in the Tower for the foreseeable future.

Whereas Jane's future remained in the balance, Northumberland's fate was more certain. In his trial at Westminster, he took the honourable step of exonerating Lady Jane, before claiming his 'treason' against Mary was merely out of love for Edward VI, a fact one might argue was also true of those trying him. Presiding over the 'guilty' lords was Norfolk who had seemingly learned nothing from his six years in captivity. Along with his two sons who had attempted to detain Mary at the start of Jane's short reign, Northumberland was condemned to death.

There followed another classic example of intrigue influenced by propaganda. Learning that his execution had been set for 21 August, the conniving Northumberland requested to hear a Catholic mass. As Somerset's ardent follower in the Edwardian Reformation, this 'change of conscience' was simply astounding. His wishes accepted, he attended mass at St Peter ad Vincula in the company of those destined to die alongside him. Taking communion, he confessed his regret at being led astray by new preachers, hoping the public confession would be enough to earn him respite. Failing to affect the outcome, other than a twenty-four-hour-stay of execution, he wrote desperately to Arundel, again without success.

On the morning of 22 August in the company of his two accomplices Sir Thomas Palmer and Sir John Gates, a defeated Dudley mounted the scaffold at Tower Hill. Frequenting the same site that had earlier witnessed the end of his father, Edmund, following the ascension of Henry VIII, he addressed the crowd, maintaining his recent view that Catholicism was the one true faith while thanking Mary for allowing him time to repent and reconnect with his true calling. Palmer, on the other hand, maintained his Protestant faith, declaring he had earlier witnessed Christ seated in a 'dark corner in yon Tower' and was pleased to be leaving a world in which he had witnessed only 'ambition, flattery, foolishness, vainglory, pride, discord, slander, boasting, hatred and malice', perhaps a passing reference to the convert with whom he had shared the scaffold. Like Dudley, he was despatched with a single blow.

The extent of recent events that Lady Jane had witnessed personally is surprisingly numerous. An account by one Rowland Lee, an employee at the Royal Mint at the time of her imprisonment who developed a connection with the unfortunate prisoner, confirms much of her later actions. Initially content to await her fate, indignant at her father-in-law Dudley's manipulations but also thankful for Mary's mercy, she, like Anne Boleyn and Catherine Howard before her, passed her time in the company of her ladies, all the while remaining steadfast to her Protestant beliefs. Keeping her company were bishops Cranmer and Latimer who, after presiding over Edward's burial, had switched places with their recently released Catholic equivalents. Included in Lady Jane's writings was a furious attack on her family's ex-chaplain, one Dr Thomas Harding, for his reconciliation with Rome after previously being a confirmed Protestant under Edward VI.

For Mary, Jane's future had to wait until the more pressing matter of her own coronation had been taken care of. After enjoying the usual proceedings at the Tower, festivities which welcomed her half-sister – the outwardly Catholic but privately Protestant Princess Elizabeth – as the drizzly November skies loomed ominously overhead, Jane was brought to trial, along with Guildford, Henry and Ambrose Dudley and the recently maligned stalwart from Henry VIII's reign, Archbishop Cranmer. It says much about the erratic see-sawing of fortunes at the time that the man who had been so productive at the heart of the previous two regimes would find himself imprisoned, whereas the exiled Reginald Pole could take his place. In contrast to every prisoner being dressed in black in a public show of penitence for past sins, Jane held a Protestant prayer book, a gesture clearly intended to display her preparation for martyrdom. As usual for a state trial at that time, the guilty verdicts were already a foregone conclusion.

The nine-day queen was sentenced to death. Better luck, however, had befallen English-born mercenary Thomas Stucley. After being imprisoned in the Tower at least once – apparently for conspiring with the French to capture Calais from the English, as well as for incurring debts to an Irishman that he had failed to repay – he was released in 1553 before successfully managing to cross to the Low Countries.

It was also at this time a third Wyatt would play his part in the Tower's dark history. Son and namesake of the poet, Thomas, by 1554 he had already suffered one period there as punishment along with his friend and social equal Thomas Howard, the earl of Surrey, after disturbing sleeping Londoners during a night of drunken carnage. Things changed, however, with news of the queen's impending marriage to Philip II of Spain. Having joined his father, who had been spared the wrath of Henry VIII, in a diplomatic mission to Spain, Wyatt's first impression of the Inquisition had been one of utter shock. Fearing the potential emergence of such methods in England, Wyatt conspired with no less than three others to lead a rebellion in Kent on Psalm Sunday the following year.

Key among his accomplices was Edward Courtenay, the same man Mary had recently freed and now earl of Devon. The reason for his involvement, apparently, was the earl's disappointment at Mary's decision to marry Philip II of Spain rather than himself, yet the recent xenophobia against the Spanish made it likely the revolt went beyond one man's setback. There is also some evidence the aim had been to secure Courtenay's hand in marriage to the Lady Elizabeth, for the Catholic Courtenay a silver medal at best. Joining Courtenay, Henry Grey – Lady Jane's father and 1st duke of Suffolk – was to operate in the Midlands with another, Sir James Croft, concentrating on the Welsh Marches.

Unfortunately for Wyatt, the ground would soon crumble from beneath his feet. Hearing of the plot in January 1554 from one of his former prison mates, Bishop Gardiner questioned Courtenay in detail. Realising their cause was lost, most of the plotters wasted no time making their escape, after which Suffolk was discovered hiding in woodland after attempting to take Coventry. Despite the reversals, the revolt did at least offer some insight into public sentiment at Mary's early reign. After gaining the sympathy of the people of Kent, and even a militia sent out by Mary to quash them, the militia-aided group marched towards Rochester, taking it. After the failure to put down the rebellion, Norfolk retreated hastily to the capital.

For Wyatt, London was well and truly in his sights. Rather than shelter in the Tower, Mary remained at Westminster, steadfastly continuing with her plans to marry Philip. After stirring her citizens into rising up to protect her, Wyatt finally ran into difficulty. Following several days of attempted infiltration, the rebellion was halted and the defeated Wyatt was dragged to the Tower, along with many of his followers, to set up home in the Bell Tower.

Despite its eventual failure, the rebellion was significant for several reasons. Apart from the outbreak of anti-Spanish feeling that would be prevalent in England over the next century, the actions of Wyatt and Grey sadly condemned Lady Jane. Although personally blameless, it was clear to Mary that as long as her cousin lived, a focal point of rebellion would continue to haunt her. Her one concession to Jane was that her sentence would be beheading.

Fresh from their recent capture, Suffolk followed Wyatt in joining his daughter in the Tower. Curiously, it seems that while imprisoned some form of communication occurred between daughter and father in the form of messages concealed within a damaged prayer book. Mary, concerned still for Jane's soul if not her body, attempted to rid her conscience of her cousin's fate by sending her own chaplain, Dr John Feckenham, to visit her at the Tower. Recently released himself after being imprisoned for resisting the Edwardian Reformation, the likeable former monk was received politely by Jane, who clung to her beliefs, claiming her fate was not a sign of error, but merely a test of strength. Deflated by Jane's stoutness of heart, Feckenham reluctantly admitted defeat.

By 11 February, Jane realised her time was up. After spending her final night alternating between prayer and writing to her family, most notably words of encouragement to her father, her destination was not to be Tower Hill, where her execution would have been a public spectacle event, but on the green in private solemnity. Ignoring the distraction of the scaffold being erected, the sight of her husband being led to Tower Hill, and subsequently his decapitated corpse returned on a litter, Jane was led from her lodgings across the inner ward to north of the White Tower where her distant relatives Anne Boleyn and Catherine Howard had died years earlier. Dressed in the same black dress and holding the book she had taken to her trial, she joined the lieutenant of the Tower in making the final journey. Addressing the dignitaries gathered there, she expressed remorse for allowing herself to be manipulated into taking a throne that was never hers. After agreeing to pray with Feckenham, she gave her prayer book to the lieutenant as a mark of gratitude, and removed her outer garments. Making the usual requests of the axe man, she tied her own blindfold and struggled sightlessly to the block. When the axe finally fell, death was mercifully instant.

Shortly prior to Jane's end, a similar fate had awaited her husband. Refused the opportunity to meet his wife one last time, such a meeting being seemingly viewed by Jane as a source of additional pain, the often petulant young man who had wept on hearing his sentence, faced death courageously. Led out from his confinement in the Beauchamp Tower – into one of the walls of which the carving of his wife's name can still be seen to this day – he made his final journey out of the inner and outer wards to Tower Hill, where an excitable crowd eagerly awaited. Refusing the opportunity of Catholic prayer, he was executed swiftly, just a few hours before Jane. Last on the list was Suffolk. Having been haplessly corrupted by the potential of the throne for his daughter before failing with his own rebellion in the Midlands, the earl was beheaded on 23/24 February.

For Mary, the three deaths eliminated one potential source of uprising, but in her sister Elizabeth, a more potent threat remained. Initially cursed by the common Tudor difficulties of producing a male heir – as she would be throughout her reign – Mary dispatched a group of some 250 horsemen to Ashridge where Elizabeth had been kept since the coronation. In contrast to Wyatt and Suffolk, the situation Elizabeth found herself in was not of her own doing. Exonerated by Wyatt, even under pressure from the White Tower's torturers, Mary could not shake the fear the intention of others to place Elizabeth on the throne was one she could not neglect. Arriving at Ashridge late one evening sometime in the middle of February, the horsemen discovered Elizabeth in bed, complaining of illness. Refusing steadfastly to disobey instructions and to return to London without her, the next morning Elizabeth, carried on a litter, agreed to go with them, bracing the cold air and what turned out to be a difficult week-long journey to the capital.

At Whitehall, the heir to the throne protested her innocence of any illicit endeavours. Finding no evidence against her, she was nevertheless transported to the Tower. For Elizabeth, there is no doubt the sudden turn of events were viewed with trepidation. For her family, most notably her mother, incarceration in the Tower had not ended well. Initially reluctant, Elizabeth braved the cold, wet conditions and was escorted by the lieutenant through Traitors' Gate. Not as a visitor, but a prisoner.

Unlike her royal predecessors, her lodgings would be neither those of the lieutenant nor the royal palace. Instead, she found herself in the upper chamber of the Bell Tower that had been famously occupied by Bishop Fisher in the reign of her father. Ironically, the Bell Tower that is now closed to modern-day visitors sits adjacent to the Queen's House and can only be entered that way. Deprived of the usual privileges, she was allowed a small area of wall walk between the Bell and Beauchamp towers for exercise, an area known thereafter as 'Elizabeth's Walk'. It may have offered some degree of solace knowing that held in the state prison was a young man she had known since her youth and one of the remaining sons of the doomed duke of Northumberland. History recalls Elizabeth would experience a very special relationship with Robert Dudley.

Treatment of Elizabeth, even for a royal at the time, paid relatively little regard for her status. As was her right, food was brought in from outside the Tower, but searched thoroughly to ensure no illicit communication took place. She later complained the guards tended to help themselves to some of it, eventually resulting in an agreement for her servants to cook the food for her in the lieutenant's lodgings before taking it up to her cell. As time passed, her walkway became less used as she was allowed access to the privy garden on the insistence other prisoners were prohibited from making contact.

On 11 April that year, Wyatt finally ran out of luck. Bravely defying his interrogators till the last while stretched out repeatedly on the rack, thus ensuring Elizabeth's life remained intact, he was executed on Tower Hill. Whereas his father and grandfather had escaped the Tower's ultimate penalty, sadly for the third generation of the family, there would be no reprieve. In keeping with his previous stance, he confirmed to the crowds that Elizabeth had been in no way involved with the ill-fated rebellion he had personally initiated. Also executed were no less than a hundred of his fellow conspirators. Sixteen days later, Lord Thomas Grey was also executed on 27 April 1554 for his part in the treason.

As Mary continued to passionately oversee her counter-reformation while consistently falling for the belief that she was with child, Elizabeth's fortunes slowly improved. After two exhausting months, she was finally granted permission to leave the Tower in May 1554 on her sister's insistence she should enjoy the rural seclusion of the royal palace at Woodstock in Oxfordshire. Joining her in leaving the Tower was the reckless Courtenay and what remained of the Dudley clan, including Robert. With her sister absent, Mary enjoyed the luxury of the royal apartments, staying there from late 1555 to 1556, still intent on becoming pregnant. Unlike her husband, who visited the Tower only three times during their marriage, Mary was not averse to its palatial charms.

Others not destined to be staying long, however, were two prisoners confined to the Tower for a rather different conspiracy. Son of the knight, Sir Edmund Peckham, Henry Peckham and his accomplice John Daniel were arrested, not on charges of heresy, but for conspiring with vice-admiral Sir Henry Dudley to rob the Exchequer as part of a plan aimed at bringing about a French invasion. Found guilty, both were imprisoned in the Tower, with Daniel in particular being subjected to close confinement. A report from April 1555 explicitly highlighted Daniel's weakening condition and his inscription in the stonework still marks an inner wall in the Broad Arrow Tower. Eventually spared of further ordeal, he was brought to Tower Hill on 7 July 1556 to be hanged.

Treason, of course, was just one of a number of ways a person could find themselves in the Tower. And throughout Mary's reign and that of her most recent predecessors, one theme which refused to go away was heresy. It was for such reasons at this particular time that the fires of martyrdom, which history would later infamously recall would burn brightly throughout Mary's turbulent reign, would begin to cast their ominous glow.

Three of the most prominent figures to be affected by the sweeping changes were the unfortunate prelates of the previous era. Deprived of their powers because of the Marian Counter Reformation, Thomas Cranmer, Hugh Latimer and Nicholas Ridley all found themselves in the company of the hordes of Protestant victims in the Tower. So tight was space, all three of these once revered clerics were forced to share a cell.

First to be relieved of the ignominy of prison were Latimer and Ridley who were burned for their heresy in October 1555. For Latimer, the fires represented a far more complex symbolism: not merely a physical pyre but a prelude to the Protestant Reformation that would eventually seal Mary's doom. Also to suffer at the stake in Oxford was the equally unfortunate Cranmer, sentenced to die five months later. After initially recanting his Protestant faith, the now broken former theological pioneer and spiritual leader should by law have been spared; however, Mary, recklessly, viewed his sins as being unforgiveable: ironically something that would confirm his martyrdom. After being offered the chance to recant publicly at the university church, Cranmer deviated from his written script and denounced not his faith but the recanting of it. At his end he adhered to his vow that his right hand would burn first and ended his life in ill-deserved pain, steadfast, nevertheless, in his belief he was entering a better world.

How bad the old world could be for a Protestant in Mary's reign is illustrated in a unique chronicle that was successfully smuggled out of the Tower. The manuscript dates from 1557 and is credited to a Protestant by the name of Cuthbert Symson, who is recorded as having 'stood in an engine of iron 3 hours within the Tower, commonly called Scevington gyves' which, as previously mentioned, almost certainly equates to the Scavenger's Daughter.

Like many a Protestant clergyman living at that time, Symson's story is a tragic one. When an Edmund Bonner spy by the name of Roger Sergeant infiltrated a Protestant congregation known to meet in one of two taverns in the Limehouse district of London, the minister John Rough was forced to flee the Catholic pursuivants, leaving the group in the hands of Symson, its only deacon. For the next year or so, the intelligent Symson kept the secret congregation together – no mean feat considering Symson's high profile jobs at the time included being paymaster to every prison in London, including the Tower. Sadly for the loyal and innovative deacon, his good fortune would eventually run out. On 12 December 1556, along with fellow Protestants Hugh Foxe and John Devenish, Symson was arrested on charges of heresy and transferred to the Tower.

It is concerning the events that followed where Symson's own writings are so invaluable. Having shown little willingness to answer the questions of the constable and the recorder, he was subsequently tortured. After an initial three-hour session on the rack caused him to faint from the pain, he was later awoken and the process repeated, by which time Symson was physically unable to stand. On leaving the rack, his fingers were bound together and an arrow was forced between them, the result of which he faced the anguish of the arrow levered back and forth. With the strange torture at an end, he was again placed on the rack.

All the evidence that survives indicates that Symson was racked at least six times, not to mention subjected to other devices including the Scavenger's Daughter. Frustrated with the lack of progress, Bonner had him relocated to the bishop's own coal shed where Symson was put in stocks and fed the most basic of diets. On 19 March, some three months after his initial arrest, Symson and his comrades were brought to trial. Despite the notable concession from Bonner that Symson was 'of the greatest patience that yet ever came before' him, he was martyred at the stake, in the company of Foxe and Devenish, nine days later at Smithfield.

As fate would have it, Mary would join her many victims in death far sooner than expected. Merely three years after the first Oxford martyrdoms and two days after the final Smithfield Fire, Mary, childless and devoid of the loving husband she had always craved, passed away from uterine cancer on 17 November 1558. Meeting his end the very same day was the once exiled Catholic Reginald Pole. In one fell swoop the Protestant fires Latimer predicted had arrived. Not only vacated was the throne but the queen's understudy as head of the church.

With no heir to succeed her or senior prelate to shepherd the scattering flock, it would prove the end of England's long history of Catholic rule and the beginning of a new era.

Chapter 14

1558–1586: Catholics, Conspirators and Clandestine Couples

On receiving news of her half-sister's death, Princess Elizabeth arrived at the Tower on 28 November, her journey delayed by a far more jovial crowd than had awaited either Mary or Lady Jane.

For Elizabeth personally, it was perhaps understandable that she arrived with mixed feelings. Her situation was far brighter than during her last visit to the Tower, but gone were the days the monarchs of England had felt any great love or affection for the castle as a royal palace. Surrounded just a few years earlier by those destined to end their lives in ignominy, it is equally of no surprise that the queen who had recently enjoyed the country lifestyle had no wish to use the Tower as a regular haunt.

As a consequence, Elizabeth would be the last monarch to treat the Tower as any form of royal residence.

Plans for Elizabeth's coronation began almost from the moment of Mary's death, mostly against the backdrop of council meetings concerning future policy. Adopting the approach of her predecessors, Elizabeth's council met frequently inside the Tower's great hall, which had at one time hosted meetings that ensured the end of her mother. Among the early changes had been the inevitable reversal of the Marian Counter Reformation, thus proclaiming England a Protestant land once more. Imprisoned clerics were released from the Tower, many taking the sees vacated by recently expelled Catholic priests and prelates, who in turn would often swap their parishes for the Tower's cells. A moderate ruler on matters of the heart, Elizabeth was determined there would be no repeat of the fires that had characterised Mary's reign. Indeed, some form of tolerance would be enjoyed throughout the next decade.

A brief glimpse at the history of the Tower during the later years of Mary's reign and early days of Elizabeth's, nevertheless, proves quite succinctly just how unstable life was during that period. For poor John Feckenham, imprisoned for resisting the Reformation before enjoying some renewed status under Mary, he would once again endure the confines of the Tower under Elizabeth despite being generally beloved as a man of goodness. Around this time, the equally unfortunate Cambridge scholar John Cheke, who had schooled the late Edward VI before failing to convert Feckenham during his first period of imprisonment in the Tower only to be converted by the same man when the shoe was on the other foot, had been himself imprisoned by Mary. Whereas Feckenham never swayed in his devotion and eventually died in prison, Cheke had converted, only to die a year before Elizabeth's ascension.

Worse fortune soon befell Mary's Catholic Bishop of London, Edmund Bonner. A somewhat controversial character since his ascension to the See of London in 1539, Bonner had already received the cold shoulder of the new queen on being received at court for the first time before displaying his own contempt by passionately refusing to acknowledge Elizabeth's outlawing of the Catholic mass, which came officially into effect on 25 June 1559. After failing to comply with the royal council's decree on two separate occasions, a subsequent order demanded he vacate the bishopric. By 20 April 1560, the queen's patience was finally exhausted and Bonner was sent to the Tower. Over the coming decade, the majority of which he spent in Marshalsea Prison, Bonner's spirits remained surprisingly high. Those who saw him often described him as a 'most courteous man', a statement that may seem somewhat at odds with the reality that no less than eighty-nine of the Protestant martyrs of Mary's reign had been sentenced by Bonner personally. He died on 5 September 1569, spared the fires of martyrdom or the axe of treason, and taken instead by the shadow of ignominy.

Early challenges to face Elizabeth included those encountered by both her father and siblings. Now in her late twenties, Elizabeth was still to wed let alone conceive, not that she had necessarily tried. On matters of succession, the problems of alternate claimants that had plagued many of her predecessors, notably Edward, were now less pressing. With Jane and Mary both dead and without issue, pretendership seemed unlikely, albeit not impossible.

Edward VI's will had been clear that succession would lie with the daughters of Frances Grey and their subsequent heirs. Though Jane, of course, had died before having a chance to become pregnant – or at least for anything to become known – she did have two sisters, the eldest of whom was Catherine. During the early days of Jane's short reign, Northumberland had used Catherine as a pawn in his plans by marrying her to the earl of Pembroke, son of Northumberland's deputy. On Jane's execution, Catherine, as sadly was so often the case in Tudor England, was dramatically cast aside by her new in-laws and the marriage dissolved by her husband on grounds that it had not been consummated.

Initially it seems Elizabeth saw the 18-year-old as little threat. Inviting her to court to become her lady-in-waiting, Catherine's future soon became somewhat cloudy after it emerged she had recently married Somerset's eldest son in a clandestine ceremony. In contrast to her first marriage, the wedding to Edward 'Ned' Seymour had certainly been consummated and the new wife was already expecting. For Catherine, marriage without royal permission was a shocking risk. Confiding her situation to Robert Dudley, the unfortunate sister of Jane was imprisoned in the same Bell Tower cell Elizabeth herself had once occupied. Joining her across the inner ward would be her husband, himself incarcerated in the White Tower.

Better news for Catherine came with the arrival of her baby boy without complication. Shortly after, her son was baptised in the royal chapel of St Peter ad Vincula – the same grim place where the bodies of Jane, Somerset and Elizabeth's foster father Edward Seymour lay. To complicate matters further, the returning lieutenant, Sir Edward Warner, under strict orders to keep Ned and Catherine apart, allowed them a brief meeting and for the second time in less than a year, Catherine became pregnant. On learning of the pregnancy, Elizabeth dismissed the errant Warner, and substituted his residence in the Queen's House for imprisonment in one of the cells.

Among Warner's neighbours in the Tower's cells at this time were two men recorded in contemporary sources solely as Pitt and Nicholls. Interrogated by Warner's replacement as lieutenant of the Tower, Sir Richard Blount, on 15 March 1559, it was penned in the council books that if necessary they were to be 'brought to the rack, and to feel the smart thereof, if as the examinees by their discretion shall think good.' It is unclear to what lengths they were actually subjected.

Ironically, considering the Tower saw a change of prisoners following Elizabeth's succession as those of the Protestant faith were released and replaced by Catholics, the Tower actually enjoyed a slightly quieter period at this time. It was almost certainly a sign of less stringent security that no less than two escapes occurred during Elizabeth's initial three years. The first of these was William Ogier, who escaped from the Tower by unknown means in 1560. A year later, 1561 saw the imprisonment of Sir Anthony Fortescue, who had been brought to the Tower three years earlier in connection with the casting of Elizabeth's horoscope. After being initially pardoned, Fortescue was arrested a second time along with Arthur and Edmund Pole as they prepared to sail for Flanders, upon which they were tried at Westminster Hall and found guilty of high treason. Notable among the facts brought to light were their alleged intention of plotting an invasion backed by a force of 6,000 men from France with the intention of replacing Elizabeth with Mary, Queen of Scots.

Despite being sentenced to death, at Elizabeth's command the sentences were commuted to life imprisonment in the Tower. Arthur and Edmund Pole both died between 1565 and 1578, but Fortescue escaped from the Tower, most likely with the aid of his brother, Sir John, whom Elizabeth held in high regard. Intriguingly, the casting of horoscopes would be a recurring theme, as the year 1561 was also notable for an impressive illustration etched into the walls of the Salt Tower by one Hew Draper, a tavern keeper in Bristol accused of sorcery – claims he refuted. The markings, which survive to this day, comprised an astrological clock and calendar, as well as several other symbols.

French naval officer, navigator and explorer Jean Ribault would one day be remembered for his role in the colonisation of the New World, yet back in 1562 he experienced a far more depressing period in the Tower. On his return from voyages of discovery he found France weighed down by the outbreak of the wars of religion, and after a short time assisting the Huguenots at Dieppe he fled to England when the town fell. Granted an audience with Elizabeth I about funding for future exploration and settlements, what began as an encouraging endeavour led to his being held for several months in the Tower, accused of being a spy. During that time, he wrote of his earlier voyage, the only known copy surviving in English.

In 1563, after five years of relative peace in England, the Tower witnessed the baptism of the second Grey/Seymour offspring. Unfortunately for Catherine, the luckless bride had lost the marriage document, meaning that as long as proof of the marriage was unforthcoming, the pair were destined to be held in the Tower, albeit in conditions in keeping with their royal status. In way of company, Catherine was permitted both a dog and a monkey – the latter most likely rehoused from the Tower menagerie. Despite living so close, it was also a case of so close yet so far. When the plague hit London and the most important prisoners had their sentences changed to house arrest, their respective destinations were Essex and Hanworth. Even on the outside world, the pair would never be reunited.

While marrying without royal permission, treason and being of potential pretender blood would be a recurring theme in Elizabethan England, it was also in Elizabeth's reign that the Tower would see a new type of prisoner. Replacing the Protestant 'heretics' whose violent ends had permanently coloured the reputation of 'Bloody' Mary were prisoners in every way their religious and political equivalent. What is now remembered as the Golden Age of England would also be the age of the Catholic conspirator.

Exactly how dangerous the average papist was in Elizabethan England is a question worthy of extended debate. Scorned in some factions as the harbingers of evil, in reality it seems highly evident most cases of papist unrest originated in retribution against those who brought harm on them, rather than any form of unprovoked zealotry. In the eyes of the English government, however, the situation was arguably more complicated. In keeping with the old adage, the enemy of my enemy is my friend, the greater fear among the privy councillors was not so much what these individuals could achieve on their own, but more could they if left to their own devices foster any potential connection with Catholic Spain or the equally Catholic, Mary, Queen of Scots. With Mary Tudor dead, and Elizabeth no closer to providing an heir, so long as Mary Stuart and Philip II remained alive, the question of succession would continue to be unresolved.

The first serious threat against Elizabeth came about in 1569 and was indeed of Catholic origin. A year earlier, Mary, Queen of Scots had been arrested and brought to England, marking the beginning of an eventful eighteen years that would be spent in various prisons. Either naïve in her planning or simply sick of incarceration, Mary encouraged the plots against Elizabeth, the first of which was the Norfolk Plot. Deviating slightly from the blueprint for previous royal conspiracies, the plan, hatched by northern royalist Catholics, included not only an intended uprising against the queen but also for Mary to be married to Thomas Howard, 4th Duke of Norfolk: son of the disgraced earl of Surrey, who Henry VIII had executed following his attempt to escape the Tower via a latrine, and grandson of the third duke, who had died shortly after being released by Mary I.

Norfolk's willingness to comply was instant. Smitten with the deposed Scottish queen, as lieutenant of the north, he had been instructed by Elizabeth to receive Mary personally. Now widowed for the third time, Howard was also of some royal stock, and, theoretically at least, a suitable match for Mary Stuart. Coupled with a rising in the north, led by the earls of Northumberland and Westmoreland, the plotters took Durham before word reached the queen of their treasonous intent. When the rising was broken up as the force endeavoured to march south, the two earls fled north of the border, whereas Norfolk was captured and thrown in the Tower.

Elizabeth decided to be lenient with the handsome courtier. Allowing him use of the east end of the royal apartments, Norfolk was kept informed of proceedings by a series of messages inserted through a hole in his chambers. After avoiding incriminating himself under painless interrogations by Elizabeth's secretary of state, Sir William Cecil, he was later freed, albeit placed under strict observation. Two who would lose their lives for their roles in the Northern Rising would be Christopher Norton and his uncle Thomas, both proud northerners. So great was the pain on having his entrails removed, Christopher is reported to have yelled out, 'Oh Lord, Lord, have mercy upon me,' before breathing his last.

Prisoners in the Tower for harbouring similar Mary Stuart-sympathies included Charles Bailly. Remembered by history for penning the useful advice that 'wise men ought circumspectly to see what they do, examine before they speak, prove before they take in hand, to beware whose company they use and, above all things, to consider whom they trust,' Bailly also carved a multi-language inscription into his cell wall, reading: *tout vient apoient quy peult attendre* – 'all comes to those who wait.' Joining Bailly until the former's release – his name also carved into the walls of the Beauchamp Tower's upper chamber – Dr John Story had made a dreadful reputation for himself 'purifying' Protestants in the reign of Bloody Mary. After spending some time as a Catholic exile in Antwerp throughout the reign of Edward VI and again on Mary's death, he was captured after being tricked on board a ship. Docking at Yarmouth, at which point the captain was cheered like a hero, Story was brought to the Tower and put on trial for a number of charges that included aiding the Duke of Alba in planning an invasion and praying for and plotting the queen's death. In response to an intervention by the Spanish ambassador, prior to Story's decapitation at Tyburn on 1 June 1571, Elizabeth is reported as having replied, 'The King of Spain may have his head if he wants it, but his body shall be left in England.' His execution is remembered as the debut of the 'Tyburn Tree', an assembly that allowed twenty-four criminals to be executed simultaneously, as opposed to the usual eight. It is also recorded that during his disembowelling, Story somehow mustered the strength to sit up and punch his executioner in the face.

Story's attempt at knocking out a royal official was not entirely unique. Imprisoned in the same tower two years later, religious fanatic Peter Burchet would receive dreadful retribution for striking dead yeoman warder, Hugh Longworth with a burning log from the fire as the latter read the bible near the window. Imprisoned already for the attempted murder of admiral Sir John Hawkins, Burchet's crimes of striking a royal official and murder saw him not only lose his right arm, but also be put to death at Temple Bar, his hand nailed to the gibbet above him as his neck was choked within the noose.

The year 1571 would mark something of a watershed in the ongoing religious diversity that had troubled England since Henry VIII's first divorce. Inspired by the papal bull *Regnans in Excelsis* which had excommunicated the Protestant Elizabeth a year earlier, Florentine banker Ricardo Ridolfi was at the forefront of a new plot, which appears to have been of similar ambition to the Norfolk one a year earlier. The major difference was reports of a foreign invasion, notably a Spanish army arriving from the Spanish Netherlands. Unsurprisingly, it was not long before the two plots were more or less merged. Either duped or inspired by Ridolfi, Norfolk agreed to pledge his own involvement, something that later became known to the soon-to-be famous spymaster Sir Francis Walsingham.

The turning of the tide came literally in April 1571, specifically in Dover. Under the watchful eye of Walsingham's spies, the plot was uncovered when the same Charles Bailly – by now a known Catholic spy having spent time in the Tower the year before – was caught red-handed attempting to deliver fresh letters concerning the foreign invasion. After the discovery of the coded letters, the duke was brought to the Tower a second time. On this occasion rather than to enjoy the use of the palace, his lodgings were the Garden Tower.

Walsingham immediately struck further. Joining the errant duke, the nearby Beauchamp, Coldharbour and Salt Towers were soon filled with his fellow conspirators. While the nobility were spared torture, for commoners like Bailly there would be no such mercy, and crucially for all concerned, it was his time on the rack that led to their downfall. Disclosing the key to Norfolk's cipher, the true extent of the letters were revealed in their entirety. For Walsingham and the privy councillors, the revelations must have seemed particularly shocking: most notably how the conspirators aimed to take possession of the Tower in Mary's name.

Though initially reluctant to pass final sentence, after six months in captivity, Elizabeth eventually condemned the duke to death. Following in the footsteps of his father, he met his end on Tower Hill in June of 1572. If just one lesson strikes hard at the heart of proceedings, it is undoubtedly the old adage that nothing is ever learned from history. The imprisonment of Howard, not once but twice, made him the fourth successive member of his line to have been imprisoned there: a stark warning perhaps of how great can be the lure of power.

The Norfolk and Ridolfi Plots were swiftly consigned to memory, yet from the similarly failed Northern Rising, more was to come. Percy and Neville, having remained initially at large since the rebellion became fragmented, met their ends with a beheading and on a Spanish pension respectively, their titles inherited by their sons and brothers. As was the case with the earl of Northumberland, the new incumbent was another who failed to heed past lessons. Younger brother of Thomas Percy, Henry, despite having initially fought against the rising in 1569, now took up his dead brother's sword. After communicating with one of Mary's agents while she was imprisoned at Tutbury Castle, Percy was discovered by Sir Ralph Sadler to have offered his services to Mary and was taken to the Tower. After eighteen months there, he was exonerated in exchange for a stiff fine and placed under temporary house arrest before being set free and gradually restored to favour.

Prior to the earl's next run-in with the Tower, the famous old building was to welcome a man who would one day become legendary for a very different reason. Famed for his scholarly thoughtfulness and resoluteness of faith, Father Edmund Campion would soon be renowned for starting the Jesuit mission in England. Captured in 1581 after visiting several Catholic 'recusant' families in secret, the unfortunate priest was placed in the cramped 'little ease' and left for some time. After suffering incessant body cramps, Campion was racked, perhaps as many as three times. So bad was his later deformity, he was unable to raise his arms during his trial. Found guilty of his crimes, the poor priest was executed.

Equal misfortune would befall Father Alexander Briant. A pupil of the infamous Father Robert Persons, Briant was placed under arrest on 28 April that year and racked in the White Tower in a bid to extract information on Persons and the Jesuit mission. Following the excessive torture imposed on him – leading to a disgraceful boast from rack master, Thomas Norton, that he had stretched Briant 'a foot longer than God had made him' – it was recorded that he was frequently starved to the point where he was forced to make do eating clay from the walls and 'loaded with irons and flung into the pit' beneath the White Tower. This may well have been the same pit that had awaited one Thomas Sherwood in November 1577, who was recorded as having been put in 'the dungeon amongst the ratts'. Ironically, in 1583, Norton himself endured a brief stint in the Tower as punishment for some form of criticism of the new faith. He would later resume his career as rack master before dying at his home in 1584.

Prosecuted along with Campion, Ralph Sherwin and three others, Briant met his martyrdom at Tyburn on 1 December and was canonised by the Catholic church in 1970. Almost six months after their executions, on 28 May 1582 Tyburn also awaited the Jesuit Thomas Ford, himself captured with Campion and whose name still decorates a wall in the Broad Arrow Tower. Rescued from Tyburn were two joints of one of his little fingers, both of which became much revered.

The arrest and maiming of seditious author and printer Stubs and Page in 1581 remind us that the purpose of the Tower was for more than just the incarceration of mischievous Catholics. Found guilty of treasonable writings, as well as insulting the duke of Anjou, a potential husband to the queen, the pair were brought from the Tower on 15 November and lost their right hands as retribution for their writings. Within moments of doing so, Stubs is recorded as having raised his hat with his remaining hand and shouted, 'God save the Queen.'

The very next year, now a decade after first being brought to the Tower, lightning was to strike a second time for Henry Percy. In league with the zealous nobleman, Sir Francis Throckmorton, in their attempts to place Mary Stuart on the throne, Percy joined his accomplice in the Tower, but was spared Throckmorton's experience on the rack. Incriminated by his papers and confession, Throckmorton's retraction proved insufficient to prevent his execution at Tyburn in July 1584, yet for Percy better fortune awaited as his incarceration lasted only a few weeks. Having faced two strikes already, the third was not far away. A year later, after inviting Charles Paget and his brother Lord Paget to his residence at Petworth to discuss the prospect of a foreign invasion to aid any English Catholic rising, news of their careless whispers reached the ears of Elizabeth's officials.

Arrested a third time, Percy was confined within the walls of the Garden Tower in December 1584. As a noble, Percy was spared the same barbaric treatment as Throckmorton, but, nevertheless, after six months in captivity, on 21 June 1585 the disgraced earl was found shot dead in his cell, with three musket balls lodged in his heart. What happened remains a mystery. Suggestion of suicide, although officially accepted as the likely cause, was simply ludicrous. As news of his death spread throughout Europe, pamphlets began to appear on mass circulation, implying a government conspiracy.

Among the accusations, sometime later it was alleged by Sir Walter Raleigh that the deed had been the brainchild of Sir Christopher Hatton on behalf of the Privy Council, using the Tower's current lieutenant Owen Hopton as the actual killer. Another possible candidate was the earl's attendant, Thomas Bailiff, who had replaced Percy's servants a short time earlier and discovered the earl around midnight, face down in his bed, the sheets red with blood. Intriguingly, Hopton later discovered a pistol outside the window – curious for an alleged suicide! The following inquiry confirmed the original verdict of death by suicide: this coming in spite of the Coroner's Court confirming he had been hit in the heart, shoulder and through the chin. Strangely, the earl was buried in St Peter ad Vincula rather than a city ditch or at a crossroads which was the usual practice for those who died by suicide.

Prior to the Throckmorton Plot, another Catholic faction had failed with the aptly named Somerville Plot. Influenced by the many criticisms of Elizabeth by the Jesuit priest Father Robert Persons, John Somerville's reputation was undoubtedly tarnished by claims that he was of a nervous, if not mentally questionable, disposition, no doubt highlighted by his open stance against the queen and his desire to murder her. Either clinically insane or naïve in his views, Somerville's attempts to carry out his plot saw his family incriminated, and his father-in-law, Edward Arden, arrested to join him in the Tower. After being delivered to Newgate, Somerville took his own life, broken following a period of torture, and Arden was subsequently executed at Smithfield. A better fate would await his wife and daughter who were pardoned after a time in the Tower.

Mirroring the Protestant onslaught that had defined much of the reign of Mary I, a similar pattern with the Catholics was now emerging. In 1585, Philip Howard, the fiercely devout 20th earl of Arundel, was arrested and taken to the Tower, seemingly for little reason other than his proud conversion to the Catholic faith a year earlier. Joining his engraved name on the walls of the Beauchamp Tower were several others of similar virtue. Over the coming decade or so, Arundel lived something of a monastic life there, surviving on little food and giving regular alms to the poor. Some three years after his arrest, also around the time of the Spanish Armada, a strange, somewhat romantic, story comes to light, concerning Arundel's loyal wife. Rather than attempt to break her husband out of gaol, she instead bribed a beefeater to leave a door open so a Catholic priest imprisoned in the Bell Tower could enter the Beauchamp Tower via Elizabeth's walkway and say mass. Hearing rumours the mass had been for the success of the Armada, the priest was tortured. Condemned to death himself on unproven charges of high treason, Arundel never made it to the block, instead succumbing to dysentery and wasting away slowly in his cell. In honour of his devotion, he was later exhumed from the saddest spot on earth, interred in the local church of his family and canonised by the Vatican.

Among the subsequent victims of the rising wind of anti-Romanism was an exiled graduate from the English college at Rheims, Gilbert Gifford, who was picked up by Walsingham's network in Sussex in 1585 after returning to England with documents concerning Mary, Queen of Scots, written in a cipher by her agents in France, Thomas Morgan and Charles Paget. News of the letters soon became known in London where the confiscated items were examined by Walsingham and his chief code-breaker. Learning of their significance, which incriminated Gifford, but hoping to turn the situation further to his advantage, Walsingham offered the young man the chance to save himself by turning double agent. Agreeing to deliver Mary her first correspondence from France in over a year, the most important player in the events that were soon to unravel was revealed: the staunchly loyal Sir Anthony Babington.

Originally a page to the earl of Shrewsbury, Babington had harboured Catholic priests throughout the decade, including Campion several years before. Travelling to France, Babington made an offer to Mary's agents to smuggle their letters back and on returning to London, hatched his own plot that would seek not only to free Mary, but also to eliminate Elizabeth. On intercepting the letters, there is indication Walsingham and his forger added to them, an endeavour that would effectively make Mary's case unsustainable.

In reality, the additions were unnecessary. Mary herself had agreed in full to Babington's plans, including the murder of her Protestant cousin. In the summer of 1586, Babington, along with fourteen co-conspirators were arrested. Almost inevitably, he was soon condemned to follow in the footsteps of many a traitor and end his journey at the Tower.

Chapter 15

1580–1603: Popish Plots, Pirate Poets and Protestant Politics

The discovery of the Babington Plot was of great significance to the government at the time. Curious about their ultimate intentions, Elizabeth, rather than stamping out the conspiracy immediately, appears to have allowed proceedings to take their natural course and followed them with great interest all the way to the irrelevant trial. Just as would be the case with the infamous gunpowder plotters in years to come, the conspirators were sentenced to be executed in two groups and spared little in the way of mercy. Bound to wooden barrels, they were dragged all the way to Holborn to be hanged, drawn and quartered. A noteworthy piece of literature to survive the period was a three-stanza poem by conspirator Chidiock Tichborne, whose tender writings to his wife give a clear insight into the realities of his plight:

> My prime of youth is but a frost of cares,
> My feast of joy is but a dish of pain,
> My crop of corn is but a field of tares
> And all my good is but vain hope of gain;
> The day is past, and yet I saw no sun,
> And now I live, and now my life is done.
>
> My tale was heard and yet it was not told,
> My fruit is fall'n and yet my leaves are green,
> My youth is spent and yet I am not old,
> I saw the world and yet I was not seen;
> My thread is cut and yet it is not spun,
> And now I live, and now my life is done.

I sought my death and found it in my womb,
I looked for life and saw it was a shade,
I trod the earth and knew it was my tomb,
And now I die, and now I was but made;
My glass is full, and now my glass is run,
And now I live, and now my life is done.

Babington's failure effectively signed Mary's own death warrant, yet it was a clear illustration of Walsingham's power that the execution came without Elizabeth's knowledge. Furious on learning of her cousin's death, she even had one of the officials, Sir William Davison, brought to the Tower for acting on the warrant without royal consent. As punishment for sending the warrant behind the queen's back, Davison would endure twenty months in the Tower in addition to a hefty fine. Before returning to his original post, he joined the large number of prisoners whose legacy involved writing, his works penned during his incarceration including a justification of his actions and a description of Ireland.

Among those penalised for Babington's failure was the Jesuit John Ballard, later racked in the basement of the White Tower. Interrogated after his 'marriage to the Duke of Exeter's Daughter', Ballard admitted to knowledge of the conspiracy without giving away further details. He would join Babington in being dragged to Holborn, along with six of their accomplices.

The Jesuit priest John Hart saw his time run out in 1586. Arrested on arrival in Dover from Douai in 1580, Hart experienced the inside of the Tower for the first time on Christmas Eve that year before encountering the rack soon after, an experience he later claimed to have 'endured nothing thereon.' After he avoided death with Campion, Sherwin and Briant by recanting when tied to the hurdle, Hart later agreed to turn informant on Father William Allen before seeing the light and joining the Jesuits while imprisoned. Sentenced to death for a second time, only to earn another reprieve, he appears to have excelled in conference with John Rainolds at Oxford concerning matters between the Protestant and Catholic faiths. Following a further period in the Tower, he was transferred to the Continent, meeting his end in Poland. His journal from the Tower was once erroneously attributed to fellow priest Edward Rishton, with whom he spent time in the cells.

Around that time further frequent mentions were made of the device known as the Scavenger's Daughter. Included in Hart's diary, the instrument apparently included 'an iron circle, which compresses the victims hands, feet and head into a ball.' Already appearing in the writings of Cuthbert Symson, in December 1580 the same object was used on Catholic priests Luke Kirby and Thomas Cottam, the horrors of which apparently caused the latter to bleed through his nose. Both were executed on 30 May 1582, after which part of Kirby's foot was recovered and henceforth venerated as a holy relic.

Hart's writings also confirmed that Skeffington's Gyves was used on John Jetter and Thomas Nutter in September 1582 and February 1584 respectively. In addition to being forced to endure the compressing, Nutter is one of many priests known to have been fettered – his legs placed in irons. So bad was the process that fellow martyr Nicholas Horner is known to have later needed one of his legs to be amputated. In 1581, Skeffington's Gyves was used on the Irish conspirator Thomas Miagh, who also suffered the rack. Carved on one of the walls of the Beauchamp Tower are the haunting words, 'By torture straynge my truth was tried, yet of my libertie denied. 1581. Thomas Miagh.'

The year 1581 had also seen the Catholic Thomas Briscous held in 'the pit' for some five months: a tragic subterranean oubliette most likely located in the basement of the White Tower. The same term has been used in old sources to describe the sub-crypt of St John's Chapel – the chapel itself being on a higher floor – and may well have been the same place. Throughout the Tower's long history stories have emerged that another chamber lies beneath it; however, this may well be speculation.

Catholic plots had already famously become a recurring theme in Elizabethan England, yet during that time the Tower walls would not be the preserve of the Romanists alone. Famed for his firm, puritanical beliefs, the prominent Parliamentarian Peter Wentworth was also held there in consequence of his position as the puritan leader, as well as his argumentative attitude when it came to matters such as freedom of speech. Renowned as being something of a perfectionist, to the point he would seldom acknowledge a mistake or shortcoming, Wentworth experienced his first of many periods in the Tower after seeing a provocative speech in the Commons cut short by the Speaker. In 1587, he was in the cells once more, along with Sir Anthony Cope, on the charge that one of their proposed amendments touched too closely on Elizabeth's prerogative as head of the Church. In 1593, he was imprisoned a third time, now for his comments concerning the succession. He would die inside the walls in 1596. During his final time, he wrote an excellent treatise on the matter of the succession.

True it may have been that those of a religious constitution contributed most significantly to the Tower's glut of imprisonments at that time, following close behind were those guilty of marrying without Elizabeth's permission. In such ways, it was not long after the failure of the Babington Plot that one of the period's best-loved sons began his own long acquaintance with the Tower. Born in Devon in 1552, Sir Walter Raleigh is often viewed as something of a quintessential Elizabethan. A renaissance man through and through, he inherited the Devonshire spirit of adventure at a young age, a trait that would earn him both great acclaim but one day lead to his downfall.

By the time Raleigh first appeared at Elizabeth's court in 1581 as a handsome swashbuckler at the age of 29, he was at the peak of his powers. Oxford-educated and fresh from several years fighting as a mercenary in the French Wars of Religion, Raleigh's combination of strength and intellect saw his stock rise dramatically. Appointed Captain of the Yeoman Guard and becoming an MP for Devon and Cornwall, Raleigh had large estates in Ireland, which had been increased by a sumptuous London townhouse and Sherborne Castle in neighbouring Dorset. In addition to control of Cornwall's tin mines, and regular plundering of Spanish and Dutch ships, his pioneering role in the colonising of the New World would make him highly successful.

The first dent in Raleigh's success, however, came with his illicit marriage to Bess Throckmorton. In 1590, with Bess pregnant, the pair married in secret, an act that would soon become known to the queen. When Bess returned to court several months later, keeping up an appearance that all was as it should be, gossip soon began to spread. Hearing the news, Elizabeth unleashed her wrath in a trademark outburst of Tudor passion and Raleigh, wife and son were all arrested and taken to the Tower.

Raleigh's behaviour here can surely be regarded as reckless at best. While it was well known that marriage to a lady-in-waiting without the queen's permission would be deemed something of an offence, his greatest error was undoubtedly his arrogance. Far from marrying a lowly family, the Throckmortons were themselves not only Catholic but also minor royals, which gave rise to Raleigh's apparent boast that he had sired a Plantagenet. Like Ned Seymour and Lady Jane Grey's sister Catherine, the secretly married couple were separated, with Raleigh setting up lodgings in the Brick Tower in the inner north wall. Consistent to his behaviour that would soon become famous, he spent much of his time writing, composing not only sonnets but also a poem about Elizabeth.

Barely a month passed before he was freed. The capture of a Portuguese galleon by the vessel Raleigh had originally intended to take prior to his imprisonment, the result of which saw a significant disagreement about ownership of the spoils, left him all but indispensable in the eyes of the head of the English navy. While Sir Walter distributed the wealth, back at the Tower, a sudden outbreak of plague saw the sad demise of his infant son. A distraught Bess was released just prior to Christmas.

The period around the time of Raleigh's release would prove far more disastrous for four other men of knightly status. Most prominent of these was Sir John Perrot, stepson of one Thomas, but believed to have been the bastard child of Henry VIII and his mistress Mary Berkley. Born in 1528, John emerged around the time Henry was negotiating his divorce from Catherine of Aragon and, from artistic representations of his appearance, seems to have resembled Henry in many ways.

Appointed lord-deputy in Ireland by Elizabeth – apparently aware, and even acknowledging, of the fact she had a half-brother – in 1584, Perrot was not without enemies. Having made the careless remark in response to Elizabeth's change of mood to him in an audience that 'now she is ready to piss herself for fear of the Spaniard, I am once again one of her white boys,' news of his arrogance, plus embellishment of his plans, saw Elizabeth send him to the Tower in 1588: the same year as the foiling of the Armada. At his trial three years later, a guilty verdict was returned, despite the lack of evidence. Livid, he was recorded as having berated

William the Conqueror, King of England 1066–1087. It was following his capture of London that William envisaged the Tower's creation. (From John Cassell's *Illustrated History of England*, 1864)

Statue of the Tower's architect and creator, Gundulf, Bishop of Rochester, located within the outer wall of Rochester Cathedral. Alluringly, the so-called 'wailing monk' proudly occupies a niche in the building whose development he oversaw while cradling in his free hand his other great masterpiece, the White Tower. (JPD)

Nineteenth-century illustration of Henry III, King of England, r. 1216–72. It was during Henry's reign that the Tower truly developed as a royal palace and castle. (Cassell)

Edward I, King of England, r. 1272–1307. Like his father, Henry III, Edward was responsible for overseeing many of the Tower's greatest developments. (Cassell)

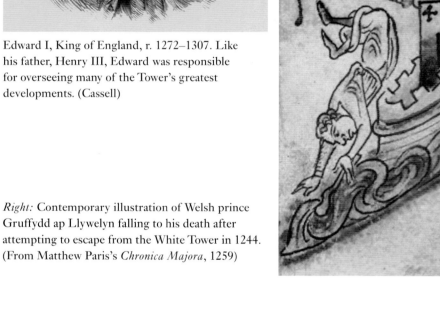

Right: Contemporary illustration of Welsh prince Gruffydd ap Llywelyn falling to his death after attempting to escape from the White Tower in 1244. (From Matthew Paris's *Chronica Majora*, 1259)

The striking down of Wat Tyler at Smithfield in 1381. (Cassell)

The execution and martyrdom of Sir John Oldcastle in 1417. (From *Holinshed's Chronicles*, 1577)

London in the fifteenth century. The illustration was designed to convey the Tower's appearance during the imprisonment of Charles, Duke of Orléans. (From Cassell; originally included in a manuscript of poems compiled by Charles, 1391–1465)

Henry VI, King of England, r. 1422–61 and 1470–71. During his interregnum, Henry was often a prisoner of the Tower and was later found murdered in the Wakefield Tower. (Cassell)

Margaret of Anjou, r. 1445–61 and 1470–71, queen of Henry VI and sometimes prisoner of the Tower. (Cassell; from an original tapestry in St Mary's Guildhall, Coventry)

The drowning of George Plantagenet, Duke of Clarence in a butt of Malmsey wine in 1478. (Cassell)

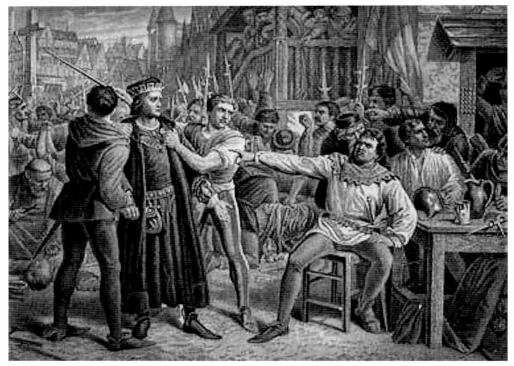

Lord Saye and Sele being brought before Jack Cade in 1450 as depicted in William Shakespeare's *Henry VI Part II*. (From an engraving of an original painting by Charles Lucy, circa 1800s)

The murder of the Princes in 1483. (Cassell)

A nineteenth-century illustration of the Bloody Tower as it appeared when viewed from the Broadwalk. (Cassell)

Richard III, r. 1483–85, earlier Duke of Gloucester. (From Caroline A. Halsted's *Richard III*, 1844; from the original portrait, artist unknown, circa late 1500s)

Anne Boleyn, Queen of England, r. 1533–36. At various times an inhabitant, guest and prisoner of the Tower, Anne became the first person to be 'legally' beheaded within its confines. (From Francis A. H. Terrell's *Anne Boleyn: A Tragedy*, 1861)

Thomas Cromwell, chief minister to Henry VIII, r. 1509–47. Following his arrest, Cromwell was taken to the Tower and beheaded on Tower Hill in 1540. (Cassell; from the original painting by Hans Holbein the Younger, circa 1530s)

Catherine Howard, Queen of England, r. 1540–41. Like her cousin Anne Boleyn, Catherine enjoyed the palatial side of the Tower before enduring a short imprisonment there prior to her execution in the vicinity of Tower Green. (Cassell; from the original painting by Hans Holbein the Younger, circa 1540)

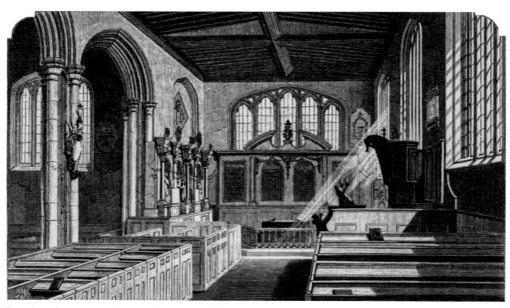

Interior of the Royal Chapel of St Peter ad Vincula, once described as 'no sadder spot on earth'. (From Lord De Ros's *Memorials of the Tower*, 1866)

The execution of Anne Askew and others at Smithfield in 1546. (From a contemporary woodcut, circa 1546)

The execution of John Dudley, 1st Duke of Northumberland on Tower Hill in 1553. Like daughter-in-law, Lady Jane Grey, Dudley would lose his head on being found guilty of treason against Mary I, r. 1553–58. (Cassell)

Edward Courtenay, 1st Earl of Devon. Brought to the Tower at the age of 11, Courtenay endured imprisonment there from 1538 before his eventual release in 1553. (Engraving by Thomas Chambers, 1762)

The racking of protestant deacon Cuthbert Symson in the basement of the White Tower in 1557. (From Foxe's *Book of Martyrs*, 1563)

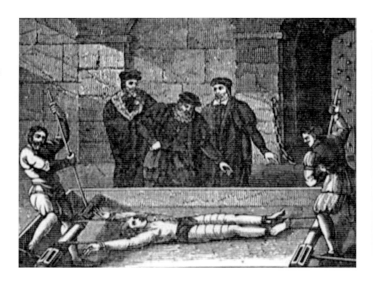

The trial of Thomas Cranmer in 1556. (Artist unknown, circa 1580)

Royal physician Roderigo Lopez engaged in conversation with a Spanish agent concerning a plot to poison Elizabeth I, r. 1558–1603. (From a contemporary engraving by Esaias van Hulsen, circa 1590s)

Robert Devereux, 2nd Earl of Essex. Once favourite of Elizabeth I, Essex suffered the Tower and a private execution as punishment for his ill-fated rising. (Cassell; from an original painting, circa 1590s)

Sir Walter Raleigh in his prime. In total Raleigh suffered three stints in the Tower prior to his execution in 1618. (Cassell; from an original painting, circa 1580s)

Eight of the Gunpowder Conspirators as depicted by a contemporary illustration by Crispijn van de Passe the Elder in 1605. (From Philip Sidney's *A History of the Gunpowder Plot*, 1905)

James VI, King of Scotland, r. 1567–1625, and I of England, r. 1603–25. (Sidney; from a print circa 1621)

Sir William Waad, Lieutenant of the Tower in the 1600s. (Engraving after a seventeenth-century portrait, 1798)

A young Sir Thomas Overbury. Overbury was in his early thirties at the time of his imprisonment and poisoning in 1613. (From an engraving by Renold Elstracke, circa 1616)

The trial of Archbishop of Canterbury, William Laud inside the House of Lords in 1644. (From a contemporary engraving by Wenceslaus Hollar, circa 1645)

The Council Chamber in Governor's House. (De Ros)

The legendary Traitors' Gate and, above it, St Thomas's Tower. It was from that tower several escapes were made or attempted. (From John Britton et al's *Memoirs of the Tower of London*, 1830)

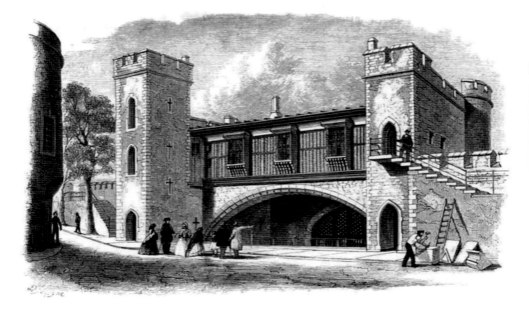

The execution of Thomas Wentworth, 1st Earl of Strafford on Tower Hill in 1641. Some estimates place the crowd around 100,000. (From a contemporary engraving by Wenceslaus Hollar, 1641)

William Penn (1644–1718), one time prisoner of the Tower and later famed as the founder of the US state of Pennsylvania. (Artist unknown, circa 1670s–1710s)

The infamous 'Colonel' Thomas Blood, who endeavoured to steal the Crown Jewels of England in 1671. (Artist unknown, circa 1670s)

The famed diarist Samuel Pepys (1633–1703). Briefly a prisoner of the Tower, Pepys was a frequent visitor throughout his life. (From the *Diary and Correspondence of Samuel Pepys*, 1867)

Engraving of Titus Oates enduring the pillories in punishment for his fabrication of the Popish Plot in 1678. (Artist unknown, circa 1670s)

The Rye House Plotters and Rye House. (The below image comprises the combining of two original engravings by John Savage, circa 1680s, and by one Forster, originally published in Francis Grose's *Supplement to the Antiquities of England and Wales*, 1772).

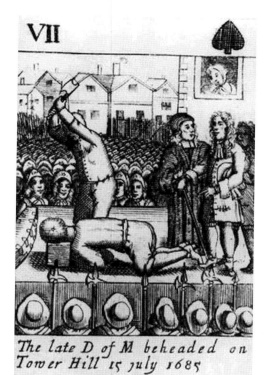

The execution of pretender to the throne, James Scott, Duke of Monmouth, on Tower Hill in 1685. (From a contemporary print, circa 1685).

The 'Hanging' Judge George Jeffreys meting out justice to unfortunate victims of the Bloody Assizes in 1685. (Artist unknown, from *The Western Martyrology: or, Bloody Assizes*, 1873)

Executioner's tools in 1715. (De Ros)

Christopher Layer. An English Jacobite conspirator, Layer was imprisoned in the Tower and later executed for his role in the Atterbury Plot of 1722. (From a contemporary engraving)

James Radclyffe, 3rd Earl of Derwentwater. In contrast to the imaginative Nithsdales, Radclyffe was executed for his role in the 1715 Jacobite rebellion. (From Mrs Thomson's *Memoirs of the Jacobites of 1715 and 1745 vol 1*, 1845)

The Tower from south of the River Thames. (From an engraving by Nathaniel and Samuel Buck, 1737)

Arthur Elphinstone, 6th Lord Balmerino. Captured after the Jacobites' defeat at Culloden, he was brought to the Tower and executed in 1746. (From Mrs Thomson's *Memoirs of the Jacobites of 1715 and 1745 vol 3*, 1846)

Simon Fraser, Lord Lovat. The 'ugly old dog' who lost his head in 1747. (From a contemporary engraving, circa 1715).

Earl Ferrers shooting Mr Johnson – the event that would lead to his imprisonment in the Tower in 1760 and becoming the last British nobleman to be hung. (From a contemporary print, circa 1760s)

John Wilkes before the court of the King's Bench in 1768. (Engraving from the *Gentleman's Magazine*, May 1768)

The Tower menagerie in 1816. (Illustration by Thomas Rowlandson)

The arrest of the Cato Street conspirators in 1820. (From a contemporary print, circa 1820)

The Tower as it appeared from the Thames in the 1800s. (Britton)

The fire of the Grand Storehouse in 1841. (From Joseph Wheeler's *A Short History of the Tower of London*, 1842)

Arthur Wellesley, 1st Duke of Wellington. Besides his crowning glories in war and serving as Prime Minister of the UK, Wellesley also held the role of Constable of the Tower 1827–52. (From an engraving by William Say of the original portrait by Thomas Phillips, 1814)

Carl Hans Lody, the first German POW put to death by firing squad during the First World War. (From a contemporary photograph)

Irish rebel and humanitarian Sir Roger Casement, who was imprisoned at the Tower before his execution in 1916. (From a contemporary photograph, circa 1910)

Deputy Führer of the Nazi Party, Rudolf Hess in 1933; from a contemporary photograph

The Tower as it appeared from the north-west in the 1970s. (Mike Davis)

Past and present. The Tower and skyline of modern London when viewed at night from Tower Bridge. (JPD, 2016)

the lieutenant with the words, 'Will the Queen suffer her brother to be offered up as a sacrifice to the envy of my strutting adversary?' Elizabeth clearly sympathised with Perrot's view, labelling the jury 'knaves' and declaring herself unwilling to sign the warrant.

As fate would have it, Perrot would die, not of the axe but from natural causes, not three months later – other sources suggest it was 1592. Adding to the intrigue, one of his officers, Sir Thomas Williams was also brought to the Tower, and met a similar end a short time earlier. Even he had not been the first. Also known in Perrot's number, Sir Thomas Fitzherbert had been transferred there back in January of 1591, under strict orders he was to remain in solitary confinement. Despite being allowed the freedom of the Tower, he perished three days before Perrot's funeral. A fourth too would follow, this time Sir Nicholas White, one of Sir John's colleagues. Faring better than the others, he survived until 1593.

Exactly what became of the luckless quartet is another of those enigmatic riddles for which the Tower has become famous. Officially all four succumbed to the same fate as Henry VI – of pure displeasure and melancholy – yet it seems highly suspicious that four apparently strong and healthy men could all die inside the Tower of broken hearts. Though the mystery remains, a wry thought emerges with the idea that had Henry VIII followed in the footsteps of his ancestor John of Gaunt and married his mistress, Perrot could well have reigned as John II. In that event, Anne Boleyn and Jane Seymour would never have been queen, and Edward VI and Elizabeth I never born.

A year after the death of White, the queen's physician, Roderigo Lopez, was brought to the Tower on being accused of conspiring with the Spanish to poison her. A Jew as opposed to a Catholic, the revelation inevitably brought an outpouring of hostility. Lopez had already incurred the wrath of the earl of Essex – at the time in Elizabeth's favour – after failing to coerce him into his intelligence service.

Accusation against Lopez may have been partly born of his status and ethnicity, yet involvement in conspiracy was not entirely alien to him. Having accepted a jewel from the Spanish on agreeing the death of Portuguese pretender, Don Antonio, he was reputedly offered more to ensure Elizabeth's demise as well. In an inspiring turn, Lopez actually gifted the jewel to Elizabeth, which she wore to her dying day. Unable to prove his innocence, however, an Essex-led court ordered that Lopez be transferred to the Tower and executed on 7 June 1594 at Tyburn. It is testament to Elizabeth's faith in the man that she refused to sign the death warrant and allowed his estates to pass to his family.

Another who would embrace the harsh realities of the Tower around this time was Father Robert Southwell, a fellow Jesuit of Edmund Campion. Having successfully evaded Walsingham's spies for at least six years, Southwell's brutal torture began in earnest in the private chamber of persecutor Richard Topcliffe and the gatehouse prison at Westminster before he followed in Campion's footsteps in being transferred to the Tower. Despite being cleansed of any infections and allowed new clothes and books, over the coming three years Southwell suffered the rack no less than three times. Like Campion, he revealed little that incriminated himself or others and went to his death confident the light of heaven would soon be shining.

Southwell would not be the last Jesuit confined to the Tower during that time. Of all the tales concerning those incarcerated for their faith, none could compare with the feats of the Yorkshire-born, Father John Gerard.

Ironically for a man who would go down in the annals of English and Catholic history as a near martyr and hero, Gerard's early path in life was far from clear. Grandson of the famed Thomas Gerrard, an early Lutheran who was purged by Henry VIII at Smithfield in 1540, his father, another Thomas, by contrast had reverted to the old religion. Like his son to follow, the Catholic Thomas had known the inside of the Tower, having been imprisoned there for his involvement in the Northern Rising of 1569 and apparently again for attempting to plot the release of Mary, Queen of Scots.

John Gerard was born in Yorkshire five years prior to his father's imprisonment. Reunited some three years later, Gerard studied at Oxford, at the time a hotbed of Catholic activity, and was apparently so persuasive in his exegesis he succeeded in converting one of his tutors to the Catholic faith. Having been imprisoned for his faith, he successfully made his way to the Continent, achieving legal permission to continue his studies and subsequently relocating to Douai, in the Spanish-controlled Netherlands, another Catholic hotbed. By the late 1570s, the English

College had been in operation for about a decade having been formed by the exiled, anti-Elizabeth scholar, William Allen, who remained fervently anti-Elizabeth throughout his life. The purpose of Douai had been to train priests as 'seminaries' after which they would begin their own mission of converting Protestants, usually back in their home country. Around that time, the Spanish Netherlands was heavily frequented by the expanding Jesuit order, who since their formation in 1540 had become renowned for both their godly devotion and hard discipline.

Gerard would famously become a Jesuit himself, but not before spending time in one of London's many gaols. There he crossed paths with the soon-to-become infamous Sir Anthony Babington, who personally paid Gerard's bail. On returning to the Continent, Gerard obtained special permission from the pope to ordain him a Jesuit priest – which he did the same week as the coming of the Spanish Armada – after which he spent the next five years moving from one recusant estate to another, saying mass for the family while hiding in various Nicholas Owen hidey-holes and converting more Protestants to the flock.

In 1594, Gerard's luck was severely tested. Having been apparently betrayed by a previously loyal servant while staying in the Essex residence of the recusant Wiseman family, Gerard had no choice but to seek refuge in another of Nicholas Owen's priest holes, armed with nothing but a jar of quince jelly and a handful of biscuits – everything the lady of the house happened to have with her at the time. Despite the constant banging of walls going on around him, Gerard survived unscathed. Subsequently sent to a London townhouse, the same servant carrying a letter for Gerard alerted the authorities of his and Owen's whereabouts. On this occasion there had been nowhere to hide.

Over the next three years Gerard's fortunes were somewhat mixed. Originally kept in the Westminster home of the notorious Catholic pursuivant Richard Topcliffe, where he was subjected to watching Owen and his servant, Richard Fulwood, being manacled, after two months they were relocated to the Clink prison which Gerard described as like a move from purgatory to paradise – a reference to the large number of Catholic prisoners kept there and more or less given free rein. The authorities remained convinced that Gerard was still intent on carrying out his original mission, and he was transferred again: this time to the Tower.

While the gallows of Tower Hill witnessed the demise of five unruly youths who were hanged and disembowelled for causing a disturbance on 24 July 1595, Gerard continued to endure incarceration in the Salt Tower that would one day become celebrated as one of the most famous in the Tower's long history. Writing in his autobiography years later, he calls attention to the engraved name Henry Walpole marking the wall of his cell in clear homage to the stay of his fellow Jesuit only two years earlier – amazingly, the engraving survives to this day. On seeing the near perfect lettering, Gerard recalls that, in addition to that of other past Catholic prisoners, it was of great comfort to him – Walpole himself having been manacled no less than fourteen times before being executed for his faith at York on 7 April 1595 after a year in the Tower – before adding that he slept very well indeed in a room 'sanctified by this great and holy martyr.'

Gerard's torture began almost immediately. His own recollection of the beginning is really quite extraordinary, stating: 'We went to the torture room in a kind of solemn procession, the guards walking ahead with lighted candles. The chamber was underground and dark, particularly near the entrance. It was a vast, shadowy place and every device and instrument of human torture was there.' After the Privy Council's first attempt at interrogation delivered little, like Owen and Fulwood at Westminster, his ordeal involved only the manacles – left to dangle by his chained-up wrists – often for up to three hours at a time. Due to his height, the manacles initially had little effect on him, as the tall priest's feet were still able to partially touch the ground. When that was changed, he remained steadfast, recording of his ordeal that he could barely have spoken even if he had wanted to.

The first day of torture revealed nothing. After being carried back to the Salt Tower, the process resumed the following day. With wrists so swollen they could barely be contained, Gerard was manacled again until he passed out. He recorded in his autobiography that he was awoken to the feeling of warm water on his face and flowing down his gullet. Interestingly, the lieutenant of the Tower, Sir Richard Berkeley, called a halt to this primitive process of 'waterboarding', considering it inhumane. Even more interestingly, he resigned his post less than a month later. Prior to doing so he wrote to Cecil personally, requesting

Gerard be allowed to walk for need of fresh air and that he was also in need of medicine.

The torture clearly left its mark on Gerard. Determinedly remaining resolute in his faith and unwillingness to comply, his swollen wrists had rendered his hands temporarily useless and he was unable to feed or dress himself without assistance. In consequence, the struggling gentleman struck up a firm friendship with his gaoler, named in his writings as Bonner. As their relationship developed and Gerard, after three weeks, recovered some movement in his hands, he managed to convince the gaoler to obtain extra living funds from his friends at the Clink, in addition to a large collection of oranges. Using what little strength his recovering hands could muster to construct a rosary from the peel, he kept much of the juice in a special container, as well as sharing some of the fruit with Bonner. On obtaining some paper from Bonner to wrap a present of a rosary for his friends at the Clink, he wrote a short legible note addressed to former servant Richard Fulwood and one of Gerard's former Clink inmates, John Lillie. Unbeknown to the authorities, also included was an invisible message written using the orange juice and a toothpick.

The secret message was clearly expected by Gerard's friends and the heat of fire revealed its content. While the recently released Nicholas Owen and his secret network outside the Tower were able to put plans in place for an attempted escape, inside the walls Gerard made another significant step. Using his knowledge of mime, he managed to make contact with fellow Catholic prisoner, the Northamptonshire recusant John Arden, who was being held in the Cradle Tower on the riverside wall of the outer ward. After initially misunderstanding Gerard's attempt to communicate via invisible ink, Bonner was soon persuaded to help him make contact with Arden more openly. As time wore on, Gerard was given permission to pay regular visits to Arden's cell, often at night, where they would pray together and make arrangements for their escape. Aided by Arden's wife, they were soon armed with exactly what they needed: a length of cord.

The night of 3 October 1597 seemed destined to go down in the annals of Tower history. Bonner – unaware of their plans – escorted Gerard to the Cradle Tower and locked them in to celebrate mass, which was now a regular occurrence. Subsequently they made their way on to the Cradle Tower's roof, the chiming of the Bell Tower's bell confirming midnight was upon them. Rowing up river, a small boat piloted by John Lillie, which also carried Richard Fulwood and possibly one other man, appeared right on schedule, immediately rousing the suspicions of a neighbour. On being questioned, they were forced to set off, following which the boat caused something of a scene when it nearly capsized close to London Bridge.

Surviving by the skin of their teeth, the following night they tried again. On receiving a new letter in invisible ink from John Lillie, Gerard prepared for attempt number two. After mooring the boat, Gerard tossed the cord Arden's wife had smuggled in over the moat with the aid of a small iron ball and Fulwood tied it to a heavy rope. In turn, Gerard pulled the rope over the moat, attaching it to a cannon on the roof.

The stage, it seemed, was set. Following Arden down the rope, the extra weight of a second man caused a sudden onset of vibrations, temporarily halting progress. Frozen to the spot, Gerard's faith was tested to the utmost. Calling on his final strength, he made it over the moat where he encountered his next obstacle, the wall that separated the moat from the wharf. Now seriously struggling, it was Lillie who came to the rescue. Frantically hoisting Gerard over, they made it to the boat and successfully to nearby Spitalfields. There, Gerard was reacquainted with Nicholas Owen who provided them with horses before meeting up with fellow Jesuit Father Henry Garnet at Uxbridge.

What Gerard and Arden achieved was nothing short of remarkable. While again testing the Tower's reputation for being inescapable, the story serves as a timely reminder of what can be achieved through a mixture of kindness and perseverance. When considering the physical, psychological and mental anguish Gerard had undergone, not just in the Tower but since returning to England, hiding out in Owen's ingenious hiding places, not to mention the failure of the first attempt, the tale is all the more inspiring. In a touching epilogue to the story, once he had successfully absconded, Gerard wrote three letters: one to the new lieutenant clearing Bonner of blame, and a second to the Privy Council doing the very same with additional mention of the new lieutenant. The final one he sent to Bonner himself, explaining the escape and warning him not to show for work that day. Taking the counsel to heart, he accepted Gerard's offer of 200 florins annuity and converted to the Catholic faith.

Rivalling Gerard for the most dramatic escape from the Tower was another Catholic imprisoned there around that time, the magnificent Edmund Neville. A truly remarkable thing it was to escape the Tower once. But in its near-1000-year history, only Neville – and the mysterious Sir John Mortimer – accomplished the feat twice.

By the time Gerard and Arden made their way upriver, Edmund Neville had spent more than twelve years imprisoned at the Tower. For the previously powerful Neville clan, the Northern Rising of 1569 had been an unmitigated disaster. With the family reputation already tarnished, Neville had spent time fighting for the Spanish in the Low Countries and developed a reputation as a soldier of fortune, not too dissimilar to that enjoyed by Guy Fawkes a decade or so later.

Neville's first experience of the Tower began in 1584. Of the many Catholic plots against Elizabeth and the state that were to occur around that time, one of the most significant had been the brainchild of the Catholic Welsh MP William Parry whose plan had been either to shoot Elizabeth in her stagecoach or else ambush her in her private quarters. Convinced, perhaps with some merit, that Parry was a double agent, Neville decided to report the MP to the authorities.

Whether Parry actually intended to carry out the plot has been the subject of much speculation. It has often been suggested that the Welsh MP lost his nerve before pulling his pistol, whereas others have claimed it was merely a ruse to bring about Neville's downfall. Irrespective of the truth, Parry was ousted from parliament and imprisoned in the Tower, meeting his end in the Old Palace Yard outside the Palace of Westminster on 2 March 1585. For the time being at least, Neville fared slightly better, albeit still confined to the Tower. Not guilty of any specific crime, it was, nevertheless, difficult for the Privy Council to believe a man of Catholic background, related to past plotters, a former mercenary in Spain and associated with recent plots should be let free.

With no clear end in sight, Neville concocted his own plan to escape. Being a man of status, and considered by no means a dangerous prisoner, he was granted many freedoms, including daily exercise outside his chambers in St Thomas's Tower. In almost perfect late-sixteenth century

Shawshank Redemption style, he assembled himself a series of items – including a small file – and patiently worked away at the bars of his window until he was able to squeeze through. Once out, a quick climb over a particularly rugged area of the outer curtain wall separated him from an unpleasant swim in the Tower moat. An accomplished swimmer, he made it across and into the darkened streets.

Neville's good fortune looked set to continue. By the time news of his escape became known early the next morning, he was already six miles out of the capital, thus missing the recently set up security checks. Unfortunately, having been forced by hunger and exhaustion to stop for food and rest, a horseman fresh from the capital took notice of his strange appearance and odour. Reported, Neville was soon back where he started.

Alone in his cell, security was inevitably tightened. In contrast to the relatively lax measures that had been in place prior to his escape, Neville now had one of his legs shackled. In 1588, the regime was relaxed a little when he was allowed visits by his wife and a couple of years after that the original freedoms were restored. This second issue of lax security measures, of course, subsequently came back to haunt his gaolers. Carrying out the same plan as before – the exact route had been blocked off, forcing him to climb a higher wall – Neville, aided by a rope that had been smuggled in by his wife, made his way out of his cell once again through the same window. Using the rope to descend the wall, he discovered his calculations were incorrect – the rope being significantly too short. Forced to drop into the moat, the resulting splash was overheard by the nearby guards, who soon saw him on the far bank. Though he did his best to blend in with the crowds, even resorting to the age-old tactic of pretending to chase a thief, one of the gaolers tracked him down.

Still undeterred, the thrice-shackled prisoner set about a third attempt. After six frustrating years of incarceration, he succeeded brilliantly in tricking his gaoler by sitting practically motionless as he gazed through his cell window before, one night, creating a straw mannequin and dressing it in his own clothes. Having also tried to change his identity to that of a blacksmith, creating for himself fake tools and a makeshift apron, he waited for his gaoler to enter his cell and then made his way towards the Tower's exit. The plan was soon discovered, his gaoler doubtlessly dismayed when he discovered that the blacksmith was in fact his prisoner.

Within two years it was decided that Neville no longer posed a significant threat and the man who had escaped twice and nearly a third time was finally allowed to walk free to be exiled to the Continent. For the story of Neville we are grateful to the autobiography of the Jesuit priest, Father William Weston, who spent time in the Tower himself after his arrest in 1598 for possession of subversive literature – notably the work of Robert Persons – as well as his failure to inform the government of the coming of the second Spanish Armada, which was dispersed by storms in 1596. He would be exiled in 1603 and lived out his remaining days in Spain.

While Neville (and Weston) finally saw the light of day, others would not be so lucky. Arrested in 1588 after being caught on board a Spanish ship, one Tristram Winslade was racked on the assumption he was a papist traitor, only to be later released after it was discovered the man had boarded the vessel against his will. Also caught up amidst the ongoing papist plots against the queen was one Catholic, Edward Squire, not a priest, but an under-groom in the royal stables. Persuaded, apparently by at least one Jesuit priest, to spread some poisonous ointment or paste on the queen's pommel, this sorry episode – later dubbed the poisoned pommel affair – would see a combination of Squire's poison failing to breach Elizabeth's heavy clothing and betrayal by a fellow conspirator acquaint him with the rack. Admitting his guilt, Squire was found guilty at his trial on 9 November 1598 and drawn, a fortnight later, on a hurdle from the Tower to Tyburn. In the usual manner for a traitor's death, he was hanged to within an inch of his life, disembowelled and quartered.

A far more civilized traitor's death would greet a man of even greater status. Following in the footsteps of Raleigh, whose fall from grace had significant effects on his status at court, the same fate awaited the man who would replace him as favourite in Elizabeth's fickle eyes.

Robert Devereux, 2nd Earl of Essex, was well known to Raleigh. Chosen to be godfather at the christening of Raleigh's son, Elizabeth had more than one reason to be displeased with Essex. Some fourteen years Raleigh's junior, born in 1565, Essex had himself been successful during his early years. Being born into aristocratic stock, he was also stepson of Sir Robert Dudley as a result of Dudley's remarriage, before cementing his place in that tight circle with his own marriage to Walsingham's daughter, also Sir Philip Sidney's widow.

Essex's downfall was in many ways intertwined with that of Raleigh's. Early friendship between the two gave way to mutual distrust, thanks in no small part to Essex supplanting Raleigh as a naval commander. In 1599, and with a revolt in Ireland brewing, Essex was sent with a large force to subdue the Irish dissidents, yet rather than doing so, he merely negotiated an awkward truce. Returning to England, thus defying his orders to remain in the Emerald Isle, he entered unannounced into Elizabeth's bedchamber. Finding the ageing queen unready for visitors, he was arrested.

Eventually he was granted his release, though the fall of Essex is nonetheless remarkable. Convinced Cecil and Raleigh had been poisoning the queen's ear, he took the fateful decision to launch his own rebellion. Unaware that Cecil and his spymasters had intercepted his letters attempting to conscript James VI of Scotland into assisting him, Essex put his ill-conceived plans into operation. On 8 February, beginning at his home at Essex House, a day after Shakespeare's *Richard II* – a play about an overthrow – had been staged at the Globe Theatre, he set out with a meagre force of some 300 that included many of his former men and Catholic conspirators, including the 3rd Earl of Southampton, Henry Wriothesley, and the later infamous gunpowder plotter Robert Catesby. Imprisoning a delegation from the Privy Council who had attempted to dissuade the rebels from their course, the party headed for the Tower. Had he known his attempts to rally the Londoners would be a waste of time – Cecil having already denounced him a traitor – history may well have been very different. Instead, the disgraced earl and his small force found themselves isolated with no additional support.

Almost miraculously, Essex and Southampton escaped the carnage, finding their way back to Essex House and successfully barricading themselves inside. Surviving until the authorities arrived with artillery from the Tower's arsenal, they later surrendered and for the second time that day, the hot-headed pair found themselves on their way to the Tower. After passing through Traitors' Gate, Essex was escorted to the north-west corner. Like Balliol and Beauchamp before him, the tower in which he was kept was renamed the Devereux Tower in honour of his stay.

Retribution was inevitably swift. Following the questioning of some eighty accomplices – most of whom were probably racked in the White

Tower – under the guardianship of the new constable, Lord Charles Howard, Essex and Southampton were tried eleven days later. Fresh from a courtroom of high drama, the disgraced earls were condemned of treason and returned to the Tower.

Left in no doubt of his fate, Essex refused to see his wife and children, perhaps fearing seeing them would further weaken his resolve. While preparing to meet his end, the doomed earl made one last desperate attempt to save his life. Many years earlier, Elizabeth had gifted him a ring, saying that if he should ever return it, his misdeed would be forgiven. Grabbing the attention of a passing pageboy, he asked the boy to deliver it to one Lady Scrope (prior to her marriage Philadelphia Carey), who in turn would pass it on to the queen. The boy, rather than follow orders, instead gave it to Lady Scrope's sister, Lady Nottingham, also wife of the constable. For Essex it was the worst possible outcome. Learning of this shortly prior to her death, the queen was characteristically furious.

Ironically, the date arranged for their deaths was Ash Wednesday, 25 February. Concerned the disgraced earls still had sufficient popular backing to cause significant trouble, Essex, it was decided, would be granted the luxury of a private execution – a fate he was in some ways entitled to due to his noble blood. Concerned there be no mishaps, and perhaps a small act of kindness, Elizabeth decreed that two executioners would be present, in case there were problems with the first attempt.

Essex's fall from grace is further illustrated by the fact he was unable to tip his guards, stating that all he had left must be given to the queen. After a night spent in prayer, he walked to the scaffold. Among those present was his former friend, Raleigh, now captain of the yeoman guards, who soon made himself scarce and watched on from a window in the White Tower. Addressing the crowd, Essex showed the typical condemned man's humility, apologising for his greed and other sins. He denied any harm was intended to the queen, and he died with full belief in God, likely a jibe against Raleigh's alleged atheism. Unbuttoning his garments, refusing a blindfold, he carried out the usual business before placing his head on the block. Elizabeth's precaution of having two executioners was not needed. After two practice swings, the traitor's head was removed with a clean stroke.

Essex was not the only conspirator to meet his end as a result of the failed rebellion. Some four weeks after his execution, the errant earl's father-in-law, Sir Christopher Blount, followed him to the scaffold, this time on Tower Hill. So weakened was Blount from an injury to his cheek during the rebellion, he was recorded as needing to be carried on a litter to his trial. Joining him was the English MP and soldier Sir Charles Danvers, who failed with a £10,000 bid for his life.

Southampton, by contrast, was to enjoy better luck. Apparently impressed by his manner in court, his sentence was changed to imprisonment. Lodged in relative comfort in an apartment to the east end of the royal palace, probably close to – if not part of – the Lanthorn Tower, Southampton saw out Elizabeth's reign in relative serenity, enjoying regular visits from his mother and medicines for his ailments. As a man of status, he also had an attendant. There is a wonderful legend that the black and white cat, with which he was painted, had entered his lodgings via the chimney and became his pet. A more fanciful, yet even more romantic tale, tells that the cat was already his pet and somehow tracked his owner down.

A year after Essex's execution, the Tower witnessed the death of the man dubbed in certain circles 'the very genius of the Elizabethan underworld'. Robert Poley was employed in the role of a Catholic sympathiser and became the servant of Sir Anthony Babington, a role that helped secure the failure of the Babington Plot – and with it two years in the Tower. Thereafter, Poley resumed his work in Walsingham's service, as a messenger for the court, and apparently witnessed the killing of the famed playwright, Christopher Marlowe. Due to his release, it is often assumed he was put there as a plant by Walsingham to spy on the other prisoners.

By 1603 the queen's health was failing. Successful in the sense that she had survived almost everything thrown at her from home-based plots to European navies, one thing no queen could conquer was time itself. In her final hours, having lost the use of her voice, she gestured her agreement to her successor, the man Cecil had in any case secretly lined up. Cursed by the usual Tudor lack of heir, the man chosen was a Protestant, yet son of a Catholic queen: the very same queen that had been put to death without her permission. The new king was to be James VI of Scotland, now James I of England.

Chapter 16

1603–1612: Gunpowder, Treason and Sop

The accession of the man destined to unite the historically warring kingdoms either side of Hadrian's Wall had initially pleased England's beleaguered Catholics. After three decades of ever-hardening recusancy laws, it was hoped that the coming of the son of the woman who had long been coveted as their saviour would bring about an end to their persecution. Less than a year into James I's reign, however, there had already been two failed plots against him.

Most prominent of those to lose station early in the new king's reign was former court favourite, Sir Walter Raleigh. Having lived a relatively quiet life in semi-retirement since his release from the Tower, Raleigh's first meeting with James is famously remembered for the king's remark, 'I have heard rawly of you, mon,' before confiscating his London house and later Sherborne Castle, in addition to stripping him of his role of captain of the yeoman guard. Raleigh's frustration was understandable but his downfall was sealed with the uncovering of the two plots, to both of which he was suspected of being linked.

The Main Plot was the more ambitious of the two, and not of Catholic creation. The Conspiracy of the Bye had been something of a joint venture between beleaguered papists and puritans to endeavour the kidnapping of the king in order to ensure that the early tacit suggestion of religious tolerance would be backed up with firm promises. In the uncovering of that plot, Sir George Brooke – an accomplice of Father William Watson, one of the main conspirators – revealed the second, 'main' plot. The brainchild of Raleigh's friend and Brooke's brother, Henry Brooke, 11th Baron Cobham and the puritan Lord Grey de Wilton, the plans here went far further than mere kidnapping, plotting instead the king's overthrow. Incriminated by some loose comments from Cobham that he later withdrew, Raleigh would join Cobham and Grey in the Tower. Relieved of the chilly conditions he had often endured a decade earlier in the Brick

Tower, the famous sailor was accommodated on the first floor of what had previously been the Garden Tower – now renamed the Bloody Tower – which would be his home for the next thirteen years. Unsuccessful in finding the king's ear and subsequently seeing the friendly lieutenant replaced on Cecil's orders, Raleigh was temporarily removed from the Tower and tried at Winchester for treason. Found guilty and returned to the Bloody Tower, Raleigh prepared for death. Curiously, Cobham, after a mock execution, was housed in the lieutenant's lodgings, within easy reach of 'Raleigh's Walk': a stretch of battlement that still connects the Bloody Tower to the Queen's House.

After considering the outcome at Winchester, Cecil decided to show leniency, commuting the sentences of all three to life imprisonment. Although he initially struggled to adapt to his worsening lot, leading to a failed attempt at suicide, over the years Raleigh's lodgings were upgraded; in addition to being allowed a servant and secretary, his second son and wife were granted unrestricted access to him. A third son also followed, born at a house on Tower Hill that Bess had recently begun renting. Adapting to his new way of life, Raleigh set to work further honing his literary skills, beginning his history of the world, which would be a bestseller in its day.

Over the next decade, Raleigh achieved something of a second legacy. Besides his *History of the World*, poems, essays, letters and political tracts flowed from his quill, but his writing was merely one of the tools of his trade. In the privy garden – the Bloody Tower was previously called the Garden Tower because of its close proximity to the constable's garden – he set up his own herb garden and converted a hen hut into a makeshift lab. For the locals, the once-hated courtier had become something of a tourist attraction. Among the visitors was the king's Catholic queen and her precocious son, Henry, Prince of Wales. An interested visitor to the Tower, Prince Henry did not share his father's sadistic streak. In watching a fight at the menagerie where three dogs were forced to fight a lion, Henry asked that the final dog be spared, citing 'he that have fought with the king of beasts shall never fight with any inferior creature.' In typical Henry-like fashion, he adopted the spared mastiff as a pet.

In a short time, a blossoming friendship developed between the prince and the prisoner, by which time Henry saw the new tourist attraction as something of a mentor. Indeed, it was down to the encouragement of the prince that Raleigh began writing his *History of the World,* leading Henry to remark that only his father would cage such a bird.

As Raleigh settled into the initially depressing confines of his new residence, outside the Tower walls two separate events were fast unfolding that would go on to leave a lasting mark on the Tower's history. In Spain, a deputation of English envoys representing England's disillusioned Catholics had failed to obtain guarantees of financial and military support from the Spanish Crown despite five solid years of endeavour. What started as an optimistic plan to put together another armada had turned into a detailed presentation regarding the benefits of ensuring the passing of the English Crown to the Spanish *infante* Isabella – herself descended of Edward III – following Elizabeth I's death without issue.

When Elizabeth died, there was still no firm plan in place and, following the swift coronation of James I, whatever dreams had once existed all but ended. Nevertheless, that did not stop two final envoys arriving at Philip III's court, named in the records as Anthony Dutton – possibly an alias for Kit Wright – and one Guy Fawkes, a Yorkshire-born Catholic who had fought for the Spanish over the past decade, and whose expertise in the art of gunpowder warfare would soon leave a very different mark on the Tower's history.

Around the time that the so-called Spanish Treason came to an end, a trio of the conspirators' comrades met together to discuss an endeavour that would later be remembered for all the wrong reasons. The mastermind was catholic landowner Robert Catesby, descended of Richard III's lawyer Sir William Catesby and himself a minor player in Essex's rebellion. Joining him were Jack Wright – brother of Kit Wright, the most likely candidate for Dutton – and Thomas Wintour, one of the original group who had earlier attempted to persuade the king of Spain of the virtues of ensuring equal rights for England's Catholics. Following a brief delay as Wintour recovered from illness, the three met at Catesby's property at Lambeth at which point the beleaguered conspirators set about a new undertaking: to wipe out the new king and his fellow anti-Catholics by way of gunpowder.

Fawkes was next to join the conspiracy. Along with Thomas Percy, a 'bad relative' of the earl of Northumberland, the five conspirators formulated their plan. Operating initially from Catesby's house in Lambeth, they rented another property in Percy's name close to the Palace of Westminster – a common occurrence at the time – and in turn planned to dig a mine beneath the parliament building, which they would later fill with gunpowder. By March 1605, work on the mine was abandoned due to a combination of slow progress and a better option presenting itself. While working on the mine, it emerged a coal cellar next door had become available, located directly beneath the House of Lords, which Percy successfully acquired. Over the coming weeks, the total number of conspirators now at thirteen, preparations were put in place for the opening of parliament that, due to plague concerns, had been pushed back to 5 November.

Things progressed smoothly until ten days before the reopening. On 26 October, a letter was delivered to the London home of one Lord Monteagle, advising he miss the parliament. On receiving it, the letter was immediately taken to Cecil who in turn showed it to the king. The wording, James noted, contained a sinister warning. Parliament would be destroyed by gunpowder.

Exactly who wrote the letter has long been a topic of debate. Many suggestions have been put forward from conspirators Francis Tresham and Thomas Wintour to Cecil himself, a false flag move reminiscent of Walsingham's sexing up of the Babington letters. Nevertheless, after biding his time, Cecil ordered that the undercrofts be checked on 4 November and among the chambers, Fawkes was found. On being questioned, he answered his name was John Johnson and he was guarding his master's firewood, something that was not entirely inaccurate. Initially placated, a more thorough second search was ordered and it was discovered that under the firewood were concealed some thirty-six barrels of gunpowder.

What happened next is worthy of any Hollywood blockbuster. Prior to his fellow conspirators still in London fleeing north throughout the next morning, Fawkes was brought before the king and questioned in his private chambers around 4am. When asked of his purpose, Fawkes answered stoutly that he intended to blow up the Houses of Parliament. When asked why, he elaborated it was his intention to blow the Scotch beggars back to their Scottish mountains.

Evidently, opinion of Fawkes was not all bad. Obviously guilty, his bravado nonetheless drew comparisons with the Roman Mucius Scaevola. Admitting his crime, Fawkes was taken to the Tower where he would alternate his time between the council chamber in the lieutenant's lodgings, the same 'little ease' dungeon endured by Campion and the torture chambers of the White Tower. Records of Fawkes's incarceration confirm the king himself put together a list of questions along with firm instructions that, if necessary, the gentler tortures should be used first – a clear reference to the manacles that had been used so effectively against John Gerard – and so by degrees proceeding to the worst. Although no definitive evidence survives, it is almost universally accepted Fawkes was racked.

In occupation of the lieutenant's lodgings at this time was one of the most famous men in the Tower's history, the notorious Sir William Waad. Replacing Sir George Harvey, the second lieutenant in two years to have taken a shine to the 'rawly' rogue, Sir Walter Raleigh, dealing with Fawkes lay primarily with Waad. How Fawkes dealt with the torture is nothing short of remarkable. After maintaining for two days he was Johnson, he finally gave his name on the 7th and began to crack on the 8th. By the 9th, he finally named conspirators, by which point it barely mattered as those who had fled had either been killed or were already in custody.

As Fawkes, at first, prepared to light the fuse and, subsequently, languished in his cell, most of the conspirators had moved north where they prepared to launch a Midlands rebellion that would culminate in the Princess Elizabeth taking her father's place on the throne. Hearing of Fawkes's capture and failing to stir the Midlands' Catholics, Catesby's conspirators were hunted down, finally surrounded at Holbeche House in Staffordshire, home of Stephen Littleton, a latecomer to proceedings. After being shot at by the sheriff and the county militia, those who were not killed were captured. It was recorded of the last stand that Catesby had said to Wintour, 'Stand by me, Mr Tom, and we shall die together.' Though die Catesby would, it was with Percy, not Wintour, succumbing to either the same musket ball or two balls from the same gunshot. As he clung to dear life, Catesby crawled back inside the house, where he died clutching an icon of the Virgin Mary to whom he had always been devoted. Injured by a shot to the arm, Wintour joined Fawkes in the Tower, along with his brother Robert, Sir Everard Digby, Ambrose Rookwood, Francis Tresham, Robert Keyes, and John Grant with Catesby's servant Thomas Bates imprisoned nearby. Also incarcerated around that time were two Jesuits, the unfortunate Henry Garnet and Edward Oldcorne.

Fawkes's fortitude in facing the rack is unofficially regarded as the longest ever a man withstood. Whether or not his cracking was of physical pain or a calculated delay that he believed would be sufficient to allow his comrades to escape is now impossible to tell. By the time he signed his name on 9 November his signature was barely legible. The popular account of his interrogation states that after some two-and-a-half hours on the rack, he collapsed midway through signing his confession, something the weakness of his signature in the surviving document would confirm.

The treatment endured by the others was similar. Over two long months, each was questioned in various parts of the Tower, and all gave confessions of their own. The lengthy declaration of Thomas Wintour, now the only surviving original conspirator, is historically the most important, confirming how Catesby had orchestrated the idea, citing 'a desperate disease requires a desperate remedy.'

Of the conspirators in the Tower, only one was destined to evade the gallows. Whether from the poor conditions or perhaps poisoned, Francis Tresham suffered a urinary tract infection and perished in his cell. For the priests, Waad's tactics were far more subtle; nevertheless, both were reported as being racked. Realizing he was in a corner, Garnet confessed he was aware of the plot as Catesby had informed him during confession, but under the laws of the Catholic church, he had been unable to break the vow of confidentiality. The plotters throughout remained steadfast in their views. A latecomer to the conspiracy and renowned for his kindly nature, Sir Everard Digby reported on the would-be deaths of the lords that there was barely three worth saving.

By late January, the surviving plotters were taken to Westminster where only Digby pleaded guilty. The others, by contrast, confirmed they had only pleaded not guilty as by doing so they would have condemned the Jesuits, a fact to which Digby himself also brought attention. There is a strange story around this time that, while placed in adjacent cells, Robert Wintour and Guy Fawkes were overheard in conversation concerning the recent capture of Nicholas Owen with Wintour stating 'God will raise up seed to Abraham out of the very stones, although they were gone.' Exactly what he meant remains a mystery.

Inevitably the verdict was guilty. Like the earlier group of rogue agents who had seen death in the Babington Plot, the remaining conspirators would be put to death in two batches of four after being dragged by hurdles to their places of execution. The first batch, consisting of Robert Wintour, Digby, Grant and Bates was taken from the Tower – Bates, as a commoner, was brought from the gatehouse prison – to St Paul's Churchyard. The greatest acclaim here must go to Digby. Having spent his final night at the Tower composing a letter for his wife and sons, in addition to a farewell poem, he faced the torment of being hanged and disembowelled. On having his heart removed he managed to refute the traditional line 'here is the heart of a traitor' with the incredible response of 'thou liest.'

The following day, the remaining four were brought from the Tower to the old palace yard, ironically in sight of the building they had attempted to destroy. Following a surprisingly short speech from the eloquent Wintour, the last original conspirator suffered a hard death, following which the crowd saw a largely unconscious Rookwood and a resolute Keyes. Last but not least was the 'devil of the vault' Fawkes. Barely able to walk from his time on the rack, he was hanged from the uppermost rung, dying instantly and saved further torture.

The thirteen were done, but the story of the Gunpowder Plot was not yet completely over. Having some knowledge of the plot, Garnet and Oldcorne were also destined for execution: Garnet at St Paul's Churchyard and Oldcorne at Red Hill, Worcester. Leaving their prison in the Bloody Tower, Garnet bade his cook goodbye, stating 'Farewell, good friend Tom: this day I will save thee a labour to provide my dinner.' When hanged, it was recorded the sympathetic crowd pulled hard on his legs, thus ending his life early to ensure he suffered less pain.

Far worse would await the incredible Nicholas Owen. The genius behind the elusive priest holes – many of which survive to this day within the walls of the great recusant houses, some perhaps still undiscovered – had still been at large early in 1606, before voluntarily giving himself up while at Hindlip Hall in the hope it might take the heat off Garnet, who at the time was hiding nearby. Taken first to Marshalsea Prison on the south bank of the Thames, he was soon transferred to the Tower where he suffered not only the questioning of the inquisitors, but also Topcliffe's torture device. Deeply troubled by a hernia, an iron plate was attached to his stomach in a bid to keep his intestines in place. Ever valiant in his attempts to keep quiet, Owen was mercilessly transferred to the rack itself, only for his hernia to give way, becoming cut up by the iron plate. Saved the ordeal of a public execution, he passed away around late 1 March or the early hours of the following morning. In light of his devotion, he was canonised by Paul VI in 1970 and regarded by John Gerard as having 'done more good of all those who laboured in the English vineyard ... saving the lives of many hundreds of persons, both ecclesiastical and secular.'

The trio's place in the Tower would soon be taken by another of Jesuit leanings. Born in York and educated at the English College in Rome, Father William Wright served as a professor of philosophy and theology at the universities in Graz and Vienna before joining the English mission in 1606. A year later, Wright was imprisoned in the Tower after being discovered as the chaplain of the recusant Gage family of Hengrave Hall in Suffolk. Eventually moved to the Marshalsea, when the plague hit the city Wright spent his time nursing the sick and burying the dead before escaping to Leicestershire. He would finally pass away in 1639 after a useful life as a prominent writer.

Arriving at the Tower a year later was the Irish chieftain Niall Garve O'Donnel. Previously taking the side of the English, ironically against his own flesh and blood, in the Nine Years' War of the 1590s, O'Donnel was one of a number from the period whose loyalties frequently changed. When fellow rebel Sir Cahir O'Doherty launched a rebellion in 1608, O'Donnel was charged with complicity and sent to the Tower, along with his son, Neachtain. Together they would avoid the noose or the block, but never again enjoy freedom.

Following in the footsteps of the many famous – if not infamous – Catholic prisoners of state to inhabitant the cold chambers of the Salt Tower was the Benedictine monk, John Roberts. Caught in 1610 saying mass for at least the fifth time, Roberts was arrested and taken to the Tower where he arrived still wearing his holy vestments. Hanged till he was dead before being posthumously quartered, Roberts's remains were placed in a nearby pit along with the sixteen criminals with which he had shared the Tyburn gallows. Like many of those who went before him, his relics were revered as prized possessions, and two of his fingers were successfully recovered from the pit.

Joining fellow adventurer Raleigh in the Tower in 1612 was the English mariner Nicholas Woodcock. Famed in history for his trips to Asia and Virginia, Woodcock was also remembered for piloting the first Spanish whaling ship to Spitsbergen in northern Norway. As a consequence of his dealings with the Spanish, he was held for sixteen months in the Gatehouse Prison and the Tower before being released to return to sea.

Notorious as a place of incarceration, it is hardly surprising that among the Tower's many stories of torture, death and despair that any hint of love frequently turned to tragedy. The following is not only in keeping with the Tower's ever-darkening reputation but also the series of misfortunes associated with two families that witnessed what could have been heaven soon descend to hell.

The tragic life of Lady Arbella Stuart is one that could have been completely different. Born in 1575, a descendent of Henry VII through his daughter Margaret, Queen of Scotland, Arbella had lost her father as an infant and her mother at the age of seven, after which she was brought up in the household of her grandmother, Bess of Hardwick. A claimant to the throne as a cousin of the king, Arbella's suspected Catholic leanings had earned her high esteem in the eyes of many of England's papist rebels whose fortunes had declined somewhat since the foiling of the gunpowder plot.

As a woman with a legitimate claim to the throne and a Catholic sympathiser, Arbella was undoubtedly of concern to the king. Discussions regarding a suitable marriage had been ongoing throughout her childhood but nothing ever came to fruition. By the end of Elizabeth's reign, reports began to emerge that she was set to marry Edward Seymour, another of that now infamous clan and a man with personal influence at court. Adhering to the long, and commonly, held view that she would never marry without the permission of the queen, the wedding never took place. Seven years later, however, she married another Seymour, without the knowledge of James.

The wedding of the 22-year-old William Seymour to the 34-year-old Arbella inevitably caused concern at court, not least to the king. The union of the fourth in line to the throne with the sixth meant any issue, especially male, would have a clear claim to kingship in the event of future uprising, especially that originating from the Catholic side. Whether inspired by genuine concern or insecurity, James acted swiftly and Seymour was sent to the Tower.

In keeping with his station, Seymour was housed comfortably, taking up residence in the house of William Waad, once again lieutenant of the Tower, before being moved to St Thomas's Tower and the infamous cell once inhabited by the slippery Edmund Neville. In hindsight it seems a strange oversight that neither James nor Waad seriously considered the possibility that Seymour would seek to emulate Neville and mount an escape. Whatever precautions were put in place, Seymour did indeed follow in the enigmatic escapee's footsteps.

For over a year the newlyweds were separated before a despairing Arbella attempted to arrange a meeting, taking a boat along the Thames as close as possible to St Thomas's Tower. Parted only by the wharf and moat, the pair are reported to have managed a brief conversation through one of the windows of Seymour's cell. On hearing of the meeting, James ordered that Arbella be sent north. Around that time, the situation became further complicated by the meddling of Arbella's aunt, Mary Talbot, the countess of Shrewsbury, who, motivated either by sympathy or personal ambition, hatched a plan to free the imprisoned Seymour and secure the couple's safe passage to the Continent.

On 3 June 1611, the highly complex plan was put into operation. Located in East Barnet since falling ill on her way north, Arbella informed her sympathetic hostess she was heading out in an attempt to meet her husband. Aiding her by dressing her up as a man, Arbella was escorted by one of the servants to a 'sorry inn' where she would collect horses for the attempted escape. So far so good, Arbella completed the fourteen-mile cross-country journey to a riverside tavern in Blackwell where, if all went to plan, her husband would join her. For the present, all she could do was wait.

From the confines of his cell, Seymour had been working on his own plan. Noting that a carter habitually left his cart close to St Thomas's

Tower most evenings, the desperate captive entered negotiations with the tradesman to aid him in his conspiracy. Perhaps taking a leaf out of Neville's book two decades earlier, a subtle change of identity was proposed with the carter's agreement. Whether the carter got cold feet or was otherwise engaged, his arrival on that evening was significantly delayed; several hours passed before they changed places and Seymour drove the horse-driven cart towards the Tower's exit at the Byward Tower with the carter hiding behind him among the hay bales. Dressed in the clothes of his associate, his new identity failed to arouse the suspicion of the guards. Sadly for the couple, the delay changed their destinies. After reaching a boat close to the point where Tower Bridge now stands, Seymour made his way towards the inn where his wife was due to meet him, only to learn Arbella had already departed.

The tale of this tragic near miss has long been cited as one of the Tower's most heart-breaking events. Convinced that Seymour's lateness was a sign all was not well, and fearing due to the late hour the tide would soon turn, Arbella was persuaded to make her way without her husband. Rowing downriver into Essex, further bad news awaited, as the tide had indeed been missed. Relying then heavily on improvisation it was, perhaps, almost inevitable that another great irony awaited. On the morning following the escape, William Seymour's younger brother, Francis, received a vaguely worded letter from a man named Edward Rodney, Seymour's cousin and the same man who had been waiting for Seymour with the boat, informing him not to expect to see his brother for some time. Alarmed by the note, Francis moved swiftly to the Tower, where he discovered that his brother was missing.

With news of Seymour's escape made known to Waad and the king, James erupted with fury. Within hours a proclamation was issued against Seymour and Arbella, along with the many unnamed others suspected of being in league with them. While Arbella and her company made their way aboard the French ship as planned, on reaching there themselves and realizing the French ship had already left, Seymour's party rowed towards a collier named, *The Charles*, a £40 bribe securing them passage to Calais. During the journey, it was recorded how they crossed paths with the French ship, but, for reasons unknown, on being asked to investigate, the captain of the collier reported back to Seymour his wife was nowhere to be seen. In truth, he had apparently witnessed her seated on a wooden hatch.

Contrary winds eventually saw Seymour and Rodney end their journey at Ostend, by which time news of their escape had been widely circulated to the authorities, including the local naval commander, Sir William Monson. While Seymour and his accomplice had luck on their side, for his wife, the opposite was true. On being ordered to search the seas, one of Monson's captains, one Griffin Cockett, spotted Arbella's French vessel from his own craft, *Adventure*. Less than a mile from port, Cockett boarded the French ship and Arbella was arrested.

James's retribution on those involved was merciless. Among the victims, Arbella's servants were sent to the Tower for questioning; the rack awaited attendant William Markham. Joining them in the Tower were Arbella and her aunt, Mary Talbot, who had orchestrated much of proceedings. Tried before the Star Chamber, Talbot was incarcerated until 1615 and then again between 1618 and 1623 after being questioned a second time concerning rumours Arbella had secretly given birth. The extortionate fine of £20,000 she was sentenced to pay on her original arrest does not appear to have been collected.

As for Arbella, imprisoned in the Bell Tower, all hope had left her. An escape plan devised by loyal servant Hugh Crompton in July 1614 was uncovered; although the culprits escaped with their lives, they would not entirely escape punishment. Within fifteen months Arbella was dead, according to official accounts she had wasted away from the same porphyria – a disease that attacks the nervous system – that had plagued her on her journey north prior to her escape; other commentators have speculated she committed suicide. If there was any consolation from beyond the grave it may have come in the knowledge that the husband she barely knew had been pardoned.

In truth, her spirit had probably died four years earlier in sight of Calais.

Chapter 17

1612–1618: Poisonings, Percys and Perilous Pirates

Another of Catholic leanings to be caught up in the aftermath of the Gunpowder Plot had been the latest earl of Northumberland, Henry Percy. Never officially found guilty of any specific crime or, indeed, any definitive connection with the plot itself, most of the allegations against him stemmed from his family ties with deceased conspirator Thomas Percy, who had worked for him collecting rents, as well as having progressed to become a gentleman pensioner thanks in large part to their being related. Learning that the pair had dined at the earl's London home on the eve of the plot, eyebrows were inevitably raised.

Taken in for questioning following the failure of the plot, Percy was himself confined to the Tower, passing the time in relative comfort conducting the scientific experiments that had already earned him the nickname 'the Wizard Earl'. As someone of noble status, he took up residence in the Martin Tower, on the opposite side of the inner ward from fellow scientist Raleigh, within which he constructed a laboratory and library, as well as a small bowling alley.

For these, perhaps unfortunate, disgraced former favourites, time in the Tower would predominantly be spent in ongoing study, during which their paths often crossed. In contrast to the Tower's ever-developing sinister image, the voluntary residence of fellow scientist Thomas Harriot as well as regular visits and correspondence from many others of academic standing made the Martin and Bloody Towers more like the chambers of Oxford or Paris than the dank cells of the Beauchamp.

In 1612, however, the playing field would change somewhat. Cecil's death, significant though it was, had been overshadowed by the premature demise of the heir to the throne. Struck down by typhoid after a summer swim in the murky waters of the Thames, any initial hope that Henry

Frederick was to be revived on sampling one of Raleigh's home-brewed elixirs sadly failed to provide a proper cure. As the prince perished, so too did the hopes of James and Raleigh; of the two, it seems Raleigh displayed the more emotion on the lad's passing. It has often been held that much of the spark that remained in the old seadog faded away with the precocious royal's tragic end.

With Cecil and Henry gone, the void that they left would see another of England's controversial figures grace the political landscape. Favourite of the king and highly rumoured to be his gay lover, Robert Carr had benefited more than anyone from Raleigh's downfall after his controversial inheritance of Sherborne Castle. Assisting Carr in his political responsibilities was his best friend, Sir Thomas Overbury, another of alleged homosexual tendencies. To add spice to the potion, the handsome Carr became sought after by the beautiful Frances Howard, who had previously been married to the son of Essex before their union was annulled on grounds of non-consummation. In response to accusations of impotence, the son of Essex refuted it, even physically proving it, before accusing Howard of various oddities, such as necromancy to ensure they never achieved carnal knowledge.

Howard's interest in Carr seems to have been largely reciprocated. Initially encouraging of the budding romance, Overbury assisted his best friend in writing Carr's love letters. This would dramatically change, however, as his willingness to participate cooled on learning the pair intended to marry. Overbury's opposition, which led to the writing of a tract entitled, *The Wife*, highlighting Frances's poorer points, caught the attention of the ageing head of the family, Henry Howard, 1st Earl of Northampton. As second son of the executed Surrey and younger brother of the also executed 4th duke of Norfolk and grandson of the loathed 3rd duke, he had long been walking a political tightrope. Concerned by Overbury's opposition, he conspired with Frances to remove him from the picture.

In 1613 Overbury, almost certainly at Northampton's suggestion, was offered two foreign ambassadorships. Refusing both, he was confined to the ground floor of the Bloody Tower for his disobedience. With Frances Howard's marriage to Robert Devereux, 3rd Earl of Essex a step closer to being annulled, the next stage of the plot involved the removal of the famously professional Sir William Waad from his post as lieutenant of the Tower on grounds that he had failed to prevent William Seymour's escape. With Waad out of the picture, the lawyer, Sir Gervase Elwes, himself a Howard lackey, took over the post and the previous lieutenant's residence in the Queen's House.

Overbury's fate was all but sealed when another of the Howard minions, Richard Weston, became his keeper in the Bloody Tower. Aided by a young widow – also Weston's employer and an acquaintance of Frances – named Anne Turner, on 9 May Weston went to work, mixing arsenic into Overbury's soup, following which the unsuspecting prisoner spent the night in agony. After three weeks of continued suffering, a letter to Carr pleading he use his influence with the king to improve his lot was met with a response that contained a strange white powder. On consuming it, Overbury's condition worsened still.

Despite the visits of several doctors, including the renowned Swiss Huguenot, Sir Théodore de Mayerne, no cure could be found for the unfortunate captive. On 1 July Weston mixed further arsenic into Overbury's food, which had been cooked in the lieutenant's own kitchen. Later that month, a second poison was added to the tarts and jellies that Overbury requested. Undoubtedly suspicious as to the cause of his developing illness, as opposed to eating the treats, he watched with hardening suspicion as they turned black and furred before his eyes.

For Overbury, the discovery only succeeded in accelerating his fate. Ironically, his recently acquired knowledge of the poison inspired him to resort to blackmail, which in turn stirred Elwes to relocate him into a dark, windowless cell in another part of the Tower. Worse still, the medicines prescribed by de Mayerne and fixed up by his brother-in-law, Paul de Lobell, did not arrive at the Tower in the condition they had been in on leaving the lab. Adding de Lobell's apprentice, William Reeve, to the endeavour, Reeve had been bribed by one of the conspirators to add the same poison used on the jellies. Within a night, and under the watchful eyes of Weston, Overbury died in apparent agony.

Northampton wrote to Elwes on hearing of Overbury's passing from Weston. The instructions in the letter, which survived despite orders that it should be burned, were obeyed and Overbury was buried in the 'no sadder spot' at sundown, his corpse apparently rank with odours. Carr

was informed of his friend's death, before the wider world was notified
that the young man had died of the pox – an excuse that from a medical
standing made sense of the use of mercury in his attempted recovery.
Despite this, rumour inevitably became rife that the young man had been
poisoned.

On Boxing Day 1613, Carr and Frances were married amidst scenes
of magnificence, yet Overbury's ghost would soon have his posthumous
revenge. In June 1614, Northampton was the first of the conspirators to
die, apparently of natural causes. Dissatisfied by his dismissal as lieutenant
of the Tower, Waad also gained his own revenge after amassing evidence
of Overbury's murder and the subsequent cover-up. Leading the inquiry
was the new secretary of state, Sir Ralph Winwood. Ironically as fate
would have it, Northampton's death had left the Howards leaderless,
whereas James's infatuation with Carr had given way to one George
Villiers. As a suspected Catholic, the late Northampton, along with the
equally guilty Mrs Turner, it was suggested had been responsible for an
intended papist coup.

The conspiracy was soon unravelled. Elwes, a man entrusted with the
responsibility of interrogating prisoners, failed to withstand scrutiny
himself and confessed to Overbury's poisoning. His career in ruins, he
was hanged, at his own request on Tower Hill, on 20 November 1615.
Also condemned was Turner, herself garrotted at Tyburn. Her end was
memorable for being ordered to wear a yellow starched cobweb-lawn ruff
– a request of the judge in honour of her regular wearing of the style
– only for her hangman to mockingly adorn a similar garb. Weston is
recorded as having made a particularly interesting speech prior to his
execution, intimating a far wider conspiracy. A fourth player, Franklin,
was taken down, but not before evidence had come to light against the
late Northampton and the recently married Carrs. In May 1615 the
newlyweds were tried before the House of Lords on the charge of murder.
Though found guilty, the sentence was deferred due to Frances's timely
pregnancy. In December she gave birth to a daughter inside the Tower.

In another great irony of this appalling affair, Frances was imprisoned
in the Bloody Tower in the cell in which Overbury had been poisoned.
So shocked had she been, it was recorded the accessory to murder gave
way to fits of laughing. At the time, the previous inhabitant, Raleigh, had

been temporarily freed in order to mount his long-awaited attempt at locating the fabled El Dorado, thus allowing her husband to inhabit the first floor lodgings. As nobles, they were granted the usual trappings of their status, including three maids assigned to wait on Frances. Carr was granted regular trips to the Martin Tower to visit the 'Wizard Earl' Percy.

A fitting end to this wretched tale of misery, deceit and hatred came with the irony that the imprisoned newlyweds soon became enemies themselves. Be it cramped together or cursed by their plight, Carr found his new love no more to his taste than Essex had. Although their original death sentences remained on record, they were pardoned and placed under house arrest, by which time their marriage had turned increasingly sour. Away from the Tower, Frances's mood turned to melancholy, her days ending with the ironic, gruelling pain of ovarian cancer. Her husband outlived her by thirteen years.

Receiving no official sentence, nor any state-approved torture, Overbury's murder provided clear evidence of how precarious life in the Tower could be. Within a year of his death, a report by Winwood, the secretary of state, concerning the interrogation of one Edward Peacham once again served to highlight the extremities of life there. Prominent among his writings were the line: 'Peacham was this day examined before torture, in torture, between torture and after torture; yet he persists in his insensible denials.'

In 1616, better fortune befell Carr's predecessor in the Bloody Tower: that old Elizabethan stalwart James had heard 'rawly of'. Confined to the Tower for the previous thirteen years, Raleigh had been ceaseless in his attempts to convince James to allow him a further voyage to the New World in search of fabled riches. Initially reluctant, James finally acquiesced in the hope that a successful endeavour would swell the royal coffers. After busily setting to work building and equipping a ship capable of crossing the Atlantic, and filling it with a trusted crew, Raleigh departed Plymouth in March 1617.

The voyage would be far from the adventure he was looking for. Cursed by adverse winds and a far from competent staff, it was not till August they finally made any real progress. After stopping off at the Canary Islands, Raleigh had to restrain one of his captains from plundering a passing Spanish ship – an occurrence that, nevertheless, led to accusations of piracy back in England. Stricken by fever, minus fifty of his men, *The Destiny* eventually completed the journey across the Atlantic, by which time Raleigh was too unwell to join his son, Wat, in exploring the mainland. While Wat led proceedings down the Orinoco River, Raleigh was left to recover in Trinidad. News from the expedition, when it came, was a nightmare. His men had attacked a Spanish settlement and Wat had been killed in a mêleé. Heartbroken, Raleigh returned to England. Worse news came when two of his men turned to piracy and Raleigh's faithful skipper, blaming himself for recent failures, shot himself in his cabin. On 21 June, *The Destiny* returned to Plymouth empty-handed.

News of Raleigh's doomed venture had reached England ahead of him. Convinced he had incited the misguided conflict with the Spanish personally, James had promised the Spanish ambassador Raleigh would be hauled to Madrid. Fortunately for Raleigh, the council saw better sense, perhaps also aware that the once despised pirate and courtier was now viewed as a loveable attraction at the Tower and a rare survivor from England's victory over the Armada. Raleigh's time in Plymouth lasted longer than expected. Mulling over his wife's suggestion of escaping to France, he remained in Devon until he was arrested and taken to London. After being duped into making another bid for freedom, this time on a French ship, Raleigh found himself back in the Brick Tower, the same tower he had first been kept in back in 1592 on marrying Bess.

Now well into his sixties, Raleigh was physically a shadow of the man he had once been. It was commented during his trial that he was a star faded as opposed to a great adventurer in his prime. In the eyes of the public, favour of Raleigh nevertheless continued to increase, just as respect for the king who submitted to Spanish pressure diminished. Fresh from his sentencing, and perhaps privately fearing public outcry, Raleigh prepared himself for death the next day in the palace yard. After an evening playing the jester to the crowds, he said his farewells to Beth and penned a final poem inside a family bible. On the morning of 29 October, after eating a hearty breakfast and sampling a pipe of his own tobacco, Raleigh is noted as having told the yeoman warder, on consuming a cup of sack prior to his leaving the Tower, that he would have enjoyed it more had he been able to take his time. Raleigh's gallows humour, it seems, saw him through to the last. Mounting the scaffold, he addressed the crowd in fine form while sipping from a glass of sherry, joking with the executioner over the sharpness of the axe, remarking, 'this is a sharp medicine, but it will cure all diseases.'

In clear sympathy with the great man, the executioner replayed the famous gesture Raleigh had once made to Elizabeth by placing his coat on the ground for the condemned man to kneel on. Refusing a blindfold, confirming he did not fear the shadow, the executioner's nerve was tested, requiring two blows to finish the job. On lifting the dead man's head, it was recorded he refrained from reciting the usual line. Instead a mournful silence, broken by words among the crowd 'we have not another such head to be cut off,' accompanied what all in attendance surely knew marked the end of the Golden Age of English history.

Chapter 18

1618–1649: A Divine Right For War

The final years of James's reign were somewhat less eventful than the early ones. Throughout his time on the throne, the Tower had undergone further subtle developments, most notably a viewing platform at the menagerie that the king himself often made use of. A career pacifist in terms of war, perversely James was far from immune to bloodlust and regularly visited the cages to sadistically watch fights between the animals. One particularly bad example, as briefly touched upon, occurred with the gift of an African lion which mauled two mastiffs, the third being adopted by James's far more impressive heir as a pet. A year later the king watched on as two cocks were torn apart by a lion and a lioness.

Perhaps the most incredible story concerning the developing zoo came with James's desire that a lamb be lowered by rope into the lions' den. Rather than being mauled, incredibly the lamb 'rose up and went towards the lions, who very gently looked upon him and smelled upon him without sign of any further hurt. Then the lamb was softly drawn up again in as good plight as he was set down.' Dissatisfied, James instead had to settle for another trio of mastiffs being devoured by the same lions. With the survival of the lamb, it was deemed a biblical prophecy had been fulfilled. A perhaps fitting performance before the man often dubbed 'the wisest fool in Christendom'.

Other parts of the menagerie also expanded throughout his reign. By 1597 it had been recorded as the home of two lions, three lionesses, a leopard, a tiger, an eagle, a wolf and a porcupine yet by the end of his reign the numbers had grown to eleven lions, three eagles, two pumas, two leopards, a tiger and a jackal. Also to develop throughout this time was the jewel house. Originally created south of the White Tower in the reign of Richard II – and rebuilt no later than during that of Elizabeth I – to operate as a permanent home for the Crown Jewels, throughout

James's tenure the jewels and plate stayed where they were. A somewhat thrifty man, unlike his Plantagenet predecessors, James never resorted to the practice of pawning the jewels for fast cash.

James's death in 1625, had the script been written differently, would have seen the ascension of his impressive son, Prince Henry Frederick Stuart, the highly gifted individual who had won over the crowds on his arrival in London in 1603 before sadly succumbing to typhoid after his ill-planned dip in the Thames to escape the summer sun. With the prince of Wales dead, the next in line was James's second son, the less confident Charles who, despite some very admirable qualities, also inherited his father's more foolish ones, including a strict adherence to the divine right of kingship.

Prominent among Charles's early critics was the puritan Sir John Eliot, who spent time in the Tower in 1626 for his criticism of James's former favourite, George Villiers, since 1623 styled 1st Duke of Buckingham. In 1629, Eliot was back on the scene, this time accompanied by eight hardened puritans who launched a string of verbal attacks on the future archbishop of Canterbury, William Laud. In a tense session in the Commons, culminating in Eliot physically laying his hands on the speaker in order to prevent him from adjourning parliament, Eliot was arrested, along with his comrades and taken to the Tower.

The hot-headed Sir Robert Strange spent time in the Tower in 1628 in direct response to threats that he made against the duke of Buckingham, resulting in his being taken to Westminster for facial mutilation. Incidentally, Buckingham was brutally murdered in Portsmouth later that year: his killer, an equally violent former officer named John Felton, who had since seen out his days within the same walls of the Bloody Tower before his execution at Tyburn on 29 November. Intriguingly, Felton had avoided being tortured after complaining it was illegal, a stance Laud acknowledged and advised the king not to incite widespread hatred by imposing it. Despite acquiescing on the point, a year later the king's wrath fell squarely on Eliot. Felton may have been responsible for Buckingham's murder, but Charles held Eliot squarely to blame for bringing it about.

On the opposite side of the political fence, Eliot was not without friends. His writings during his imprisonment demonstrated that he had as many as forty key allies and listeners with whom he would correspond. Nevertheless, his lack of favour with the king made release unlikely: so much so, Charles not only sentenced him to life in the Tower, but also fined him the substantial amount of £2,000. On hearing this, Eliot's outstanding response was that if the king could pluck such a figure out of his two cloaks, two suits, pairs of boots, galoshes and books, much good might it do him.

Charles's wrath at Eliot's tenacity knew no bounds. Concerned by his prisoner's writings, most notably his essays in favour of parliamentary control – a stark contradiction to the divine right of kingship – in 1631 Eliot was removed from the tower that had once lodged Raleigh, Overbury and Carr, thrown into a series of dark cells and prohibited from receiving visitors. Contracting TB, Eliot faded fast. On 27 November 1632, he died and was buried not in his native Cornwall but with his head intact in the saddest spot on earth.

A year prior to Eliot's death, Mervin Tuchet, 2nd Earl of Castlehaven had become the first man of the new reign to lose his head on Tower Hill. In 1630, Tuchet, known more widely as Lord Audley, had been tried by his peers for raping his wife and sodomising two of his male servants. Despite a stern rebuttal, most notably that the charges were born of a joint conspiracy by his wife and son on matters concerning the family inheritance, Audley was found guilty on all of the charges. He was beheaded on 14 May 1631.

Better luck was to be enjoyed by the diplomat, MP and agent to Charles's sister – Elizabeth of Bohemia – Francis Nethersole. In December 1633, Nethersole received a letter from Elizabeth's private secretary, imploring him to help secure aid from England for her son, Charles Louie, now heir to the Electoral Palatinate – previously the County Palatine of the Rhine – who was currently living in exile in The Hague. Elizabeth and her husband Frederick had lost both the Palatinate and the throne of Bohemia in around 1620. For forwarding an extract from the letter to Sir John Coke, the king's secretary, in addition to his own correspondence suggesting failure to comply might lead to future conflict with Charles Louie, a furious Charles transferred Nethersole to the Tower. He was released after about four months, but not before Charles received a firm promise from his sister that Nethersole would never again be used in her service. A free man, Nethersole later found work as a Civil War pamphleteer.

Returning to political matters, Eliot's determination would inspire many on the Republican side. Sadly for Charles, his own defensive stance against wider influences in turn began something of a vicious cycle that would ultimately culminate in the English Civil War.

As the nation's slide into its sixth major domestic conflict to date gathered pace, leaders would soon emerge on both sides of the political divide. One who would appear in support of the king, yet was also destined to die at the Tower, was native Yorkshireman, Thomas Wentworth. Made earl of Strafford by Charles in recognition of his support of royal authority, and subsequently the king's enforcer in the north and lord deputy in Ireland, his hard approach had already successfully quelled a Catholic uprising. Also on the Catholics' side was the conservative archbishop of Canterbury, William Laud. Lenient with regard to the ancient traditions, Laud had become deeply concerned by the increasingly puritanical nature of the Church of England and attempted to stem the flow with something of a minor counter-reformation. Whereas Laud's policy resulted in many Puritans taking refuge overseas, mostly following the Pilgrim Fathers to the New World, many who stayed viewed his movements as a further call to war.

Rioting in the capital in May 1640 saw the archbishop's palace at Lambeth violently attacked. Arrested as a result had been one of the mob leaders, John Archer, who had led his charges with the beating of a drum. When questioned by lieutenant of the Tower, Sir William Balfour, Archer is recorded as having been racked in order to produce a list of accomplices. From the evidence that survives, it appears that Archer holds the distinction of being the final person to have been 'married to the Duke of Exeter's Daughter.'

By 1640, Charles's grip on his kingdom showed signs of failing. Having ruled without parliament for eleven years, his need for funds was heightened by the so-called Bishops' War: a rising in Scotland that had come from widespread discontent at Laud's attempts to enforce England's religious ways on Scotland's diehard Presbyterians. When parliament met, the anti-royalist faction had the daggers out for Strafford and Laud. Learning that the chief of the opposition, the puritan John Pym, sought to impeach Strafford for high treason, Strafford in turn plotted to arrest Pym and his key supporters. Unknown to Strafford, Pym was already aware of this.

The knowledge of Strafford's plan ironically contributed to his downfall. Knowing that time was of the essence, Pym struck hard, circulating accusations of treason against Strafford the day he reached London. On 25 November, two weeks after his initial arrest, Strafford was relocated to the Tower, taking up residence in the lieutenant's lodgings like so many prisoners of status before him. As usual for a man of noble stock, he was granted many freedoms, most notably attending church every day and taking regular exercise with the lieutenant.

While all was quiet within the Tower, outside the walls, the citizens of London called for blood. As a stern upholder of absolute authority, Strafford, himself not without his own tyrannical reputation established on the back of his actions in Ireland, was very much viewed in such ways among the poorer classes. By the time he was taken upriver to answer his charges before the lords, it was noted this previously impressive figure had notably diminished despite the regular exercise.

Initially optimistic about his chances, Strafford wrote to his wife and maintained a cheery bearing throughout his long trial. On 1 March, Laud joined him within the famous walls – by now equally hated by London's anti-Catholic faction – taking up residence in the Bloody Tower. Concerned the tide was turning from a united Commons, Strafford found far more success amongst his peers in the Lords and by the time the trial was over, he had satisfied most of the charges. It was at this point, however, Pym endeavoured to implement a new strategy. Inspired by a loophole in the English law that had famously allowed kings to behead wives and rid themselves of key challengers for several centuries, Pym sought to ensure Strafford's doom by act of attainder. Passed by the Commons, it fell before the Lords, itself now under increasing pressure from both the lower house and an angry city to make the bill an act.

Aware of recent developments it was Charles who moved next. Pressured to put his own signature on the document and thus condemn the man whose safety he had personally assured, he sought to spur Strafford to freedom by bribing Lieutenant of the Tower, Sir William Balfour, to allow the earl safe passage. Buoyed by his own Scottish loyalties, Balfour rejected the suggestion and kept the Tower gates shut when a troop of 100 soldiers arrived by boat on 2 May to escort Strafford to freedom. As a consequence of the king's folly, the earl's position had become vastly weaker. Learning of the deceitful ploy, the Lords united behind the Commons and signed the attainder in numbers. In addition to the lords, further difficulty came from Lord Newport, the Tower's constable, who had also refused to accept a bribe to ignore Strafford's escape. Still attempting to spare Strafford, Charles now found himself the target of the angry mob. Realizing that the king had backed himself into a corner, Strafford wrote to inform him of his intention to relieve him of the escalating problem. In a sad highlight of the weaker aspect of his character, Charles buckled and soon gave in to peer pressure. Like Simon Sudbury and Richard II in the Peasants' Revolt, Charles had found his scapegoat.

Knowing he was to die, Strafford spent his final days in repentance, helped in doing so by the Calvinist primate of Ireland, James Ussher, who praised Strafford's valiant end. On 12 May, dressed all in black, Strafford accepted the escort of Balfour to Tower Hill. On passing through the archway of the Bloody Tower, he paused to receive a final blessing from Laud, who spoke down to him from the chambers above. On making his way from the Middle Tower to the scaffold, where a crowd some estimates place as large as 100,000 had gathered, having declined the offer of a blacked-out coach, it was reported Strafford's angry stare reduced the baying crowds to silence. Making his final speech and comforting his mournful brother, he accepted his fate. While word spread through the kingdom that the head of the tyrant was off, diarist John Evelyn remarked of the 'fateful stroke' that had severed 'the wisest head in England'. Whether an exaggeration or not, what cannot be doubted was that it contained knowledge Charles could certainly have later done with.

The English Civil War proved an eventful time for the Tower. During the conflict years, a story circulated that a desperate Royalist was chased up the White Tower's main steps by a Roundhead, only to drop to his knee and trip his pursuer before sending him to his death on the Broadwalk below. Exactly who those men may have been is unrecorded, if indeed the event actually happened. Sadly, many Tower records were lost or destroyed during the chaos, at which time the primary focus of the castle was to incarcerate imprisoned Royalists.

The years 1643 and 1644 both witnessed escapes from the Tower, all of which were of Irish connection. Initially successful was the head of the MacMahon faction, Hugh Oge MacMahon, who ruled over the Kingdom of Oriel. In recent years, MacMahon had become a lieutenant colonel in the Spanish forces, a post that would eventually lead to his capture. After entering a conspiracy with Cornelius Maguire, 2nd Baron Enniskillen, to capture Dublin Castle on 23 October 1641, things took a turn when the plot was revealed and the pair brought before the council. Subjected to the rack, he was transferred to the Tower of London and by 1643 both men occupied either the Martin or Devereux Tower. After attempting to enter communication with potential sympathisers in the city, two apparent priests from the Spanish embassy visited them in the Tower, resulting in an escape plan. Then sometime in August 1644, among the food sent in, one particular loaf of bread hid the instructions that a length of rope had been hidden for them on the outer battlements. Using already smuggled in tools, the pair sawed open the door of their cell and headed for the north wall of the Tower. Locating the rope, they descended noiselessly into the moat and to their allies on the other side.

Their time at large, however, was temporary. Discovered a month or so later in Drury Lane, by the lieutenant of the Tower, they were returned to captivity and held under far closer confinement. Found guilty of treason, MacMahon was sent west and hanged at Tyburn on 22 November 1644. Asked if any should pray for him, he responded, 'None but Roman Catholics.' On 20 February the following year, Maguire followed him to the afterlife.

The year prior to MacMahon's escape and death saw the imprisonment of Irish Royalist, Daniel O'Neill. Having followed in similar footsteps to the now infamous Guy Fawkes and gained experience taking up arms in the Low Countries, O'Neill was imprisoned after fighting for the Royalists in the Bishops' War. On his release, he entered dialogue with the king about bringing the royal army to London to combat the radical Parliamentarians. However, the plan, now known as the Second Army Plot, was uncovered, and he was imprisoned in the Gatehouse Prison at Westminster. Subsequently transferred to the Tower, in 1643 he successfully escaped through the classic combination of tying together a rope of bed sheets and disguising himself as a woman, duping the guards into believing he was his gaoler's wife. Away from the Tower, O'Neill's successful travel to Brussels was of notable benefit to Charles, for whom the fiery Irishman fought bravely in the forthcoming conflict.

The early 1640s would see a number of other imprisonments as the shadow of civil war fell over the Tower. An MP was sent to the Tower for his lenient views regarding Strafford in 1641, whereas another was taken the same year for opposing an armed guard. Sir Ralph Hopton was imprisoned for leading opposition to the Grand Remonstrance – the grievances against Charles I – and Lord Edward Montagu for unequivocally defending the king's integrity. Similar was true of the lord mayor of London, Sir Richard Gurney, and the bishop of Ely, Matthew Wren – uncle of the famous Sir Christopher – who spent his time in church administration and writing until his release in 1659.

Balfour was dismissed as lieutenant of the Tower at Christmas 1641 and replaced with the Cavalier Sir Thomas Lunsford. The move was undoubtedly part of a wider strategy, one long considered important in England, that the Tower held the keys to the kingdom. Unfortunately for Charles there were other considerations: most notably the threat that widespread dislike of Lunsford would lead to merchants refusing to supply the Mint with bullion, thus potentially leading England to economic ruin. As fate had it, Newport remained in place as constable and refused the incoming lieutenant access. Ironically, he returned as a prisoner of war in 1645 until his release on the condition that he emigrated to Virginia.

Charles's second attempt at bringing in his own man was difficult. Appointing the equally Royalist Sir John Byron as the replacement, Byron soon found himself at loggerheads with a new unit of City Trained Bands who had been brought in as part of the Tower garrison. The conflict was arguably the first of the Civil War and left Byron little choice but to hand in his resignation. He was replaced by a loyal Roundhead.

Still imprisoned throughout the early conflict was Archbishop Laud. Apart from maintaining what control he had over the church – most directly what went on within the Tower's chapels – Laud found himself in direct opposition to Pym's replacement, the puritanical William

Prynne with whom Laud had already clashed before his arrest. So great was the hostility that Laud had Prynne physically mutilated, including the cropping of both ears and having the letters SL – seditious libeller – engraved into his face. Now in command, Prynne began his own assault on Laud in dramatic fashion by visiting him personally in the Bloody Tower in 1643 with a band of musketeers to confiscate his defence papers.

Appearing at his trial in the spring of the following year, Laud nevertheless presented a good case, thanks in no small part to his excellent memory. Not guilty in the eyes of the law, his death sentence came again through another dubious act of attainder. In his small abode in the Bloody Tower, Laud drew up his last will, reporting how he was leaving this world 'weary at the very heart at the vanities in it.' On 10 January he addressed a large crowd at Tower Hill, declaring that by his faith he was destined for the Promised Land. His death was unique in the sense that noticing several spectators gathered beneath the scaffold, he requested further sawdust be added to ensure none would be splattered with his blood.

Edward Martin, President of Queen's College, Cambridge and later dean of Ely, was another of the religious life who saw time in the Tower in 1642. According to at least one source, he escaped after six years, whereas other sources state that after being transferred to a series of other prisons, he escaped Ely House before being recaptured. He was eventually released and pardoned in 1650.

Also caught up in the changing fortunes of war were Sir John Hotham and his son of the same name. Parliamentarians by nature, the younger Hotham had sought to convince his father to defect after encountering disagreements with his fellow Roundheads in Yorkshire and entered negotiations to hand over the City of Hull to the Royalists. On discovery of their planned defection, both men were sent to the Tower and executed in early 1645. A similar fate had also recently befallen Sir Alexander Carew and the City of Plymouth. Angered by the act of attainder that led to Strafford's execution, Carew was betrayed by a servant and held in the Tower for a year until he was beheaded on Tower Hill two days before Christmas.

One of the many Royalists doomed to languish in the Tower's cells around this time was the soon-to-be revered, George Monck. Born into poverty in 1608, the future general gained experience as a mercenary on the Continent before fighting on the king's side until his capture by General Fairfax in 1644. Initially Monck had been kept in Hull where Fairfax attempted to persuade him to defect. Stubbornly resisting, Monck was transferred to the frequently breached St Thomas's Tower and offered the ultimatum of staying there or change sides. Over the coming two and a half years, Monck bided his time, the majority of which he spent writing a book, entitled *Observations upon Military and Political Affairs*. He stayed in the Tower until 1646 at which time he reluctantly concluded the king's cause was lost.

One of the stranger stories from the period concerns the poet Edmund Waller. Famed for his middle ground political views, in parliament's eyes making him the perfect candidate to oversee peace negotiations with Charles in 1643, the often gentle poet on meeting Charles subsequently became the brainchild of a Royalist plot. Created with the intention of taking over the Tower and freeing the king's Royalist sympathisers, Waller's Plot failed to come to fruition after a servant betrayed him. As a cousin of Oliver Cromwell, Waller was spared death despite being found guilty of treason and instead exiled and fined after several months in the Tower. A worse fate awaited Waller's brother-in-law, Nathaniel Tomkins, and Richard Chaloner, however, who were summarily executed on 5 July 1643 for their roles in the conspiracy.

Another poet made to endure the inside of the Tower was the highly acclaimed Sir William Davenant. Apparently a godson of Shakespeare, after taking up his sword for the Royalist cause before being forced into exile with the future Charles II, Davenant, later named lieutenant governor of the American state of Maryland, was captured by a parliamentary ship as he attempted to make his crossing. Originally imprisoned on the Isle of Wight, he was moved to the Tower in preparation for his trial. Spared largely as a result of the lenience of Cromwell and the pleading of fellow poet, John Milton, Davenant would play a prominent role in post-Civil War high society.

A year prior to Davenant's incarceration, the Tower had hosted a different type of writer in the form of critical pamphleteer Clement Walker. Previously an MP who had been expelled from the House during Colonel Pride's infamous purge after agreeing to support the king's concessions, he was later arrested and committed to the Tower. He would pass away in 1651, prior to any form of trial.

At the height of the Civil War, the Tower was arguably every bit as crowded as it had been during the infamous papist plot days. Estimates from the time suggest that over the course of the war, as much as one third of the House of Lords may have filled its cramped cells. Not helping the situation was the increasing divide between the Presbyterian-dominated parliament and Puritan-led army that threatened a splinter conflict between the Roundheads. The divide was remedied on Cromwell's dismissal of the Long and Rump Parliaments, which saw the establishment of the 'Commonwealth' with himself installed as lord protector. In consequence, several important Parliamentarians were imprisoned in the Tower for their radical views.

One of the most important of this new wave of political prisoner was the notable John Lilburne, revered in some circles as the leader of this group of so-called 'Levellers'. Vehemently anti-royalist, the group was making a mark as strong advocates of the rights of the common man – beliefs that were viewed as threatening by the Parliamentarian heavyweights. Rather than lead to further military conflict, the rising feud occurred mainly through use of the written word. Following a sudden influx of Leveller pamphlets, highlighting their radical beliefs, discipline in the army suffered, leading to several mutinies and skirmishes. In 1649, Lilburne was himself brought to the Tower – his second experience there having criticised the earl of Manchester's performance as a military general two years earlier. Joined by three other senior Levellers, he went to work in a Raleigh-like manner and was exiled to the Netherlands before being imprisoned once more on returning to England. He was eventually released and became a Quaker.

Better luck had previously fallen upon the Royalist lord mayor of London, Sir Richard Gurney, who was freed in 1647 after four years in the Tower. In a near identical example to the see-sawing of fortunes witnessed during the Tudor period, his successor as Tower lieutenant, Sir Isaac Pennington, was imprisoned there at the Restoration. A similar story was true of loyal Royalist, Michael Hudson. Arrested on attempting to reach France and examined by a parliament-led committee regarding the movements of the king, Hudson successfully mounted an escape before being captured again at Hull and brought to the Tower. After passing his time largely in isolation, during which he attempted to form a plan to alleviate the Tower of its Roundhead overlords, he escaped in 1648 after disguising himself with a basket of apples on his head.

Following Hudson to the Tower was a Royalist of even greater status. Famed for his prowess as a leader on the battlefield, Lord Arthur Capel had been instrumental in the Royalists' initial withstanding the siege of Colchester by General Fairfax on the resumption of hostilities in 1648. When Colchester fell after two months, however, Capel found himself at the famous 'hound's' mercy. Along with Lord Norwich, he soon swapped the hard conditions of Bishop Gundulf's battered castle for the more civilised lodgings that surrounded the wailing monk's original Norman citadel north of the Thames.

As usual for a peer imprisoned in the Tower, Capel's privileges were extensive. Lodged between the Queen's House and the Beauchamp Tower, during the many visits he received from family, he was persuaded to follow in the footsteps of Edmund Neville and William Seymour and plan his escape. Inspired by previous successes, a suggestion was put forward that the imprisoned lord could swim the moat after ascending the outer wall, something Capel dismissed because of his poor ability as a swimmer. Ironically all was not lost; indeed, it was partly for that reason the fully developed plan was to become unique in the Tower's history. A tall man, it was decided he could cross the moat without his feet even leaving the ground.

In reality, the essence of the plan differed little from previous endeavours. Using his noble privileges to their advantage, Capel's family smuggled in much of what was needed, including a rope with a grappling hook to assist him over the outer wall. After deciding which area of the moat would be most appropriate, he used two sets of rope to get out of his cell and over the outer curtain wall before proceeding to descend from the battlements. There, he entered the chilly waters of the moat and, despite a momentary alarm when the water level came up to his beard, was able to make it to the safety of his gathering friends and by private coach to a sympathiser's house.

Unsurprisingly, news of Capel's escape caused uproar among the authorities. Concerned the future direction of the nation could depend on such things, London's houses were searched while Capel was relocated from Temple to somewhere south of the river. On being ferried safely across the Thames, the unscrupulous ferryman alerted the authorities, collected the reward money and ensured the unfortunate peer was returned to the Tower.

For Capel, his personal fate now mirrored that of the Royalists. Having successfully smuggled letters out to his fellow Cavaliers about fresh attempts to liberate the king, news of his dealings became known to Cromwell. Condemned to suffer the same fate as the king, Capel was brought from the Tower to the old palace yard and spoke passionately to the gathered crowd, urging them to put their faith in Charles's exiled son. Under the watchful eye of one Richard Brandon, the man suspected as having been responsible for the execution of the king five weeks earlier, he awaited the fall of the axe.

Like the doomed king himself, his head was removed at a single stroke.

Chapter 19

1649–1662: Parliament, Protectors and Dependable Protestors

A short time after Capel's daring escape, the Scottish Parliamentarian, Lieutenant General John Middleton – later 1st Earl Middleton – also achieved a similar feat. Originally a Roundhead who changed sides following the king's regicide, Middleton was taken to the Tower after his troops were defeated at the Battle of Worcester.

Middleton's tale must surely count amongst the strangest of all of the prisoners in the Tower. Confined there under the security of 'three lockes', it is said that he was awoken one night by the ghost of his friend Laird Boccani. After answering Middleton's enquiry concerning his mortality, Boccani predicted the earl would escape in three days, at which point he vanished without a trace. Either inspired by the phantom Cavalier or perhaps the actions of the Irishman O'Neill, Middleton duly escaped three days later by dressing up in women's clothes smuggled in by his loyal wife.

Far less fortunate were several others who had fought bravely in the Civil War. Colonel Eusebius Andrews was beheaded on 22 April – or August – 1650 after his involvement in a bogus plot against the army. A year later, the colourful Browne Bushell was executed on 29 March after a complicated pattern of events that had seen Hugh Cholmeley surrender Scarborough Castle to the Royalists. At the time Bushell had been sent on an errand to Hull, but was captured and granted release on the specific condition he recover Scarborough for the Roundheads. Returning to find Cholmeley had gone with the queen to York, Bushell kept his promise only to defect two years later and once again pass the garrison over to the Royalists. On 19 April 1645, Fairfax – Bushell's own father-in-law – took him to London to be court-martialled. Somehow convincing his accusers of his loyalty, he was granted his own ship which he later delivered to the prince of Wales. He was taken to the Tower and executed in 1651, apparently on the grounds of being both a turncoat and a pirate.

Also to face death in 1651 were the Welsh Presbyterian preacher Christopher Love and a man named John Gibbons who were executed on 22 August for plotting the restoration of Charles II. In honour of that, the Puritans of the time celebrated Love as a martyr.

Thomas Dalyell, who was imprisoned on 16 September 1651 experienced better fortune. Revered as a general major of foot and another who had been brought to the Tower after the defeat at Worcester, he escaped the following year by unknown means and fled abroad before returning to Britain for the Highland Rebellion of 1654. A similar tale is true of Lieutenant General Sir Edward Massey, who, upon being injured at Worcester, convinced Charles II to flee the battlefield without him. After being forced to endure a short time in the Tower, the recovered Royalist is reported to have successfully made his way up one of the chimneys to freedom and later crossed the sea to Holland.

The third prisoner to follow suit was Major General Robert Montgomerie. Successfully breaching the Tower's defences in 1654, he evaded arrest several times, as well as later escaping from Edinburgh Castle, before crossing to the Continent. He was made Lord of the Bedchamber on the Restoration before losing favour as a result of his hard Presbyterian beliefs.

Good fortune, at least initially, also befell George Cooke who was imprisoned in the Tower in 1651. Recorded as a member of Gray's Inn, Cooke made his escape when summoned to attend the council. Captured, he was later returned to his cell. Similarly, a man named Thomas – other sources say John – Tudor was imprisoned, escaped, recaptured and later released in 1654. His escape was not, however, without consequence to his warders William Tasborough and John Gillet, both of whom were locked away in Tudor's place.

Major John Wildman, a former Leveller, had made his fortune purchasing the estates confiscated from convicted Royalists only to be imprisoned for a time in the Tower after Cromwell learned of his attempts to unite the Levellers and overthrow him. Thanks to his moneymaking skills, raising the £10,000 needed to purchase his release proved little obstacle, though he was once again imprisoned in the Tower after the Restoration.

Victory for the Roundheads in the Civil War might have been successful in ending the life of one king, but in reality the ramifications ran far deeper. With Cromwell's ascendancy confirmed, defeat for Charles I's son and heir, the future Charles II, would see the temporary end of the monarchy and, with it, the liquefying of the Crown Jewels. Even before Charles's death, large quantities of the plate had already been smelted down to fund the Cavaliers' war effort, yet worse was to come. When Cromwell ordered the destruction of the Crown Jewels, the gold was converted into coins, at the Tower Mint, and entered circulation. It is perhaps one of the Tower's greatest ironies that within the same set of buildings where the jewels had for so long been protected, they were later destroyed and converted into the currency of the realm.

For the lord protector, the ceremonial trappings of kingship that had been worn by all the previous rulers may have no longer been necessary, but having eradicated the monarchy, the man now king in all but name was unable to escape the same threats and challengers they had endured. Hated by the Royalists, on taking over as lord protector Cromwell soon became the target of those who had earlier fought alongside him. As a career military leader, not immune to human failings, there was growing evidence in his later years of the old adage that power corrupts. Having successfully survived the Levellers' mutinies of 1649, discontent in the decade that followed saw numerous threats on his life.

Imprisoned in 1654, Colonel John Gerard had been a Royalist ensign throughout the Civil War before secreting himself in the Royalist underworld on the establishment of the Commonwealth. In November the previous year, Gerard had appeared as a witness at the trial of Don Pantaleone Sá, brother of the Portuguese ambassador, who was himself imprisoned in the Tower for the murder of an Englishman, apparently who he had mistaken to be Gerard after a street altercation the night before. Early the next year, Gerard travelled to France where the planning of what became known as Gerard's Conspiracy was put into operation. Returning to England, he was arrested on charges of conspiring the murder of Cromwell as the protector rode to Hampton Court Palace followed by the seizing of the Tower. Gerard's trial commenced on 3

June. He was swiftly condemned and beheaded on Tower Hill on 10 July 1654, ironically on the same scaffold as Pantaleone Sá.

Within two years of the foiling of Gerard's Plot, a new threat emerged when two of Cromwell's former soldiers, Edward Sexby and Miles Sindercombe, successfully fled to the Continent and began to produce their own subversive papers against him. Among the literature they produced was a pamphlet entitled, *Killing no Murder*, which spoke in defence of the justified murder of tyrants. Fresh from this, Sindercombe returned to England in 1656 with the aim of initiating a plot to have the lord protector shot. Quickly finding that the houses they had rented near Whitehall Palace lacked a good view of any of Cromwell's routes in London, they moved to Hammersmith, which Cromwell frequently passed on his way to and from Hampton Court. As fate would have it, Cromwell failed to turn up on the day they had expected and a third attempt near Hyde Park also proved abortive.

With three failed plans already behind them, the rashness of the plotters accelerated bringing about their downfall. Chancing instead to kill the protector by means of arson, Sindercombe successfully infiltrated Whitehall Palace, at which point he set fire to the chapel. On the discovery of the fire, Sindercombe was immediately surrounded, losing his nose in the mêleé that led to his arrest.

Inevitably the Tower beckoned, as it did for Cromwell's would-be assassin, disloyal soldier John Cecil, who had lain in wait at Hyde Park. On being sentenced to death, Sindercombe took matters into his own hands. Having failed in his attempts to bribe his gaoler, he died the night before his execution after swallowing poison provided by his sister. In spite of this, the next day his lifeless corpse was dragged by horse to Tower Hill. Due to his suicide, he was deprived of an honourable burial, his naked corpse instead left in the dirt while a pit was dug to receive it. As a final insult, a long stake was hammered through his heart, part of which still showed above the ground and was plated in iron, to serve as a warning to any future would-be insurgents.

Following Sindercombe to the Tower was Sexby. With one plot already failed, on returning to England a year later Sexby soon realised discovery would be inevitable. As he attempted to return to Flanders, he was arrested and interrogated. He contracted a fever and died in the Tower in 1658.

Prior to Sexby's demise, 1657 was notable as the first of three periods in the Tower for the charismatic duke of Buckingham, George Villiers. An infant when his father was murdered, the young duke had been a companion of Charles II during their childhood, which had included regular stays at the royal residences. In adulthood, their bond was so strong it was commented that the pair were practically brothers. After fighting for Charles at Worcester in the final battle of the Civil War, Buckingham had joined the future king in exile.

Though firm friends, they were equally famous for their arguments. After six years in the Netherlands and growing increasingly impatient with the rising power of Cromwell, Buckingham attempted to return to England and reclaim his lapsed estates. The most prized of his lost assets was his birthright in Yorkshire, which had become the property of Cromwell's revered general, Thomas Fairfax. Rather than attempt any form of military coup, the once affluent duke set his sights on marrying Fairfax's 19-year-old daughter. Despite significant opposition, Fairfax himself seems to have been encouraged by the idea. So great was Buckingham's effect on his daughter, she even broke off her engagement with the earl of Chesterfield to accept his proposal.

Hearing of the marriage in September, it was debatable what had annoyed Cromwell more: that the marriage had occurred or that Buckingham had apparently claimed that if the plan failed, he would seek to marry one of Cromwell's rather plain daughters instead. Angered by the slight, Cromwell placed Buckingham under house arrest. On hearing of the lord protector's actions, Fairfax was furious at Cromwell's intervention. In contrast to the many times they had fought so valiantly together, their meeting at Whitehall ended with Fairfax storming out. After a short time at his London house, Buckingham managed to evade his gaolers and escape to Kent. Within days, however, he was rearrested and moved to the Tower.

Joining him there was a Colonel Mallory. Like many involved in the Civil War, Mallory successfully escaped the Tower, only to be apprehended for a second time. How he achieved his initial liberty is unclear but fortunately for him, he was released on the Restoration.

Also released around that time was the former Royal Naval officer, Major William Rainsborowe. A valuable member of the New Model Army throughout the Civil War and interregnum, the puritanical sailor was one of a number who emigrated to the early settlements of New England. Returning to England in time for the beginning of the Civil War, Rainsborowe served predominantly as a captain throughout the conflict before being made a colonel by the Rump Parliament. Infuriated by the decision to revoke his promotion, he attempted to sell the arms he had recently acquired for his proposed militia, an act that soon came to the attention of the authorities. On the restoration of the monarchy, Rainsborowe was taken to the Tower as a tactical move in case of possible treason and released on bail two months later. After leaving the Tower, he returned to New England and died in Boston, Massachusetts in 1673.

When the war was finally over, Cromwell made the decision to modernise elements of the Tower that had become severely weakened after a century of neglect. His first measure was to dismantle the once alluring royal apartments that had fallen into disrepair south of the White Tower, followed by the Coldharbour Gate, the old Wardrobe Tower – prior to which the contents were valued and relocated – and the redundant Jewel House that adjoined the White Tower. To his credit, Cromwell did away with animal cruelty at the menagerie, to which many more animals had been added, including an 'Indian cat from Virginia' most likely a cougar, since the time of James I. By these means the site that had once been celebrated among the most important royal palaces in Europe had been forever changed.

Despite Cromwell's firm grip over British politics, throughout the 1650s, discontent at his government had steadily increased. Blighted by the curse experienced by previous kings, the threat of Royalist insurrection was always at hand.

Bearing the brunt of the latest failure was Yorkshireman, Sir Henry Slingsby. Ever a true Royalist, Slingsby was drawn out of retirement on hearing news from the earl of Rochester that the future Charles II was again planning to overthrow the Commonwealth. The original plan was for Slingsby to seize the city of Hull to pave the way for a Royalist invasion; however, after a planned rising in the West Country failed to gather momentum, the plan was aborted. Arrested and kept in Hull, possibly only on the strength of rumour, Slingsby's attempt to draw the captain of the garrison into the plot ensured his downfall. He was taken to the Tower and tried for treason before being executed on 8 June 1658. Executed with him was fellow conspirator, and former chaplain to Charles I, the Reverend John Hewett.

Another figure of status to face time in the Tower in the aftermath of the Civil War was the Yorkshire gentleman, John Lambert. Second only to Cromwell and Fairfax at the head of the Roundhead hierarchy, his hardline puritanical leadership style had secured for him many great victories but also many enemies, including the lord protector. Lambert was arguably the natural choice to eventually replace Cromwell; however, having been one of the main opponents of Cromwell's intention to take the crown a year earlier, he had been dismissed the following year, only to re-emerge at the downfall of the new protector, Cromwell's son, Richard.

It was here once again that power would reveal or corrupt. Fresh from the establishment of a new council of state, Lambert's puritanical autocracy was instantly met with disdain. With the wind of change blowing heavily in the favour of Charles II, Lambert attempted to prevent the members of parliament from taking their seats, temporarily leading to his gaining control of the army. On 26 January, Lambert was accused of mutiny and, in March, after failing to deal with the charges, led by General Monck, he was sent to the Tower.

Ironically, Lambert was shut up in the same St Thomas's Tower chamber that had earlier witnessed interesting escape attempts by Surrey, Neville and Seymour. Inspired by their successes and a desire to prevent the imminent return of the monarchy, Lambert attempted to follow in their footsteps by way of a combination of smuggled rope woven from silk and successful breaching of the loosened bars of his cell window, before making his way to a specially arranged barge on the river. Unlike the tower's previous inhabitants, suspicion of his escape was avoided thanks to the voluntary assistance of his bed maker – a girl named Joan – who had taken his place, adorned his nightcap and even answered the warders in a gruff voice as they did their rounds.

The delay presented Lambert his opportunity to head north, where a rising was planned at Edgehill – the site of the earliest battle of the war. On hearing of this, Monck, in command of the Royalist forces, attempted to intercept him. When the man assigned the specific task, Colonel Sir Richard Ingoldsby, arrived at Edgehill on 22 March to find Lambert leading six troops of horse, he put the question to them: did they really want to restart the Civil War? Embarrassingly for Lambert, few did and his attempts to flee came unstuck in boggy ground. Unlike Capel, Lambert was not destined to die just yet. Tried for treason, he was sentenced to life imprisonment, far away from the Tower, firstly on Guernsey and, later, Plymouth.

Struck down by a combination of malaria and urinary infections, Cromwell died on 3 September 1658. With his death the realm initially had no leadership. The man dubbed 'iron side' had succeeded in augmenting his rule, but his well-meaning son Richard had no such skills. As the warring generals wrestled for power, a victor emerged in the form of former Royalist, turned Roundhead, turned Royalist again, General George Monck.

Already familiar with the Tower from his earlier prolonged stay, Monck had fought busily since 1646, putting down rebellion in Ireland. For the devoted Royalist, Monck viewed the task as a compromise of conscience as he had been fighting the king's enemies rather than promoting the Roundhead cause. Appointed chief of Cromwell's forces north of the border, he completed the conquest of Scotland before leading his charges south. He would return to his true Royalist cause on Cromwell's death.

Cromwell's death had not only been good news for the future Charles II. In scenes reminiscent of the 3rd duke of Norfolk and Henry VIII over a century earlier, after languishing in his own cell inside the Tower, the duke of Buckingham later recalled that he estimated himself to have been only three days from execution when Cromwell died. Fortuitously reprieved, Buckingham was transferred to Windsor Castle and later bailed by father-in-law Fairfax. After swearing an oath before the Commons, the great manipulator was freed. Buckingham's good behaviour, however, would not last. Forgiven by the new king for deserting him and making peace with the institution that had beheaded his father, he later became embroiled in a minor scuffle in the House of Lords with the Marquess of Dorchester. With Dorchester a few hairs of his wig lighter and Buckingham minus a few real ones, both were sent to the Tower and subsequently released after a week of cooling off.

As always with the ending of one era and the beginning of the new, reprisals for what had come before were inevitable. North of the border, the end was nigh for the prominent politician and peer, Archibald Campbell, 1st Marquess of Argyll. The *de facto* head of the Scottish Government in the English Civil War following Charles I's execution, he had previously fought prominently against the king over the preservation of Presbyterianism in Scotland. Deploring the regicide, however, Argyll initially supported the future Charles II, even personally crowning him Charles II of Scotland at Scone on New Year's Day 1651, before experiencing personal ruin with the Royalists' failure and facing little choice but to commit to Cromwell's Commonwealth. At the Restoration, he was arrested by Charles and sent to the Tower, released and then rearrested to be tried at Edinburgh. Found not guilty of regicide, he was, nevertheless, later condemned when a series of letters in his hand, written to Monck, confirmed his alliance with Cromwell. With this, he was beheaded on the maiden – the Scottish equivalent of the guillotine – before Charles had even had the chance to pen the execution warrant.

Originally a prominent ally of Cromwell, Sir Henry Vane (the Younger) had also opposed the act that saw the beheading of Charles I and subsequently withdrew from power completely on Cromwell's dissolving of the Rump Parliament after becoming lord protector in 1653. With Cromwell dead, Vane had re-emerged in the post-Cromwell Commonwealth, a fact that had not gone unnoticed by the new king.

Joining Vane in being targeted were the others responsible for either the regicide of the new king's father or opposing the Restoration. Prominent among them were Lambert, not as a regicide but for his recent role in attempting to restart the Civil War: Major General Thomas Harrison, who had known the interior of the Tower since the later days of the Protectorate after he had apparently conspired against Cromwell; and Sir Isaac Pennington, a confirmed member of the court that tried Charles I. After much debate, parliament passed the Indemnity and Oblivion Act, shortly prior to which Vane was brought to the Tower. Despite being spared accusation that he had played any part in the regicide itself, Vane, for now, remained incarcerated and was later transferred to the Isles of Scilly where he engaged his time in writing. In April 1662, parliament passed a resolution demanding his return to the Tower amid charges of high treason against the newly crowned Charles II, most notably concerning his activities during the interregnum. He was executed on 14 June 1662 on Tower Hill, almost two years after Harrison. Despite not having signed Charles I's death warrant, Pennington endured incarceration until December 1661 when he died of natural causes.

In attendance at Vane's execution, writing positively on his conduct, was another of history's famous figures who would enjoy a somewhat unique relationship with the Tower. Famed in later years for his journaling, most notably his observations around the time of the Great Fire, Samuel Pepys rose through the ranks of the English civil service, working primarily for the naval officer, Lord Montagu – more recently earl of Sandwich. Already well familiar with the Tower from his visits as a tourist, Pepys returned there on Montagu's orders after hearing a story that the previous lieutenant of the Tower, Sir John Barkstead, had amassed a fortune potentially as great as £50,000 worth of gold coins. Exactly how he managed this is unclear, besides it involving extortion of the Royalist prisoners, the proceeds of which he later buried in wooden barrels somewhere within the walls before fleeing to Germany prior to the Restoration.

With this began another of the Tower's unique tales. Though later imprisoned in the Tower himself and hanged, drawn and quartered along with two others for their role in the execution of Charles I, his body interred, his head spiked above St Thomas's Tower, Barkstead had served as a goldsmith in the Strand at the outbreak of the Civil War – a fact that lends some credence to the possibility of the amassed coins. Whatever had become of the alleged treasure, however, was still unknown. Inclined to believe the story to be in keeping with Barkstead's maverick personality, Montagu sought permission from Charles II to conduct a search, responsibility for which was delegated to Pepys.

By the end of October 1662, Pepys arrived at the Tower and presented himself to famed governor Sir John (Jack) Robinson – the same man who would later serve as lord mayor of London. Escorted by, among others, a Mr Wade and Captain Evett – the two men who circulated the original treasure story after apparently hearing it from a Mary Barkstead, who claimed to be the dead man's wife – Pepys and his party made straight for the Bell Tower. There, in the same cell in which Sir Thomas More had been incarcerated over a century earlier, Pepys concentrated his early efforts, convinced after learning they were heading for 'a cellar' within or nearby the Queen's House, it was the most likely location.

After a disappointing first day, the party returned. Frustrated at the lack of leads, digging was adjourned, at which point Pepys questioned Wade and Evett more closely. During the resulting conversation, the pair promised to bring Barkstead's alleged wife along to the next session. On 7 November, the third session began with the mysterious woman in their company, giving Pepys directions where she had seen the former lieutenant dig. Despite their best efforts, the day proved fruitless, leaving Pepys little choice but to conclude that either the barrels had since been moved or the woman had been hoodwinked.

A month later, the search was unexpectedly resumed. In a visit from Evett and Wade, Pepys was informed that the woman now believed the Bell Tower had been the wrong location and that the barrels had actually been buried in the garden outside the Bloody Tower. Undeterred by the cold December weather, Pepys decided a last search was in order. Watching from a window in what is now the Queen's House, the budding diarist oversaw a final fruitless effort. The treasure was never found. Whether it ever existed remains a mystery.

Chapter 20

1660–1672: Black Death, Burning Buildings and Bloody Burglaries

Master of the Tower Mint Thomas Simon was one particularly unfortunate example of the many who lost out in the see-sawing of fortunes during the collapse of the Commonwealth and the Restoration of the monarchy. Since Charles I's execution, the Mint had continued with its primary purpose of serving the British economy by producing new coins – albeit now without the monarch's head. With Cromwell at the helm, the new coins were designed in his image and subsequently minted. Unpaid by the thrifty lord protector, Simon was soon out of pocket by some £1,700, and eventually forced to accept only £700 in recompense. Writing in desperation to Cromwell for payment, his requests were ignored.

With Cromwell dead and Charles II crowned king, Simon started work once more, only to be devastated a second time. Finding himself in competition with the Roettiers family, goldsmiths from Antwerp, the new king decided to pass on Simon's design. In 1665 his miserable lot ended when he fell victim to the plague.

William Gouldbee, John Rathbone and William Lea were just three of many men gaoled in the Tower around the time the plague broke out. All were arrested for what appears to have been the same purpose – described in the records as 'treasonable practices' – yet all suffered very different fates. Gouldbee was acquitted, Rathbone executed, most likely at Tyburn but Lea became one of the celebrated group who successfully managed to escape the Tower. Exactly how he achieved this, little information has survived; only that it occurred 'in the plague time'.

It was around the so-called plague time that the Tower faced what could quite easily have developed into the greatest challenge in its entire history. Stirred from his slumber by the outbreak of a fire on the night of 2 September 1666, less than a mile to the west in a bakery in Pudding

Lane, Samuel Pepys initially showed little interest in the conflagration before making his way to the Tower and watching with developing alarm from a window in one of the western turrets of the White Tower as the inferno began to spread to the west.

After three days of relative calm around Tower Hill, a change in the wind made the threat suddenly imminent. With the White Tower currently used as the nation's principal gunpowder store, the effects of the Great Fire could have been truly catastrophic. Fearing the worst, a combination of soldiers and local volunteers attempted to move the gunpowder to nearby ships to be transported to Woolwich or Greenwich. Ironically, at the same time, huge quantities of treasure, that the local goldsmiths had deposited for safekeeping inside the Tower at the outbreak of the fire, were also evacuated.

As fate would have it, that very gunpowder would actually help save the Tower. With alternative firebreaking tactics proving insufficient, the demolition of nearby buildings by detonating the powder created the necessary breaks to ensure that the flames would not spread. The fire ended on 5 September from a combination of that firefighting measure and the onset of late summer rains, much to the relief of all concerned. Twenty-five years later Tower employees would witness a brief glimpse of what might have been when some 2,000 barrels of gunpowder fell through the rotting wooden flooring in July 1691. Like the Great Fire itself, a disaster was avoided when the powder failed to leave the barrels or ignite.

One of the prisoners whose life would end in the Tower in the year of the Great Fire was the lawyer and former colonel, John Downes. Though Downes never took up his sword during the Civil War, he was noted for profiting from the confiscation of Royalist estates, and as a friend of Cromwell had been encouraged – or possibly bullied – into acting as a commissioner at the trial of Charles I. On the Restoration, Downes was one of a number of 'regicides' brought to the Tower in retribution for his part in the king's beheading. His death sentence, however, was commuted to life imprisonment and he lived out his days in the Tower.

Within a year of Downes's death, another notable prisoner arrived in the form of the philosopher Henry Oldenburg. A German theologian and diplomat who was also a founder member of the Royal Society,

Oldenburg's large network of acquaintances saw him arrested on suspicion that he was operating as a Dutch spy. Fortunately for the German, his incarceration was brief.

While the struggle between pro-Royalist and pro-Parliamentarian factions was largely over by the time of the Great Fire, the opposite could be said of the ongoing religious disagreements that had contributed so greatly to the original conflict. Prominent among the rising factions in late-1660s England were the Quakers: a militant puritan sect whose pro-social equality stock was rapidly rising.

Influential among their number was the son of a wealthy London couple named William Penn, who would one day be remembered for playing a dramatic role in the development of the fledgling United States of America. A prominent writer, like so many of the Tower's stalwarts, Penn endured an unwanted experience inside its cells as punishment for composing an anti-Anglican diatribe, *No Cross, No Crown*. Arriving in the Tower, the young revolutionary, in scenes reminiscent of that experienced by the unfortunate Lady Jane Grey over a century earlier, was visited by many of the religious life, who endeavoured to convert him out of his heretical ways. Taking them on in theological discussion, Penn remained unmoved. In response to their attempts, the young man was recorded as having stated: 'the Tower is to me the worst argument in the world.'

Penn's time in the Tower was relatively brief as he was released following the intercession of his wealthy father. His freedom bought, Penn left Protestant England for good and crossed the Atlantic to seek his own fortune. He would later be officially acknowledged as the founder of the State of Pennsylvania.

By early 1660 and with the eleven-year interregnum at breaking point – characterised primarily by the governing of Cromwell's Commonwealth and further dissolution of parliament – very little had stood in the way of England's constitution returning to where it had been before the Cromwellian revolution. With the Houses of Commons and Lords both structurally sound and many key Royalists still alive, the process of making Charles II king had only one significant obstacle. The jewels that had been used for the coronations of his predecessors no longer existed, meaning for the king to be crowned a new set would have to be created.

The source of the modern-day jewels has been the topic of much discussion. Although the Crown Jewels had been destroyed following the death of Charles I, the gold that was then used for coinage could possibly have been further reused in the construction of the new crown jewels, most notably the Crown of St Edward – something that tradition has long depicted. By the time Charles was brought to Westminster Abbey, the replacement crown had been sumptuously recreated, following which it was moved to a new home in the Martin Tower. Though kept at the Tower regularly since the 1230s, only once in the castle's long history have any of the jewels been the subject of an attempted robbery. That time would come in 1671, the endeavour steeped in blood. Specifically, one Thomas Blood.

Thomas Blood, or Colonel as he often went by, was himself something of a character. Born in 1618 in County Meath in Ireland, Blood had already made his name fighting for the crown in the Irish risings that proved more than a minor distraction to England's authority already under pressure from the Roundhead/Cavalier tension that eventually led to the English Civil War. When the Civil War finally began, in need of troops to combat the Roundhead opposition, Charles ordered his vassal in Ireland, the duke of Ormonde, to negotiate a truce with the rebels and increase recruitment for the war in England. Angered by recent developments, Blood, a devout Protestant, made his way to England where he would join the mostly Protestant Parliamentarians in their conflict with the king.

Famed for his achievements as a lieutenant in Cromwell's forces, Blood's talent for deceit and his effectiveness as a spy was allegedly demonstrated in the way he successfully waylaid Royalist shipments of arms, essentials and gold, securing good portions for himself before handing in the remainder. Known to have profited further from a combination of monetary rewards and lands in Ireland, as well as his dealings in the lawless and dark taverns and cellars of London's underworld that flourished on the fringes of Cromwell's puritanical Commonwealth, Blood's life may have been different had the dying Cromwell been replaced by a stronger man than his ineffective son. A hardened republican, Blood had been active in several minor risings against Charles, and come 1664 was recorded as having evaded arrest after an abandoned effort to storm the Tower.

As fate would have it, Blood's affinity with the Tower was far from over. After losing his lands as a consequence of his opposition to the king, in 1667 the hostile colonel returned to England to aid the escape of Captain John Mason – one of his co-conspirators from a plot conceived four years earlier to drive the English from Ireland – as the guilty man was transferred from the Tower to face trial in York. Further to this plotted rising in the north, Blood had previously been party to two other plots in 1663 and 1665 respectively, both of which had concerned the kidnapping – or murder – of the duke of Ormonde and the taking of Dublin Castle.

Securing the escape of Mason, on 6 December 1670 Blood finally oversaw a successful kidnapping of Ormonde from his carriage in London before losing him in the chaos that followed. It has long been suggested such acts had been the brainchild of the dubious duke of Buckingham, who, like many of his predecessors, needed little excuse to further his own cause; however, this has never been proven. As a Parliamentarian, Blood would have needed little incentive to hate Ormonde, not least as it was his job as lord lieutenant of Ireland to carry out Charles's command and strip the Parliamentarian rebels of the rewards they had received from Cromwell.

There has also been much suggestion that it was Buckingham who was the brains behind Blood's most daring scheme. After spending significant time around the Petty Wales area of London – a seedy location close to Tower Hill – in the spring of 1671, the Tower received one of its strangest visits. Dressed as a clergyman, Blood – now with a bounty of around £2,000 on his head – came with one purpose in mind: to see the Crown Jewels of England, which were once again being kept in their special depository in the Martin Tower.

At the time of Blood's visit, access to the jewels was, unlike today, by no means completely restricted. Now a paying visitor enters a specially designed bank vault in the Waterloo Block and views the valuables behind thick bulletproof glass and under observation from both Tower officials and numerous unseen cameras. In Blood's time the paying visitor could be given a personal tour from the assistant keeper who lived permanently in the chambers above. The man entrusted with the safety of the jewels at that time was one Talbot Edwards, a kindly man of military background in his late seventies who escorted such visits to help make ends meet.

Although he noticed the slightly unusual appearance of the roguish cleric and the hired actress introduced as his wife, Edwards graciously showed the couple to the basement of the Martin Tower and, once there, unlocked the reinforced door to the jewels, which were on show behind a metal grille in a cupboard built specifically into the inner wall. The actress thereupon faked an upset stomach, at which point Edwards momentarily left to fetch some water, allowing Blood the opportunity to assess the surroundings before building up further rapport with Edwards on his return. As an act of gratitude, Blood paid a second visit several days later, presenting Edwards with some fine gloves as a gift.

Unbeknown to the kindly host, Blood made good use of these visits. By making himself known to the Tower guards and achieving an in-depth reconnaissance of the area, he had a clear idea of what barriers stood in the way of his taking the jewels. After his second visit, Blood returned with his pretend wife to dine with the family on several more occasions, culminating with discussions about a potential marriage proposal between his 'eligible nephew' and Edwards's daughter. With the offer accepted, Blood, to Edwards's delight, arranged to bring his nephew to the Martin Tower in order that the young couple could meet. In return Edwards organised the sale of a brace of fine pistols to Blood.

The role of nephew was taken by one Thomas Hunt, a professional highwayman and almost certainly an alias for Blood's own son, who would soon join the colonel and other members of their criminal gang with a final accomplice piloting a getaway carriage outside the Tower's walls. After dining with them again on 8 May 1671, Blood informed Edwards he had two friends in the city that would love to see the jewels, but were short on time. Learning that Edwards would be delighted to escort them, it was agreed that the visit would take place at dawn the next morning. In keeping with Blood's impeccable planning, everything that had happened had been at least in part effectively organised. While one of the gang, Robert – or Richard – Halliwell, stood lookout, excusing himself that he had seen the jewels already and apparently being mistaken by Edwards's maid for the lady's fiancé, Blood and the other criminals, Hunt and Robert Perrot, made their way inside the Martin Tower. Completely ignorant of what the villains had planned, Edwards was set upon with a cape the moment he prepared to unlock the cage. Unwilling to go down quietly, the startled keeper was viciously attacked with a wooden mallet and stabbed with a long knife.

Whatever affection Blood had developed for the ageing keeper had clearly been overcome by avarice. After all but killing the unfortunate man, the trio set to work to free the Crown Jewels. According to the official report of what happened next, after successfully removing the metal grille, the imperial crown – other sources suggest the Crown of St Edward – was flattened with the same mallet used to attack Edwards and placed under Blood's cassock. Further damage would be inflicted on the sceptre, which Perrot filed in half before attempting to force it inside a travel bag, while tucking the orb down his breeches.

What happened next defied belief. With Blood's mallet attack on the crown knocking free some of the jewels, including Edward the Black Prince's Ruby, a stranger entered the Martin Tower, none other than Edwards's son, returned from Flanders to witness his sister's betrothal. First seen by Halliwell, the lookout did his best to stall the newcomer before hurrying to the jewel room to inform Blood that the new arrival was presently paying his respects to his mother and sister. At that point Blood clearly feared the worst. Leaving the sceptre, they made off with the flattened crown and orb and attempted to exit the Tower. As they closed in on their escape, the stricken Edwards managed to remove his mouth gag, and shout at the top of his voice that the crown had been stolen.

The first person to find him was his daughter, beholding not a dashing future husband, but her father in a pool of blood. Immediately leaving the Martin Tower, she raised the alarm across the inner ward, at which point the thieves were still attempting to flee. The first to hear her was her brother, accompanied by a Swedish military man named Captain Beckman – according to most sources a friend of Edwards Junior – who set off in pursuit. Whereas Blood Junior and Halliwell had already made it beyond the Middle Tower and were preparing to set off on their horses, back near the Bloody Tower Perrot and Blood were in serious trouble. Fearing they were about to be locked in, Blood opened fire on a yeoman warder near the Byward Tower who had been preparing to shut the gates. Miraculously, they survived not only the chase of Edwards and his

Swedish companion but also their shouted orders at the roused warders to raise the drawbridge.

The final scene is worthy of any comedy. In an attempt to lose their pursuers among the busy nearby wharf, Blood accused his pursuers of being thieves, a tactic that succeeded in fooling some of the locals into setting upon Edwards Junior and Beckman. Delayed but not stopped, the pursuing party caught up with the conspirators at Iron Gate. Missing with his second pistol shot, Blood subsequently lost a short struggle at which point he and Perrot were arrested. Soon to join them was Hunt, who, despite reaching the final accomplice – named either William Smith or Desborough – and the horses, collided with either a cart or an inn sign. While the fifth man fled the scene, Hunt was taken to join his accomplices in the basement of the White Tower to be later joined by Halliwell.

The outcome of this affair is perhaps every bit as important as the event itself. With the criminals apprehended, the younger Edwards informed Sir Gilbert Talbot – keeper of the jewels – who in turn rode straight to Whitehall to inform the king of what had happened. At the same time, Edwards in the company of several officers of the Tower attempted to question Blood in the White Tower, who apparently 'lay in a corner, dogged and cowering and would not give a word of answer to any one question.' After being brought shackled before the king, his brother, the duke of York, and cousin Prince Rupert for questioning, not only was Blood spared the axe but pardoned altogether.

Exactly what became of Blood, or why he was spared, has never been fully explained. Having partially succeeded in absconding with the jewels, a charge of treason and execution on Tower Hill should surely have awaited. Writing a year or so later, John Evelyn himself reported, 'How he came to be pardoned ... I could never understand ... the only treason of this sort that was ever pardoned.' Of equal intrigue, during the conversation at Whitehall, Blood informed Charles that years earlier he had declined the chance to pull the trigger on the 'merry' monarch – at the time just a 'merry' prince – after witnessing him swimming naked in the Thames at Vauxhall.

Two months after the audience, Blood was officially pardoned and actually granted the return of his lost lands in Ireland, worth approximately £500 per annum. Rumours about Charles's reasoning unsurprisingly soon surfaced. Among them was that the famously impoverished monarch had actually commanded Blood to steal the jewels in the first place, in order that the precious stones could be sold on the black market. Another suggestion was that Charles had wagered a bet as to whether it could be done. Far more likely is that the man, reputed to have been a government spy, had access to information with which he was able to blackmail the king into granting him his freedom. By contrast, Talbot Edwards, who recovered physically, had to wait far longer for his pension which amounted to only £200, of which he cashed about half to fund his medical fees. As fate would have it, his daughter married not the thief but the friend of the brother who had helped to foil the theft, Captain Beckman.

Incredibly, the Blood saga did not end there. After apparently becoming a Quaker, Blood was once again in trouble after making accusations against the duke of Buckingham – the man accused of being the brains behind the robbery – landing him in a debtors' prison. After his death, and burial in Westminster's New Chapel Yard, there were reports that his demise had been faked and, eventually, his coffin was exhumed. Finally, the matter was resolved and both colonel and conspiracy were finally laid to rest. His legacy as the mastermind behind the only attempt to steal the Crown Jewels lived on. As the man himself said, 'It was a gallant deed, even if it failed. It was, after all, to gain the crown.'

Chapter 21

1673–1688: Postulated Princes, Corrupt Commonwealth and Hanging Judges

The escape of imprisoned spy William Arton – or Alton – was one of the major talking points of 1673. Arriving at the Tower a year earlier, the Dutchman was successfully sprung in October before returning home across the North Sea. As usual in such instances, the prisoner's escape turned out to be bad news for his warder, as well as at least two others.

It was around this time a gruesome discovery was made that would leave a permanent mark on the Tower's history. By 1674 the demolition of the royal apartments decreed by Cromwell was still to be completed and, while parts of the masonry had indeed been demolished, most of the wreckage still littered the inner ward. Tired of the constant complaints and unruly sights afflicting his citadel, in July of that year, Charles II ordered the completion of the long overdue work, including the demolition of Henry III's fifth, and by then superfluous, turret on the south wall of the White Tower. In its time, the turret had contained a private staircase, used solely by the monarch to enter St John's Chapel, which had remained largely un-investigated by outsiders. On removing the turret, work began to dismantle the staircase, during which a startling discovery was made. Beneath one of the steps, a wooden chest was found to contain two skeletons along with pieces of velvet rag.

No one learning of the discovery doubted the identity of the deceased. Missing for nearly two centuries, the remains had been found almost exactly where Thomas More claimed the two princes had been buried; strangely, More had suggested that the box had later been moved by a priest, whereas the actual find corresponded with the original claim. Subsequent to their discovery, Charles's physician, as well as many other antiquaries of status, examined the bones in detail and agreed that they were almost certainly those of the vanished sons of Edward IV. They were then placed in a stone coffin and for a time left close to the site where they had been discovered. There are reports, sadly, that many of the original bones and other remnants were taken by souvenir hunters; when some were taken to the Ashmolean, they subsequently disappeared, replaced by those of animals.

Incredibly it was around four years before Charles, moved by conscience or complaints, finally ordered the long overdue burial of his forebears in a manner befitting their royal status. Appropriately the ceremonial urn that marks their final resting place was designed by Sir Christopher Wren, who at the time was still overseeing the rebuilding of London following the Great Fire. A Latin inscription confirms the belief that within the wall into which the urn was placed lie the remains of the sons of Edward IV, one of whom had been not only a prince, but also king of England in his own right.

Ironically, it was also around that time that the successor to the man who was widely regarded as having been responsible for the death of the princes, the errant duke of Buckingham, made his final trip to the Tower. Charged with the bizarre crimes of necromancy and predicting the famously superstitious king's horoscope, Buckingham initially evaded arrest, before making a reckless decision to visit Charles personally to plead his case. At the completion of his audience with the king, the duke was apprehended and imprisoned for two days.

Of far greater consequence to Buckingham was the fate endured by Sir William Coventry in 1668. Insulted by Buckingham in a play the duke had written – Buckingham had clearly based a character on him – Coventry's rash decision to challenge Buckingham to a duel – illegal between peers – had seen Coventry removed from public life and confined within the walls of the Brick Tower. Among those who visited the peer was Samuel Pepys. No friend of Buckingham, he was as pleased as anyone when Coventry's influential friend, the duke of York, helped ensure his release. Ironically, Pepys himself was soon to endure a period of enforced stay within the ancient walls. Already no stranger to the Tower from his countless pleasure visits, fruitless treasure hunt and monitoring of the Great Fire, by 1678 the now chief secretary of the admiralty had been caught up in yet another anti-government plot.

The Popish Plot must surely go down as one of the strangest in England's history. Devised by former Protestant clergyman Titus Oates, who had converted to Catholicism after visiting the seminaries, Oates had been expelled as a navy chaplain and from the Jesuit school for accusations of homosexuality and blasphemy. Following time abroad, on his return to England, Oates spread word of a fictitious Jesuit plot that, if successful, would have seen not only the murder of the king but also all Protestants. As part of Oates's propaganda, countless accusations were levelled, usually against English Catholics, many of whom were falsely imprisoned and even sentenced to death.

Despite the fictitious pedigree of the plot, the person bearing the brunt of the Protestants' hatred was the king's Catholic younger brother, James, Duke of York, himself next in line for the throne. Forced into temporary exile, Pepys, as James's close servant and friend, found himself directly in the firing line. As the anti-Catholic momentum, championed largely by the Whigs, against James gathered pace, Pepys was accused of using his position in the navy to leak secrets to the French court – a terrible slur in any age. On 20 May 1679, the accusations against Pepys were brought to the attention of the House of Commons and, when answering the charges, Pepys denied them vehemently. Even with no direct evidence against him, having been accused of treason, he had no choice but to resign from the admiralty, and was held in the Tower. After a month in a cell, he was released on bail, and a year later finally cleared of any wrongdoing.

Public opinion of Charles II on the restoration of the monarchy had initially been overwhelmingly positive. By the late-1670s, however, due in part to James's Catholicism and murmurs that Charles himself harboured similar sympathies, certain elements of dissent began to be voiced. It was views such as those that helped in no small part to assist the rise of Whig culture, itself inspired by memories of the Cromwell era.

The fabricated Popish Plot of 1678–79, despite proving to be little more than an exercise in fearmongering, had nevertheless succeeded in cementing the execution of several Catholic peers. Among them was William Howard, Viscount Stafford: another of that famous family whose number had known both the rigours of power and the interior of the Tower since the days of Henry VIII. Contrary to the deserved punishment of many of his ancestors, William Howard was harshly implicated by Oates and beheaded on 29 December 1680 for allegedly plotting to kill the king. At his execution, the jeering of the crowd led him to appeal to the sheriff to intervene. In response, he merely heard the ironic words, 'Sir, we have orders to stop nobodies' breath but yours.'

The Popish Plot had also proven a disaster for the Yorkshire Tory, Thomas Osborne, Earl of Danby, who Charles had used to raise subsidies to help foot the cost of his war with France. Acquiescing to Charles's hopes would sadly see the principled politician on a collision course with parliament, most notably the Whigs under the leadership of Anthony Ashley Cooper, the earl of Shaftesbury. In 1677 Danby used a technicality to his advantage to see Shaftesbury and Buckingham, as well as James Cecil, 3rd Earl of Salisbury and Philip, 4th Baron Wharton found guilty of contempt of parliament and imprisoned in the Tower until the following year – Shaftesbury was forced to experience the longest period due to refusal to show remorse.

Following the murder of Protestant Sir Edmund Berry Godfrey in October 1678, panic gripped the capital as rumour of the Popish Plot seemed to have been confirmed. In an act that must be considered somewhat devious, especially considering his hatred of Oates, Danby was accused by Shaftesbury of being part of the conspiracy and used his knowledge of Danby's dealings in France to see him brought to the Tower. In April 1679, a pardon from the king failed to avert his journey to the Tower, the product of a typically dubious act of attainder.

In February 1681, the Irish Catholic Edward Fitzharris penned a particularly damning letter advocating the dethroning of Charles and the exclusion of James from the succession. Rather than describing his own views, however – views that would have seen him charged with treason – his plan was instead to plant it in the home of a prominent Whig, in the hope it would be conveniently uncovered. Betrayed by an accomplice, the Irishman was imprisoned in the Tower and subsequently impeached. Around that time, he also betrayed Danby by implicating him in Godfrey's murder. Intriguingly, the Tower chaplain at the time, Francis Hawkins, offered Fitzharris a pardon on the grounds he had implicated one of the members of the Commons in writing the original letter, confession of which swiftly saw Fitzharris's execution.

Shaftesbury's revived fortunes were short-lived and lost for a second time as a consequence of his support of James Scott, the duke of Monmouth in his endeavours to replace Charles as king. Charged with treason, Shaftesbury was returned to prison in the Tower, after which support for the exclusion bill was exhausted. Struck down by a stroke, the king's health declined. When Shaftesbury was brought to trial, he was acquitted. Rather than tempt fate again, he fled to Holland where he died in January 1683.

Further to various plots against the king himself, the most significant element of anti-Royalist collusion focused more on plans to bar James from the succession as opposed to attacks on Charles himself. The Whigs' momentum may have faltered after the banishment of Shaftesbury, yet things changed when Charles and James were both targeted in the same year by a conspiracy of Roundhead veterans in what was called the Rye House Plot. The idea was simple in its ingenuity, consisting solely of a scheme to capture the two at Rye House Farm, itself on the royal route, as they returned from Newmarket races.

As the facts became known, five Whig leaders, including Lord Russell and Algernon Sidney were taken to the Tower, following which, the earl of Essex, Arthur Capel – son of his namesake who had earlier escaped the Tower – was also accused of being part of the endeavour. Previously a loyal follower of the king, in recognition of which he had been made lord lieutenant of Ireland, Capel had since endured the hot tongue of Charles's mistress, Barbara Villiers, for foiling her attempt to enrich herself of Dublin's Phoenix Park. Perhaps of some consequence, Capel was arrested on 10 July 1683, accused of being in league with the Rye conspirators, and placed in the same cell where his tall father had languished some thirty years earlier. Intriguingly, the same room had housed Lady Essex's grandfather, the murdered Henry Percy, 7th Earl of Northumberland, in the reign of Elizabeth I.

What happened next, even in the context of the Tower's long, dark history is worthy of detailed investigation. Three days after Capel's arrival, the same day on which Lord Russell was taken to trial at the Old Bailey and sentenced to death by Judge Jeffreys, the royal barge arrived at the Tower Wharf, mooring at the monarch's private entrance, known then as the King's Steps. Having arrived at the Tower, partly for purposes of Ordnance, but also seemingly to interrogate the Whigs currently incarcerated there, on reaching the river as they sought to return to Whitehall, cries of 'murder' were heard from inside the walls. The victim was none other than Capel himself. On investigation it was discovered that the easily recognisable lord was dead in his room, his throat clearly slashed by a razor. So great was the cut, he had almost been beheaded.

Ironically at the time, news of Charles and James's arrival had become known to two schoolboys, both of whom had made their way into Tower Green and had seen the razor fly through an open window only to be almost instantly retrieved by a maid. In addition to the young boys, a passing manservant had also been present. Those who argue the 'suicide' verdict are correct to point out that Essex had only recently asked for a razor, while also citing that by committing suicide before being sentenced, the usual act of attainder disinheriting his family would no longer come to pass. Far more surprising is the fact that the king and duke showed little interest in the ensuing commotion and instead returned peacefully to the river.

Unsurprisingly, rumours of their involvement has been prevalent. In later years a print displayed three well-dressed individuals attacking the earl, even pushing his body into the position it was apparently later found. Furthermore, one soldier by the name of Lloyd was sentenced to Newgate prison for confirming he had seen at least two such individuals that day, as well as hearing shouts of, 'My Lord is dead.' Another accusation by sentry Robert Meek was never taken seriously; he would later turn up in the Tower moat. A third individual, Lawrence Braddon, who questioned Lloyd and the boys, would also vanish without trace. The revelations piqued the curiosity of the renowned diarist John Evelyn, who later commented, 'His Majesty is very melancholy.'

Irrespective of the exact cause of Capel's death, murmurs of foul play continued. Ironically, the events would have more than a passing effect on England's lord protector Judge George Jeffreys, who concluded the genetic fallacy that Capel's suicide was a sign of guilt, thus making Russell and Sidney also guilty. Like the missing princes, the case of Capel remains officially unsolved. As for Russell and Sidney, both died by the axe, Russell suffering the indignity of requiring at least three blows at the hands of, the now infamous, Jack Ketch. Sidney was executed on

7 December 1683 for alleged complicity in both that and the Popish Plot. In the absence of sufficient witnesses, the council called upon his writings, *Discourses Concerning Government*, which was cited as dangerous propaganda potentially capable of inspiring insurrection.

Another unsolved mystery concerning the Tower that year had been the fate of the unfortunate Yeoman Warder, Edmond Halley. A beefeater for some nineteen years at that time, Halley had served as a shepherd of the inner and outer wards during the period 1675–78 when the first royal astronomer John Flamsteed complained about the effect of the ravens on his stargazing in the north-east turret of the White Tower to Charles II – something that was undoubtedly of great interest to his son, Edmond Halley junior. Some five years after the observatory's removal, Halley senior's journey in to work on 5 March 1683 appears to have run into difficulties. Five weeks later he was found dead in a field in Stroud.

The cause of his death has long been the subject of speculation. Despite a suggestion he had been depressed about debts he had incurred through his ownership of a local tavern, the resulting inquest delivered a verdict of murder. Some conspiracy theorists have conjectured that he knew more about the death of Capel – which was fallacious, as Halley appears to have died first. What is known, however, is that the yeoman warder's son of the same name outshone his father intellectually and grew to become a fine mathematician and astronomer, eventually succeeding Flamsteed at the new royal observatory at Greenwich. The crowning achievement of Edmond Halley Junior was undoubtedly his correct forecasting of the solar eclipse of 1715 and the discovery of the famous comet, which was named in his honour and last passed our planet in 1986.

One of Capel's fellow arrestees was the prominent Whig, Lord Grey de Werke. First held in the Tower in 1682 on charges of eloping with his sister-in-law – he was released as evidence came to light that the woman in question was already married – Grey had been a frequent champion of Charles's bastard son, the duke of Monmouth, and a stern anti-Catholic. On his arrest by Henry Denham, his captor faced the dilemma of taking his prisoner to the locked Tower at night under strict orders from Charles that he must hand over the prominent Whig in person. Not one for playing by the rules, he acquiesced to Grey's suggestion they pass the time in one of the nearby inns.

Needless to say, it was a decision Denham would regret. In a move worthy of the Tower's first prisoner, Ranulf Flambard, Grey waited till his captor was in a drunken stupor before he attempted to flee the city. Unfortunately for him, he had chosen an inn frequented by Tower personnel and effectively led himself up a blind alley. With dawn breaking, and Denham awakening from his awkward sleep, the pair entered the Tower to learn the lieutenant was still to rise. Incredibly for Grey, all was not lost. Finding himself beyond the Byward Tower and now alone with Denham, Grey took advantage of the man's hung-over condition and slipped away through the door of the Sally Port that led to the wharf. From there he was able to make his way out of the Tower and then, by a stroke of good fortune, to board a wherry boat.

While Grey made it to Holland, as punishment for his failings, Denham spent six months in his should-be prisoner's place in the Tower. Nevertheless, as fate would have it, Grey was destined to return one day. Having failed with his fellow conspirators in killing the merry monarch, the conspiracy against the Crown was renewed at the coming of his Catholic brother and successor, James II of England.

Charles's death, just like many of his predecessors without a legitimate heir, proved problematic in terms of deciding who should succeed him. Despite possessing some extremely noble qualities, most notably his sound performance as head of the Royal Navy and for his excellence in combating the Great Fire of London, James II was never destined to be a popular monarch. A diehard Catholic in an age where Catholics were treated with either distrust or disdain, it was hardly surprising that the man who had already been the target of countless anti-papist plots during the reign of his brother should continue to be the subject of unrest on the throne.

As usual in England's history, cometh the new monarch, cometh the pretender. Unable to father a legitimate heir during his marriage, Charles had nevertheless been far more fruitful outside the marriage bed. The eldest of Charles's acknowledged sons was the ambitious James Scott, whom he had made duke of Monmouth. Over the years there has been much debate about whether their mother, the famously licentious Lucy Walters, really knew Charles was the father, or whether Charles or Monmouth were completely sure themselves. Irrespective of the truth, in the eyes of England's anti-James faction, Monmouth was seen as the most appropriate successor.

Though making no secret of the fact he coveted the throne, Monmouth, like many of his princely predecessors, operated under the support of the king's enemies. Under their influence he had set himself up in direct opposition to his father, becoming involved in the Rye House Plot that forced him to flee to the Netherlands. With his father dead in 1685, Monmouth wasted little time in spreading rumours that his uncle had hastened Charles's demise by poison and with support of only eighty-two rebels, he launched a three-ship assault on Dorset.

Initially, what on paper seemed such a reckless venture was successful. Joined by some 6,000 locals, Monmouth defeated the local militia before leading his troops into Somerset. There, he ran into difficulties. Bogged down in the marshy Somerset Levels, his troops were defeated at Sedgemoor on 6 July by the Royalist forces led by John Churchill, the future duke of Marlborough. Failing to build on early promise, the seventh civil war in England's history was over before it had even begun.

His force seriously depleted, Monmouth's prospects of success now looked increasingly bleak. Championing his claims, the frequently elusive Lord Grey de Werke had lined up on the wrong side at Sedgemoor and fled with Monmouth towards the south coast, only to be arrested two days later. Granted an audience with his uncle, Monmouth's apologies fell on deaf ears. In a letter to his son-in-law William of Orange – the man who ironically would overthrow James three years later – the king explained how Monmouth had acted in a manner unsuitable for a royal and would be executed the following day.

Comparable with Clarence two centuries earlier, Monmouth's end is surely one of the most bizarre and disgusting of all in the Tower's long history. Transferred there on leaving Whitehall, his incarceration lasted less than two days. After an awkward goodbye with his wife and sons, he made a final attempt at acquiring his freedom by asking the commander of the Tower guard, coincidentally his wife's cousin, to send a message to James which was subsequently intercepted by the secretary of state, the earl of Sunderland. Deprived of that crucial last chance, Monmouth's time at the Tower ended with visits from several clerics. Showing no remorse for his love for his mistress, he nevertheless did mourn the bloodshed on his account while acknowledging Charles and his mother had probably never been married. After offering a better goodbye to his wife, during which he apologised for his mistakes, he prepared himself for the short coach journey to Tower Hill. At the scaffold, he addressed the crowd before laying eyes on his executioner, Jack Ketch, who had needed multiple blows of the axe to finish off Lord Russell. Learning of this, Monmouth was worried. As it turned out, with very good reason.

Finishing his speech to the large crowd and acknowledging his many sins, Monmouth tipped Ketch with six guineas, passing a sceptical eye over the sharpness of the axe, and making the promise to have the executioner's fee increased should the job be completed instantly. On feeling the first blow, Monmouth rose his head in indignation. On the second, the cut was deeper but by no means final. After losing his way, and having to be ordered by the sheriff of London to finish the job amidst the booing of the crowd, Ketch required three more strokes to end Monmouth's life. The botched job was then finished with a butcher's knife.

If the ridiculous spectacle was not enough, the ignominy was far from over. Perhaps a sign of things to come, there is a remarkable story that returned to the Tower for burial in the Chapel of St Peter ad Vincula, it was – incorrectly as it turns out – murmured that no portrait of the duke had ever been commissioned. Incredibly, so the story goes, the recently executed duke's head was sewn back on so his portrait could be taken. Today a strange picture of a man, lying awkwardly in slumber and displaying a uniquely morbid and soulless expression, is kept in the National Portrait Gallery and was once credited as being of the duke. Though two earlier paintings of Monmouth certainly exist, the previous designation of the painting, now titled *unknown man*, may well confirm the legend, or at least have given rise to it. Interestingly, a more far-fetched theory argued that Monmouth had changed places with a double and was later remembered to history as the Man in the Iron Mask.

A better end would await Monmouth's most important deputy. Two years after escaping the drunken Denham, Lord Grey de Werke was once again back in the Tower, only now in very different circumstances. Having backed Monmouth's rebellion to the bitter end, after a short period in the cells, whether in an attempt to save his own neck or because of rumours that Monmouth had seduced Grey's own wife, Grey agreed to turn informant against the rebels. Although James agreed to spare Grey's life, in three years' time it proved a decision he would regret. With frustrations at James's rule reaching a peak, Grey became involved in the Glorious Rising that would cause James to lose his throne.

Back in 1685, however, James's position on the throne had been relatively secure. As such, it was an England ruled by James II that Edward Gove would visit on being transferred to the Tower. An Englishman by birth, Gove had not seen England since emigrating to the New World as a 17-year-old in 1647, after which he eventually set up home in New Hampshire.

It was in the new colony in later years that a series of events would shape his destiny. An outspoken and honest man, Gove became a member of the opposition party in the New Hampshire assembly, a role that brought him into opposition with hot-headed bully and businessman Robert Mason. Complicating the matter, New Hampshire had been made a royal province in 1679, at which time Mason pushed a dubious claim for landownership that had already been the subject of a longstanding legal wrangle. In Gove, the people found a voice of opposition to Mason's tactics, prompting Mason to use his influence back in England, which saw a new lieutenant-governor appointed by Charles II and sent to New Hampshire to rule with an iron fist. Taking up his sword against the newly appointed Cranfield, Gove initially flouted the new authority and evaded arrest until an underwhelming attempt at a coup forced him to surrender. Tried on the crime of leading a rebellion, Gove was found guilty and sentenced to being hanged, drawn and quartered, his lands forfeit to the British Crown. Struggling however to find anyone willing to carry out the execution, Gove was transferred across the Atlantic to the Tower.

His ship arrived in England on 6 June 1683, also carrying a letter from Cranfield which explained the crimes on which Gove had been convicted and the fear, due to the importance of the man, of insurrection if he had been executed in his home colony. Initially shackled, he was later granted the freedom to walk the Tower grounds, before James II eventually pardoned him, the original crimes no longer deemed relevant to his present situation. To the joy of Gove's neighbours, Cranfield was subsequently removed from his appointment, and suffered the indignity of leaving his jurisdiction with his neck loosely garrotted and his legs tied to the rear of a horse. Gove returned to New Hampshire in 1686, his estates restored. Strangely, as he approached death in 1692, he held steadfast to his belief that he had been poisoned in the Tower, and experienced physical decline ever since. Whether this was true or not, the hero of New Hampshire passed away at 62, his reputation salvaged.

In contrast to Gove and his supporters – all of whom were pardoned for their roles in the insurrection against Cranfield – the lot of Monmouth's supporters, most notably those who had marched with him in the West Country, was looking every bit as bleak as Monmouth's portrait. In retribution for their crimes against the king, James set up a moving court that would become forever demonised for its inherent cruelty. Led by the infamous 'Hanging' Judge George Jeffreys, vehemently cited by his critics as a sadistic bully who loved inflicting misery on criminals, the Bloody Assizes would leave a deep stain on England's history every bit as dark as anything that went on inside the Tower. After seeing some 330 victims being led to the gallows – some of which he was reputed to have watched while dining – as well as sentencing over 800 to deportation to the West Indies, where they would be sold as slaves, Jeffreys was rewarded by being promoted from lord chief Justice of England, a position he had held since 1683, to lord chancellor, and given a seat in the House of Lords. Such terrible decisions were unsurprisingly detrimental to James's reputation in the eyes of the population, especially as Jeffreys's promotion effectively married the executive and judiciary branches of British Law.

Bloody ends in James's reign were by no means restricted to the such-named assizes. An incident at the menagerie in 1686 involving a woman named Mary Jenkinson and one of the Tower lions saw her arm hideously mangled and later amputated before finally succumbing to her wounds. Accused of deserting, Royalist soldier Richard Cane was hanged on 15 April 1687 as a stout reminder that a soldier must always keep to his post.

While more would follow throughout the year, by 1688 James's grasp on his kingdom was looking far less secure. Helped in no small part by Jeffreys's brutal behaviour in exerting justice against Monmouth's rebels, opposition to the king's reign had reached a height. Despite his recent fathering – or apparent fathering – of a son by his second wife, Mary of

Modena, an intriguing set of rivals for his throne emerged in the form of his married Protestant daughters. On hearing that James had issued a declaration of indulgence, more or less repelling the anti-Catholic laws that had been in place since the Gunpowder Plot, no less than seven Anglican bishops were imprisoned in the Tower in direct consequence of their unwillingness to comply.

Supported by the city of London at large, the prelates were removed from the Tower a week later to stand trial at Westminster Hall. Acquitted, the news was followed by a group of peers making contact with William of Orange and his wife, James's daughter Mary, inviting a Dutch invasion. On 5 November, an ironic date by all accounts, this anti-Catholic coup was put into operation. Backed by a professional force of some 15,000 who landed in England at the same time James was being deserted by John Churchill – later 1st Duke of Marlborough and famously an ancestor of Sir Winston – James was defeated. Arrested on attempting to flee to Dover, he avoided imprisonment in the Tower and was instead exiled to a country estate in France, where he would see out his days in noble splendour.

Chapter 22

1688–1715: Hapless Hollanders, Jealous Jacobites and Happy Hanoverians

The Glorious Rising was inevitably bad news for many of Royalist persuasion. Yet of the many affected by James's overthrow, recent developments would prove especially bad for one who had come to prominence during the Monmouth Rebellion. Disguising himself in preparation for crossing the Channel, the alcoholic Judge Jeffreys became the architect of his own downfall when recognised in a tavern in Wapping and set upon by an angry mob. Spared death by the narrowest of margins, the former voice of the law was taken to the house of the lord mayor and afterwards imprisoned – apparently at his own request – in the Tower, citing it as the one place he knew he would be spared. Correct in his prediction he was kept safe from physical harm, but nothing could spare him from verbal attacks. Heckled by angry visitors, the level of vitriol aimed at him reached its pinnacle when he received a barrel, which he believed to be filled with oysters, only to discover they were in reality empty shells used to cover a smuggled-in noose. After a miserable four months, during which time he had been granted permission to buy as much brandy as he could afford, Jeffreys died of kidney complications at the age of just 43.

Following William and Mary's accession, the dark cells of the Tower became filled with those who had wielded power during the previous regime. With the Protestant Dutchman tending to favour appointing officials of his own nation, the brunt of the change fell primarily on James's Catholic loyalists.

One of the first to lose station at this time was the Tower's former lieutenant, Sir Edward Hales. Failing in his attempts to flee, he was arrested and locked up inside his old fortress. An even more significant prisoner during this time was Richard Graham, Lord Preston. A confirmed Protestant, he nevertheless remained true to his Jacobite loyalties and had attempted to follow the stirrings of Louis XIV in France and raise a rebellion in the north. Imprisoned for a time in the Tower, he was arrested once more when he attempted to cross the Channel carrying letters confirming a French invasion was being prepared. Brought again to the Tower, and sentenced to death at his trial, he avoided the axe in return for informing on his fellow conspirators, including Henry Hyde, Earl of Clarendon; Admiral George Legge, 1st Baron Dartmouth; Francis Turner, the bishop of Ely, as well as William Penn.

Of those mentioned, the conspirators who paid most for their actions were the earl of Clarendon and lord Dartmouth. Clarendon was James's brother-in-law from his first marriage, thus also uncle of the new queen, yet this did not stop his name coming up in connection with the purported invasion. Relocated to the Tower, Clarendon was eventually released on condition he kept to his estates. The former Tower constable Dartmouth, however, was less fortunate and suffered a stroke in his cell.

Defection by James's hero of the defeat of Monmouth, John Churchill to William, by contrast, had been something of a mixed blessing. Though spared the inevitable imprisonment, death in battle or being exiled on William's accession, the now earl of Marlborough nevertheless failed to obtain any significant office in William's government. The circumstances that led to his arrest were unusual. In May 1692, four years after James II's dethronement, a skilled forger crafted a letter in an almost identical hand to Marlborough's, demanding James's restoration. Signed – in fake signatures – by several other rebel peers including the former archbishop of Canterbury, William Sancroft, and Thomas Sprat, Bishop of Rochester, on discovery of the letter in a flowerpot at the residence of the bishop of Rochester, Churchill was arrested. After a month languishing in the Tower, suspicion fell on the forger – one Robert Young – as well as the planter, Stephen Blackhead. In light of the fresh evidence, the duke was released on bail. Curiously, the Churchill family would not be altogether finished with the Tower. Charged on suspicion of taking bribes, John's brother George was imprisoned in the cells whereas another brother, Charles, was eventually made lieutenant after Marlborough's career peaked when he led the English forces to victory at Blenheim.

Another of Howard connection incarcerated in the Tower was Edward Griffin, 1st Baron Braybrooke who was arrested in 1690 on charges of treason against the new rulers. After initial success in escaping, the peer was later caught and returned there. Spared the axe, he died as a prisoner in 1710.

Better luck, however, was to befall English Catholic William Dorrington who had risen to the rank of Major General fighting in the Irish Army. Remaining loyal to James following the Glorious Revolution, Dorrington replaced Ormonde as commander of the Irish Guards before seeing action at the infamous Battle of the Boyne in 1690. On being captured and brought to the Tower a year later, he successfully escaped – other sources say that he was released – to retake control of the Irish Guards.

Another to escape the Tower during the Williamite conflict was English army officer, Colonel John Parker. Another proud survivor of the Boyne, Parker had made it to London by 1693, at which point he became party to a plot to assassinate William in Flanders. Evading initial arrest, Parker was captured the following year and sent to the Tower. Despite being kept in close confinement and deprived of any writing utensils, in league with Sir John Friend who bribed a yeoman warder, his escape from the Tower was achieved on 11 August 1694. Although he enjoyed some eight years of freedom, Parker later joined an exclusive list of those imprisoned in both the Tower and the Bastille, where he was sent for insulting Mary of Modena.

Following Parker out of the Tower was the 4th Earl of Clancarty, Donough MacCarthy. Imprisoned around 1690 for his role in the Jacobite resistance in Ireland, MacCarthy escaped from the Tower on 27 October 1694 and successfully made his way to James II's court in France. Exactly how he achieved liberation is unclear. Entering MacCarthy's cell on the day in question, his warder discovered his wig on its block and placed upon his pillow, attached to a note, 'This block must answer for me.' Answer for himself, however, he would as the reckless earl later returned to London to see his wife. Betrayed by a relative, he was retaken, only to receive mercy from King William who banished him for life.

Less fortunate was conspirator Sir William Parkyns. Despite taking an oath of allegiance to William, inspired primarily by his continued desire to practise law, on the death of Queen Mary, Parkyns joined a conspiracy with several others to assassinate the Dutch usurper. In consequence of his limited part – his suffering of gout diminished his role – Parkyns was implicated and tried. On 13 April 1696, he was executed alongside Sir John Friend on being found guilty of conspiring the king's assassination. On 28 January 1697, Sir John Fenwick was also beheaded for being privy to the plot. Better fortune, however, befell the 2nd Earl of Ailesbury, Thomas Bruce, who attempted to maintain his fitness by walking the length of his cell for some five hours a day, achieving an average of 'fifteen London miles'. He was released on bail a month after Fenwick's execution.

Away from the intrigue of Jacobite conspiracies, the year 1699 was of particular importance in the history of the Mint, primarily for finally seeing the end of professional rogue William Chaloner. A subordinate of Sir Isaac Newton during the great man's stint as Warden of the Tower Mint, Chaloner had grown up in poverty in 1660s Warwickshire. On reaching adulthood, he became apprenticed as a nail maker and used those talents to amass an ill-gotten fortune through various questionable enterprises not limited to counterfeiting, coin clipping, unlicensed surgery, female love potions and sex toys and even posing as a psychic medium. After creating for himself what could be regarded as an enviable lifestyle, highlighted by the purchase of luxurious accommodation in Knightsbridge, through the conducting of such scams, Chaloner set about targeting the Tower Mint.

It was there under Newton's watchful gaze that the esteemed scientific mind gradually gathered evidence against Chaloner. After purchasing himself a quiet house in the Surrey village of Egham, Chaloner proceeded to acquire the machinery he needed to create his own mint and began work counterfeiting further coins. Realizing from early calculations that as many as one in ten of Britain's coins were fake, Newton began scouring the local inns and taverns, successfully uncovering one of Chaloner's co-conspirators. A short time later, Chaloner was arrested and held in Newgate Prison.

Nevertheless, the story was far from over. Furious at his capture, the crafty counterfeiter put his talents to use writing on monetary policy, practically lecturing the government how to deal with the crisis for which he had been largely responsible. Accusing Newton and the minters of a host of crimes, Chaloner found a listener in the form of Charles Mordaunt, the earl of Monmouth, himself an enemy of Lord Montagu, the present chancellor of the Exchequer and Newton's patron. Brought before the Privy Council, his words did at least lead to an inquiry, undoubtedly less than Chaloner had hoped. When Chaloner appeared at the bar of the Commons in 1697 to expose the fraud, he received permission to conduct an experiment at the Mint. Newton refused the proposal and instead offered his own evidence of coins grooved by Chaloner's recently suggested methods. Chaloner also turned his attention to the new Bank of England, successfully counterfeiting the new banknotes. On this occasion, retribution was swift. Seized after his printer was accused of creating a dud note, he defended himself with the claim that the forgery had been an experiment in security. Incredibly, the bank accepted it and rewarded him with £200 for his research.

In response to accusations of incompetence if not embezzlement from Chaloner, Newton sought to complete the charlatan's downfall. Overseeing the re-coining process, he also returned his focus to exposing the resourceful criminal. Setting the bait by offering a reprieve to two gaoled lesser criminals in exchange for information, Newton discovered that a pair of coining dies from the Tower Mint had been sold to Chaloner. Empowering select informers, in his role as a magistrate he brought many into the Tower for questioning.

As Chaloner's wealth from recent failures dwindled, he was caught in his attempts to mastermind a final scam, more or less the set-up of a national lottery yet without the offer of a final prize. Arrested and returned to Newgate, Newton personally oversaw a ten-day session conducted inside his house on Mint Street within the Tower's outer ward, culminating in full trial. Ending this incredible episode, Chaloner was found guilty at the Old Bailey of treason and taken to Tyburn and hanged on 22 March 1699. Newton, meanwhile, was promoted from the Mint's warden to its master.

A year after the fall of Chaloner, 19 July 1700 saw the end of three Dutch prisoners for the murder of one Oliver Norris. Named in the trial papers as Michael van Bergen, Katherine Truerniet and Gerhardt Dromelius, they were hanged at East Smithfield, a place also known as Little Tower Hill due to its close proximity to the area. The following year, the crime of peculation would come back to haunt one Samuel Shepherd who was imprisoned in the Tower for bribery during the parliamentary election for Newport on the Isle of Wight. That same year, two commissioners of the Prize Office – concerning goods and ships captured at sea – were sent to the Tower for failing to make up their accounts.

Just as the Tower frequently played host to many an English king and queen, it is somewhat ironic that the same should be true of Britain's first official prime minister. Born in Norfolk, Robert Walpole, famous for his quote that 'every man has his price,' lived almost exactly as he preached, successfully deepening his own pockets and his Norfolk estate before swapping his prosperous home for the depressing walls of the Tower. Accused of embezzling government funds, Walpole spent six miserable months in the Tower before resuming his political career as if nothing had happened.

Queen Anne's death in 1714 ended a remarkable era in British history. Plagued by ill-fortune and the usual lack of a male heir, Anne's death gave rise to a problem not faced by an English government since the death of Elizabeth I. With no obvious successor, discussion on the matter laboured on for some time. With no better alternative, accession to the throne passed out of England to traditionally hostile Germany.

Unsurprisingly, discontent at the beginning of the Hanoverian era was writhe. Whereas the Williamites had criticised James II's unwavering Catholicism, there was now a feeling even among the Protestants that a Catholic of English blood was still better than a German. Within a year of George I's coronation, rebellion was raised under the flag of the 'old pretender', James Edward, son of the late James II. Support in raising rebellion for James Edward led to the beginning of the first Jacobite Rebellion and almost enabled the Stuarts to reclaim the throne.

It was after the failure of the rebellion that an incredible event occurred, destined to go down in the Tower's history as quite possibly its most inventive escape. Born in 1676 and forever a Stuart loyalist, William Maxwell, 5th Earl of Nithsdale had personally visited the exiled James Edward in St Germaines and also proclaimed him king in the Scottish borders before joining the Jacobite rebellion for their heavy defeat at Preston. Along with six other Scottish lords, Nithsdale was captured after the battle and taken south to the Tower.

Aged 36, Lady Winifred Nithsdale learned of her husband's capture around Christmas 1715 and immediately set about to secure his release. Having made every effort to ensure the family papers, as well as anything incriminating among their possessions, were safely hidden, she, accompanied by loyal maid Evans, left their home and made her way south through the dreary wintry conditions.

A fortnight passed before they reached their destination. Forced to undertake most of the journey on horseback, the snow-laden roads being impassable for a carriage, they arrived in London in a state of ignorance about recent events. Buoyed by news her husband was still alive, albeit soon to face trial, Lady Nithsdale took up lodgings with a Jacobean sympathiser referred to simply as Mrs Mills before visiting her husband at the Tower and preparing a formal appeal to the House of Lords. On learning that six of the seven prisoners were to be condemned, she took her appeal before the Commons; the act failed by only seven votes. Learning that three of the six imprisoned lords had been offered stays of execution by the king, Lady Nithsdale endeavoured to secure the same for her husband and incredibly tricked her way inside St James's Palace, posing as a maidservant. Despite reaching the king, her grovelled attempts at securing a similar stay of execution fell on deaf ears and the palace servants eventually rounded her up.

Devastated, the aggrieved lady visited her husband in the Tower, informing him of recent developments. Like many a man of important stock, Nithsdale was lodged inside the Queen's House, in a room off the council chamber that had once been used to interrogate Guy Fawkes. While her husband prepared his speech for the scaffold and composed correspondence that he prayed would ensure his son's birthright would not be confiscated, his wife began plotting their escape.

Lady Winifred's plan was as simple as it was ingenious. Dealing with an area of the Tower that was often a hubbub of noise and activity, she conspired with her maid that she would dress her husband up in women's clothes and attempt to get him away unnoticed. Aided by the assistance of several sympathisers, including one Miss Hilton – a friend of Evans – a woman named Mrs Morgan – sources vary as to whether she was a friend of their landlady from Drury Lane or alternatively an alias for Miss Hilton – and the landlady, Mrs Mills, herself to acquire necessary costumes, they visited Nithsdale again the day before his execution. Informed she could only take in one visitor with her, Lady Nithsdale entered with Mrs Morgan, who, wearing an additional gown, removed her outer dress. Dressing Lord Nithsdale up in the woman's clothing, Lady Nithsdale got frantically to work on adding appropriate make-up as well as exchanging her husband's white periwig with a red one that matched the hair colour of Mrs Morgan – or Mrs Mills. While Evans replaced Mrs Morgan, all the while Lady Nithsdale spoke loudly of her plans to submit a request for a reprieve. With Mrs Mills leaving, Mrs Morgan returned, leaving a cloak with a hood to be used by Nithsdale.

After a sustained period of coming and going, the Nithsdales were finally left alone. Convinced the costume might work, Lord Nithsdale left the room in the company of his wife and joined the maid in walking together out the Byward Tower to the prearranged coach. All that remained was a fitting encore. With the nervous couple gone, Mrs Morgan, now alone in the room, staged a mock conversation with herself, under the pretence Lord Nithsdale remained present. On Lady Nithsdale's return, Mrs Morgan departed, leaving Lady Winifred to continue the charade with an apparently excellent ventriloquist act. After a time had passed, she became the final person to leave the cell. Bidding her husband good wishes, she asked a servant approaching the cell with fresh candles not to disturb him, insisting he needed time alone to rest and prepare. Within thirty minutes she had joined her husband inside the safe house, the dreary setting soon to be left far behind them.

Nithsdale's stroke of fortune was incredible. Other associates, however, were less fortunate. The morning after the escape, on 24 February 1716, Nithsdale watched from an attic window as the other two Jacobean peers, James Radclyffe, 3rd Earl of Derwentwater, and William Gordon, 6th Viscount Kenmure, were executed for their role in the doomed rebellion. Being so far from the black-draped scaffold on Tower Hill, it is unlikely the absconded lord was aware of the conversation between Radclyffe and the executor concerning a large splinter on the block before he was dispatched with one strike on reciting the words, 'Lord Jesus, receive my soul.' After being placed in a Catholic chapel at Dagenham Park, the earl's body was later moved to Dilstan Castle in Northumberland, and in 1805 the vault temporarily opened to visitors.

The commotion following the sounding of the alarm on learning of Nithsdale's escape aside, officials at the Tower would never know what had become of the missing earl. No less than five warders were dismissed on grounds of negligence and forced to swap their positions of importance for the cells. Placing of a guard at every road and gate leading out of the city failed to stop a magnificent coach bearing the arms of the Venetian ambassador that included the errant lord. Lady Winifred too was not stopped as she travelled north to secure the family papers before returning south. Whether or not there is any truth in the suggestion the king ordered a late reprieve, it matters not. Having successfully made their way out of the Tower and then the country, they ended their lives happily in Rome.

Chapter 23

1715–1820: Bonnie Battlers, Loathable Lords, Aggressive Gordonites and Yorktown Yankees

S uccessful defeat of the risings of 1715 was of course bad news for all who had lined up on the losing side. Among the many to have been captured was Sir William Wyndham, a man whose own affinity with the Tower would contribute another unique tale.

As a young boy, William had apparently become the subject of a travelling fortune-teller who prophesised the simple portent, 'beware of the white horse.' Bizarre as this may have been, the story became stranger still years later when a Venetian fortune-teller made the same bold claim when the Scot explored Italy. Following his capture in 1715, Wyndham was one of many Jacobites taken to the Tower. Curiously, as his stagecoach prepared to pass under the Middle Tower, a group of workmen had been fixing an emblem above the archway – one that remains to this present day. The sign was a white horse, the coat of arms of George I.

Incredibly, Wyndham soon escaped the Tower, only to be persuaded to surrender and then released on bail. He finally died in 1740, many miles from the Tower, on a hunting trip when his horse slipped from under him. Somehow inevitably, the steed had been white.

Another who would succeed in achieving liberation from the Tower was fellow Jacobite, George Seton, 5th Earl of Wintoun. After he had taken the rare step of pleading not guilty at his trial – regardless of the plea, a death sentence usually awaited a condemned man at the time anyway – he was granted a small stay of execution to prepare his defence. Through a combination of successful pleas, bribing the warders not to disturb him late at night and the acquisition of a file, he managed to remove at least one of the bars and made his way to the Continent. Never recaptured, his warder, Adam Mason, was severely punished on charges of negligence.

The failure of the Jacobite Risings under the flag of the Old Pretender, for the present cemented George I's place on the throne. Within seven years of the first rising, that would change when a second attempt was made to restore the House of Stuart. Led by the Tory Bishop of Rochester and leader of the High Church Party, Francis Atterbury, the so-called Atterbury Plot came about as a direct consequence of both the decreasing popularity of the Whig government and the widespread release from prison of the original rebels under the Act of Grace and Pardon. After communication with the Old Pretender, a new rising was prepared for 1722, coinciding with the expected date of the next general election.

One of the key players in the development was a man named Christopher Layer, a barrister of the Middle Temple who, with the agreement of his fellow conspirators, travelled to Rome in 1721 to meet with the Old Pretender personally. Convinced of the possibility that the plotters could raise a sufficiently powerful army, mount an effective attack on key sites like the Tower and the Bank of England, and finally capture the royal family, Layer left Rome with James's blessing.

Things ran into difficulty the following year. On the death of Charles Spencer, the earl of Sunderland, news leaked that the Jacobites had been endeavouring to amass a large army, and among Spencer's confiscated papers was correspondence with James himself. Determined to hunt down those responsible, Prime Minister Walpole brought charges against the likely suspects, including Atterbury, Layer and the duke of Mar's agent in England, the Irish deacon George Kelly. Arrested, Layer initially absconded from a London gaol before being lodged with Atterbury in the Tower. So seriously was Layer's ability to escape taken that he was shackled in leg irons to ensure no further oversights. At that point proceedings against the pair began in earnest. Found guilty of treason, both Atterbury and Layer were taken west and met their end at Tyburn on 17 May 1723. Among his accomplices, George Kelly was held at the Tower twice. Imprisoned there in October 1722, he escaped in 1736.

In Kelly's great escape, another special tale was found. Recorded as having occurred sometime between seven and eight in the evening on 24 October 1736, notice of a reward of £200 for information that would lead to his capture accompanied the literature concerning his disappearance. Born in the county of Roscommon in the same year as the Glorious Rising – 1688 – the intelligent young future Jacobite was educated at

Trinity before becoming a deacon and fleeing to Paris. Indeed, it was there he would make the acquaintance of Atterbury.

Kelly was Atterbury's secretary when in 1720 the pair secretly returned to London. Unknown to them both, word of their arrival had leaked and they were both surveyed discretely by the government officials, resulting in their arrest two years later. On being detained, Kelly was recorded as having drawn a sword on the officer in question and with his free hand burnt any incriminating documents. Released on bail after his initial imprisonment in May, by October his continuous plotting for the Jacobite cause saw him relocated to solitary confinement in a cell of the Beauchamp Tower.

After two years of immense patience, he protested of his harsh treatment, including constant surveillance, his allowance being taken and his declining health – he probably had smallpox. His complaint successful, he was relocated to Number 8 Tower Green, the home of resident warder Richard Madox. Partially liberated and enjoying access to the grounds, in 1730 he wrote again concerning his health, requesting he be allowed – escorted – regular trips to Hampstead for better air. Aided by an accompanying medical report, by 1736 he penned a further letter about his asthma and requested some five hours a day to be allowed into the city. Granted access, the regular trips included the opportunity to browse the capital's retail outlets, allowing him the purchase of a horseman's coat. At around two in the afternoon on 24 October, carrying the recently collected coat over his arm, he left for a regular jaunt with his warder and returned to the Tower after dark. Informing warder Fowler he planned to visit a friend of his – a son of another warder – the unsuspecting Fowler wished him good night, oblivious as the red-coated Kelly about turned and walked unchallenged out of the Tower, mistaken for an officer.

A few days after achieving his remarkable feat, the cunning deacon boarded a ship bound for Calais. Inspired, perhaps, by the antics of the legendary Jesuit, Father John Gerard, he penned a letter to the duke of Newcastle apologising for the escape, as well as one to the Tower officials, insisting that his books become property of his friend. In 1745 he joined the Jacobite rebellion and, after its failure, fled to France to become secretary to the Bonnie Prince, living until the age of 74. Whether reports of him as a 'general favourite' or a 'notorious raskall' take precedence, his exploits serve as another timely reminder of what can be achieved through hard work, planning and extreme patience.

The year 1743 would be another memorable one for the Tower. Whereas execution of commoner and noble alike had been witnessed on Tower Hill, Smithfield or Tyburn since the days of the appellants, until that time only seven executions – eight including Clarence – had been carried out inside the walls, none of which had been commoners. That all changed in an event that would forever blacken not only the reputation of the Tower, but also the soldiers employed to protect Britain's shores. Ordered to march south from their native Scotland to London, apparently at the request of the king who had never seen a Highland regiment before, the well-disciplined soldiers of the Black Watch made the trip with appropriate trepidation. On arriving in London, their suspicions were confirmed when they learned that the monarch was abroad and had no interest in seeing them personally. Rather than arrive at the king's pleasure, they instead learned they would be reassigned to the Caribbean.

News of the relocation was received badly. Critics of the Scots have condemned what happened next as clear neglect of their duties, but their stance is far less surprising when recognising that the regiment had signed up solely for duties of Highland watch. On 17 May 1743, approximately a hundred highlanders deserted the garrison and headed north for their homes. On being intercepted by General Wade's regiment of horse, the deserters were swiftly court-martialled. Of the 100 or so found guilty, the sentence of being shot by firing squad was only carried out on the ringleaders. On 18 July 1743, Corporals Samuel and Malcolm MacPherson, as well as Private Farquhar Shaw were all executed near St Peter ad Vincula.

Within two years of the Black Watch executions, trouble north of the border again threatened to stir. Refusing to be deterred by the failures of the Jacobite Rising and the Atterbury Plot over twenty years earlier, attempts to rid Britain of its Hanoverian rulers were once again put into operation. With James Edward's hopes damaged from past failures, the rebellion would occur on this occasion under the banner of his son, the 'Young Pretender', Charles Edward, better remembered in history as Bonnie Prince Charlie.

After making a strong start that culminated with the taking of Edinburgh and a long march south into England, the army was forced into a retreat. The rebellion was effectively ended after being routed by the Royalists at Culloden in April 1746. Among the prisoners taken were General William Boyd, Earl of Kilmarnock and Arthur Elphinstone, 6th Baron Balmerino. Initially mistaking a group of Hanoverian troops for his own, Boyd's arrest was largely the product of his own fatigue. He was taken to London and found guilty of high treason.

There is a strange story that at the trial, the Whig Lady Townshend fell in love with Kilmarnock and later adopted a stable boy, who she had been told was the man's son. Tried alongside him, Balmerino was also found guilty. Balmerino's story is also unique for having asked the coach to stop at Charing Cross after his trial to buy gooseberries. Around the time he and his wife were eating them at dinner, the lieutenant of the Tower entered with the death warrant, causing his wife to faint. When the pair were beheaded on Tower Hill on 18 August 1746, Kilmarnock greeted him with the words, 'My Lord, I am heartily sorry to have your company in this expedition,' to which Balmerino replied, 'I am only sorry that I cannot pay this reckoning alone.' In contrast to Kilmarnock's instant dispatch at the hands of his gentlemanly executioner, for Balmerino, the nervous axe-man would need three attempts before finally ending his misery.

Following them to the block was Charles Radclyffe, 5th Earl of Derwentwater. Walking in the footsteps of his brother, the 3rd duke – Nithsdale's accomplice who the cross-dressed lord saw being executed in 1715 – and, himself, one of only a handful of Englishmen to be involved in both the 1715 and 1745 rebellions, Radclyffe was executed on 8 December 1746.

Unquestionably the most glamorous prisoner to grace the Tower in connection with the Jacobite rebellions was the Scottish heroine, Flora MacDonald. At the time of Bonnie Prince Charlie's defeat at Culloden, MacDonald had been living on the island of Benbecula in the Outer Hebrides, where the prince had sought refuge in the aftermath of his defeat. Despite being under Hanoverian control, MacDonald, swayed by her Jacobite sympathies and her distant family connection to the prince's companion, Captain Conn O'Neill, dressed the prince up as her maid and sought permission from her stepfather – also the head of the island's militia – to take a boat to the mainland. After helping the prince flee to the Isle of Skye, MacDonald's actions aroused the suspicions of the watchers, leading to her temporary imprisonment in the Tower. She was released a year later and forever immortalised in song.

Another prisoner taken to the Tower in the aftermath of Culloden was Simon Fraser, Lord Lovat. Labelled something of a despot, this particularly unique character is remembered primarily for having forced his aunt to marry him on his uncle's death in order to obtain the family estates. He had been raised a Catholic in France and was one of a select few to have been imprisoned in both the Tower and the Bastille. Brought to the Tower, he aroused contempt by seeking to bribe the lieutenant that by sacrificing his eldest son in his place, Lovat would allow the lieutenant's niece to marry his second son. It is undoubtedly in keeping with such actions that it was said of him in 1706 by Lord Belhaven that he could justly have deserved to be hanged five times in five different places, being not only an English traitor but 'a traitor to the Court of St James … St Germaines … Versailles and … to his own country of Scotland.'

After four months inside the famous old walls, Lovat's end came on Tower Hill in predictably lamentable circumstances. Described as being of unflattering disposition, his carriage ride to his trial at Westminster on 18 December 1746 will be forever remembered for the rampant attempts of the mob at vandalising the stagecoach, culminating in the aggressive comments of a bystander, 'You ugly old dog, don't you think you will have that frightful head cut off?' to which Lovat brilliantly replied, 'You ugly old bitch, I believe I shall.'

Sentenced to death a day later, his request to be granted a Scottish death and be executed by the Maiden was denied, following which he would become the final man of noble status to be dispatched by the axe. In almost typical Lovat fashion, further ignominy would precede the execution as overcrowding resulted in somewhere between eight and fifty innocent spectators losing their lives when a stand collapsed.

It was, perhaps, hardly surprising the man's death was not the end of his story. After his execution, his head was stitched back onto his body in scenes reminiscent of Monmouth – albeit for different reasons – and a mystery would soon ensue regarding its future whereabouts. Placed in a ceremonial coffin immediately after his beheading, Lovat had made lavish plans for his funeral that included a tomb at the church of Kirkhill, a lead coffin and several pipers. In contrast, however, to the instructions of his close relatives and secretary of state, the duke of Newcastle, that the body would initially remain at the Tower, the undertaker requested it be taken to his funeral parlour, following which he profited from the payments from curious onlookers to see the infamous lord's corpse. Hearing of the indignity some four days later, both the constable of the Tower and duke of Newcastle were inevitably furious. Hearing that a ship moored in the Thames would soon be sailing north, Lovat's cousin requested that the body be put on board but that was rejected in favour of it being interred in the 'no sadder spot' of St Peter ad Vincula. By 17 April, the lead coffin was back and apparently interred, remaining undisturbed until 1876 and the reinterment of several others discovered in the crypt; since 1841 others had also been found in the old cemetery where the grand storehouse once stood.

It was at this time the true mystery came to light. Despite apparent certainty he had been buried inside the Tower, a strange letter written by one of Lovat's descendants suggested the body had in fact made it to Kirkhill. According to tradition, the head had been held in a separate vault. Whether a switch was made in honour of Lovat's wishes is unclear. To this day, questions regarding the head, the lead coffin at Kirkhill and the one at the Tower remain unanswered.

Following Lovat to the Tower was the equally despicable Laurence Shirley, 4th Earl of Ferrers. An unashamed womaniser and spendthrift, Ferrers added murder to his list of sins when, after running into financial troubles – which caused his estates to be placed in the hands of a trust – he shot and killed one of the trustees after his request for an interview was denied.

Ferrers was detained in the Middle Tower on his arrest in 1760 and later tried for the trustee's murder. His plea of insanity being somewhat at odds with his ability to present his own defence, a guilty verdict soon followed. After being denied a final visit of his mistress by his elderly aunt, the countess of Huntingdon, who had visited Ferrers in his cell, the disgraced earl set about preparing for his execution. Engrossing himself in listening to one of his specially assigned warders read *Hamlet*, he wrote his speech for the gallows and set off in a horse-drawn carriage to Tyburn as though dressed for a wedding. Honoured with a cord made of silk as opposed to rope in acknowledgement of his status, the unrepentant earl went to his death on 5 May.

As fate would have it, his death was memorable for several reasons. With the concept of the Tyburn Tree now somewhat outdated, Ferrers was subjected to the new method of hanging by standing on a slightly raised section, release of a lever resulting in the area sinking and leading to instant decapitation – or so was the plan. Unfortunately for the ill-reputed lord, in the absence of thorough checks being made it was discovered to the horror of those involved that the tall Scot's toes still touched the ground. In pity for the abhorrent spectacle, the executioner and his assistant hastened the earl's demise with the humane pulling on his legs. Once the body was removed from the gallows, it was taken to Surgeons' Hall and dissected. At the time of writing, he remains the last – and likely final – peer to die through hanging in England.

Within three years of Ferrers's death, another well-known personality suffered at the Tower. Recorded as both an MP but also a member of the infamous Hellfire Club, John Wilkes was every bit the anti-Royalist as had been his Leveller predecessors a century earlier. Equally liberal with his writings, a vehement attack on George III's government in Wilkes's own newspaper landed the hot-headed MP in the Tower. After a week of incarceration he was released and later enjoyed a stint as lord mayor of London.

A contemporary of Wilkes was another lord mayor of London, Brass Crosby. A prominent lawyer from the north, Crosby was joined in the political sphere by London alderman Richard Oliver who became MP for the city in 1771, the same year of Crosby's own election. Intellectually tethered by their mutual views regarding civil liberties, both endured time in the Tower that year after a series of newspaper stories reported the debates openly, a breach of the parliamentary privilege. After two of the printers were imprisoned and later released, largely as a result of Crosby and Oliver's intervention, the two politicians were themselves incarcerated in the Tower for challenging parliamentary authority. After Crosby spent some time lodged in the vicinity of the parade ground, receiving regular visits from Wilkes and other supporters, the pair were released – a victory, it was deemed, for the common people.

During Wilkes's tenure as lord mayor, one of his close associates made trouble for no good reason. An American living in London, Stephen Sayre was a merchant and city sheriff who in 1775, and with the aid of a London mob, sought to kidnap George III. Meeting with a fellow American, Francis Richardson – at the time also a lieutenant in the British Army – Sayre attempted to conscript Richardson into his stand to capture the king on his way to the State Opening of Parliament and hold him prisoner in the Tower while the mob helped themselves to the spoils of the armoury. Informing Richardson that Wilkes himself was part of the conspiracy, the American soldier was asked to bribe the yeoman warders to grant access to the Tower the day in question.

Seeing better sense, Richardson made news of Sayre's conspiracy known to Lord Rochford, the eighteenth-century equivalent of the modern-day defence secretary. On Sayre's arrest, he denied all knowledge of the plot, but was nevertheless taken to the Tower. Despite widespread criticism from the tabloids that Rochford was creating a prison state by believing rumour without full investigation, he kept Sayre in a cell until after parliament's reopening had passed. He was later released after paying a bail of £1,000.

Another Scot to endure the Tower's cells was the ageing aristocrat, Lord Gordon. Staunchly Protestant, he had been vehemently averse to attempts to relax the stringent anti-Catholic laws that had been in place since the time of Guy Fawkes and his fellow conspirators. Following the presentation of a petition before parliament, accompanied by a strident anti-Roman diatribe, violence spilled out onto the streets in scenes reminiscent of those witnessed four centuries earlier during the Peasants' Revolt, culminating in attacks on the Bank of England and the Royal Exchange. Also attacked were the houses of several peers and the bursting of a distillery causing the deaths of several rioters.

Besides those drowned in booze, it was estimated as many as 850 rioters lost their lives at the hands of the authorities, including soldiers from the Tower garrison who were brought in to help regain control. Escaping death at the hands of the rioters or soldiers, Gordon was imprisoned in the Tower for his part in the troubles. Though charged with treason, it was later concluded the horrific scenes, albeit in his name, had resulted from spontaneous emotion rather than anything premeditated. Whereas a one-armed soldier named William McDonald, a Charlotte Gardiner, and a Mary Roberts were all hanged on 11 July 1780 for their roles in the Gordon Riots, after eight months in the Tower, Gordon was released and later converted to Judaism.

Around that time, another prominent person confined in the Tower was one remembered to history, like Penn a century earlier, for leaving his mark on the developing New World. Born in Charleston, South Carolina, Henry Laurens had previously served as President of the Continental Congress, famously responsible for drawing up the Declaration of Independence, and had been recently appointed the US's first ambassador to the Netherlands by the time he fell into the hands of the Royal Navy. Captured at sea in 1780 after attempting to reach Holland in the hope of ratifying a trade deal with the Dutch and drumming up financial support for the new nation, the politician's attempts to discard his papers overboard saw them retrieved by a British sailor with a boarding pike. As a result, Laurens was brought to Whitehall for questioning where accusations regarding the exact nature of his mission were levelled in full.

Found guilty of treason as a result of the recovered draft treaty, Laurens was relayed by boat to the Tower where he was greeted by a boisterous rendition of 'Yankee Doodle' by the yeoman warders. In total, Laurens spent about fifteen months at the Tower, during which he received regular visits from his estranged son. A stranger to the Tower's dingy cells – even his lodgings off Tower Green he saw as substandard – and required to pay for his keep, the American revolutionary kicked up a fuss about the expenses and was grateful to the generosity of local sympathisers, as well as his warder, James Futerell, who brought him food and comforts. Spared the axe or the gallows, Laurens was exchanged in return for Lord Cornwallis who had been captured following the British defeat at Yorktown and soon began his new role as ambassador to Great Britain – or the court of St James.

Laurens's story was not completely finished. A man with a morbid phobia of being buried alive, he insisted on being cremated following his death – according to some variations of the story, he was first beheaded and his head rolled down into the nearby river. Remembered fondly for his pioneering role in the young United States of America, he went to his death with the unique accolade of being the only American to be imprisoned there and, potentially, for having avoided Tower Hill only to lose his head back home after he had died. He recounted his experiences at the Tower in an autobiography entitled, *A Narrative of the Capture of Henry Laurens, of his Confinement in the Tower of London.*

France's role in the same war inevitably saw a number of French prisoners held in the Tower, including the suspected spy, Francois Henri de la Motte. A former officer in the French army, in 1781 de la Motte was found guilty of such crimes by his jury and audaciously expressed the wish that his head be immediately struck off if that be permitted. Around that time, the Tower received another prisoner of foreign birth. Involved in an attempt to kill the Swedish king in Finland in 1788, Johan Anders Jägerhorn spent more than two years in the Tower from 1798 for his close friendship with Irish revolutionary Lord Edward Fitzgerald, as well as acting as an intermediary between the Irish and the French prior to the Irish rebellion against British rule. In 1801 he was released and deported back to Finland.

The final decade of the eighteenth century would see the Tower's cells once again filled with those who sought political reform. Horne Tooke, himself a notable member of the Society for Constitutional Information, was arrested and sent to the Tower in May 1794 after government spies intercepted a dubious letter intended for his eyes only. Also suspected of high treason were John Thelwall and Thomas Hardy of the so-called London Corresponding Society. Fortunately for the trio, all were cleared, with Tooke using his time in incarceration to keep a diary. Similar was true of a fourth prisoner, Stewart Kyd, who penned the second instalment of his *Treatise on the Law of Corporations.*

One who campaigned in defence of such prisoners incarcerated in the name of political reform was Sir Francis Burdett. In 1810, the reformist politician himself endured two months in the Tower as punishment for his views that the recent imprisonment of the radical John Gale Jones by parliament itself was a step beyond the power of the executive branch. Deemed a breach of privilege, a warrant was issued for Burdett's arrest by the Speaker, leading to his transfer. On returning to Westminster by boat on his release, he missed a planned demonstration in his honour and began legal proceedings against those who had caused his imprisonment. Incidentally, his lawyer was none other than former Tower prisoner Samuel Shepherd.

Of greater concern to the yeoman warders than the sojourns of these largely harmless prisoners were a series of events that would follow the infamous Gordon Riots – now seen by some as a precursor to the French Revolution. By 1820 two and a half decades of war with Republican France had led to further propaganda and politically induced rioting. One accused of bearing responsibility for the new violence was Arthur Thistlewood whose Cato Street Conspiracy would leave its own mark on England and the Tower. Having already failed in one endeavour, the latest of a long line aimed at capturing both the Tower and the Bank of England, Thistlewood became the brains behind an even more radical conspiracy: the genocide of the entire Cabinet.

Fortunately for those in government, Thistlewood's plot never came to fruition, not least due to his failure to recognise his right-hand man was secretly a government spy. Having assembled his group of plotters, they were taken off guard as they gathered around a stable on Cato Street in London, leading to a skirmish and the killing of one of Thistlewood's apprehenders. Caught, he was taken, along with seven of his co-plotters to the Tower.

While Thistlewood was destined to follow in the footsteps of the missing princes, Raleigh, Overbury, Carr and Laud, and take up residence in the Bloody Tower, the remaining plotters were held in various other locations: John Brunt in the Byward Tower, James Ings and William Davidson in St Thomas's Tower, with Richard Tidd and the others in the Middle and Salt Towers. Renowned for his revolutionary, anti-slavery views, Thistlewood was subsequently condemned to death and hanged with his allies either at Tyburn or outside Newgate Prison. With this, the Tower would, for almost 100 years, see the last of its prisoners, thus ending a long unbroken chain of events that went back to the slippery Flambard.

1800–Present: Iron Dukes, Iron Crosses and Iron Ostriches

A raging inferno lit up the sky above the Tower's inner ward on 30 October 1841. Breaking out as a result of an overheated flue in the Bowyer Tower, the conflagration was first seen around half past ten as it spread unhindered to the seventeenth-century storehouse, which failed to survive despite the best efforts of the Tower's fire brigade. The thick palls of smoke, accompanied by the inevitable sight of the fiery inferno over the outer walls, provided a rare glimpse of what might have been had the Great Fire of London penetrated the eastern reaches of the city almost two centuries earlier. The spectacle occupied the attention of the thousands of locals who gathered in the moat to watch as the Tower was engulfed in flames accompanied by the noise of collapsing walls.

Fire at the Tower was rare, yet this was by no means an isolated incident. In 1774, Henry III's Lanthorn Tower had suffered a conflagration that demolished much of what remained of the somewhat dated royal apartments, but that was relatively trivial compared to what happened on this particular evening. Once the city's fire engines were eventually granted access through the Tower's outer gates, evacuation of the Crown Jewels, as the flames threatened the Martin Tower, became complicated when it was learned that the keeper of the Jewel House had access only to the outer room, the key to the inner barred area in which the jewels were kept being held by the lord chamberlain. With time running out and the fire closing in on the jewels, a second attempt in the Tower's history at removing them by use of force was required. A hero of the evening was a brave policeman who gained access to the place where the jewels were held and passed them out in conditions so ferocious that his uniform was charred. By the time the fire had been dowsed, the storehouse and the Bowyer and Brick Towers had been permanently lost with the White Tower and royal chapel also receiving a few scars of battle. The scene was forever immortalised in a famous painting by the artist J.M.W. Turner.

Occupying the old site, the storehouse had been one of the Tower's more imposing constructions. Designed to contain three storeys, including the attic, some of which had been used as lodgings for the Tower guard, it had predominantly been used as the central weapons depository and was reputedly capable of holding sufficient arms and ammunition for 60,000 men. In addition it was also the primary depot for a potentially priceless collection of historical artefacts, ranging from banners, musical instruments and weaponry to the infamous devices used to torture prisoners. Of the estimated 100,000 stands of arms kept there, only 4,000 were saved. Among the greatest losses were the recently rediscovered rack and the Ordnance Survey's map office, after which the department was moved to Southampton.

The history of that particular part of the inner ward is intriguing. Prior to 1694, the area had served as the cemetery of the royal Chapel of St Peter ad Vincula, which to this day lies tucked away inside the north-west corner of the inner wall. What exactly had become of the remains of those who had been laid in rest in its consecrated ground at the time of the storehouse's construction remains unknown. Some believers in the paranormal have suggested that it was the disturbance of the area that led to a high level of supernatural activity in the years that followed. The clearing of the wreckage for the foundations of the storehouse's replacement led to the discovery of several bodies whose remains were later reinterred.

Work to replace the storehouse began later that same year with the Tower's constable, the legendary Arthur Wellesley, 1st Duke of Wellington, placing the foundation stone of what would in appearance command similar stature to its predecessor. In Wellington's honour, the new building was also named after his most outstanding military achievement. While the arsenal was moved to the White Tower, the three-storey Waterloo Barracks, completed in 1845, was designed to house the Tower's ever changing garrison, in addition to providing accommodation for members of staff and a number of offices and storerooms. Since the 1960s, it has also incorporated the Jewel House, which was relocated from the damaged Martin Tower.

Life at the Tower even ten years prior to the execution of Thistlewood and his key allies had been a far cry from that of its earlier days. No longer the cold place of incarceration of political prisoner and violent traitor alike, whose incessant groans had become the typical backdrop, the Tower's role as a depository of arms and munitions would continue beyond the end of the Napoleonic wars. Day-to-day life at the Tower evolved with a core acceptance that the ancient site's primary uses belonged more as a living museum rather than having relevance to modern military strategy. Similar was true of the Mint, the ordnances and the menagerie. So long co-existing as centrepieces, those three functions would soon be relocated to sites beyond the walls.

Security was always of paramount concern, but throughout the 1700s, just as had been true throughout its earlier history, regular breaches continued to occur. A particularly bad example was in 1798 when one of the garrison soldiers abandoned his professional responsibilities and entered the press room at the Mint, armed and in full uniform. Initially unperturbed by the presence of the soldier, the atmosphere changed after the AWOL guard threatened the staff and absconded with some 500 guineas of loose cash. Though the issue was largely dealt with internally, this strange event effectively marked the beginning of the end of the Tower's use as a depository for bullion. With the expansion of the Bank of England in the latter half of the eighteenth century occurring simultaneously with the City of London's growing evolution into banking and commerce, the Tower's long-time purpose as a stronghold for storing physical monetary deposits was gradually scaled down. In 1812, the Mint was finally moved after a series of boiler fires were viewed as a major risk to the wider fortress. With this, the former mint buildings were converted for use as barracks and storehouses and today serve primarily as homes for the yeoman warders.

Accelerating the rate of this largely predictable evolution was the personality of Arthur Wellesley himself. The menagerie, long celebrated as the Tower's main tourist attraction – at its prime the saying, 'going to see the lions,' became synonymous with visiting the Tower – was one of the main sources of unrest for the battle-hardened constable. Not least of his reservations was the behaviour, often outrageous, of some of the day trippers, whose antics included baiting the lions and feeding iron nails to the apparently iron-loving ostriches, resulting in the deaths of at least two of them.

By the time of Wellington's arrival as constable, there were signs that the menagerie was enduring a period of decline. Already a far cry from the site that had been founded as the royal menagerie in the thirteenth century, by 1805 it was recorded as having twenty-three animals, falling to just eight by 1821. The decline here seems all the more dramatic considering between 1704 and 1741 it had included six lions, two leopards – or possibly tigers – a bald eagle, at least two other eagles, two Swedish owls, two mountain cats, a jackal, a panther, a racoon, a porcupine, an ape, vultures, and some form of bird of prey. Writing in 1753, the anonymous author of *An Historical Description of the Tower of London and its Curiosities* included biographies of the lions, as well as an overview of the other animals kept there. Reasons for the decline are somewhat unclear; however, some insight can perhaps be gauged from a variety of unfortunate happenings, including a story from 1780 of a small boy being mauled to death by an excitable monkey and from the knowledge that revered scientist John Hunter had entered an agreement with the keeper to use the bodies of dead animals on which to perform scientific experiments.

Within a year of its seeming demise, however, the attraction enjoyed something of a revival with the appointment of new keeper, Alfred Cops. Among the early changes, Cops increased the collection to some forty mammals, including four bears, fourteen birds and a kangaroo, as well as over 100 reptiles. For Wellington, however, the constant threat of accidents loomed large. After Cops himself narrowly avoided strangulation by a snake, a cleaner was nearly mauled by a leopard before a wolf escaped captivity to cause chaos in the sergeants' apartments. The founding of the Zoological Society in 1826 saw the establishment of the new attraction at Regent's Park two years later and on the death of George IV, it was agreed the royal collections should be moved there. By 1835, exactly six centuries after the gifting of three leopards to Henry III, the Tower menagerie followed that of Windsor to what would later become London Zoo.

As the century progressed, so too did other changes, many of which successfully built on the work accomplished during the previous century. No longer a site concerned with the nation's money supply, jewels, animals and prisoners, it was decided instead that the armouries collections would be used as part of a bigger theme: one that would accelerate the Tower's transition into becoming a living testament to history. Within a decade or so of the menagerie's closure, this transition had entered its next phase, with visitor numbers reaching close to 100,000 per annum. Much to the dismay of Wellington himself, who abhorred the tourist boom and remained steadfast in his beliefs the garrison was of pivotal importance – not least his fear that allowing mass entry had the potential to be used as the catalyst of rebellion or unrest – revenue was also up, a fact largely attributable to the social range of the visitors. The destruction of the grand storehouse had already removed one of the key eyesores of the old castle and in 1858 the architecture of the Norman chapel of St John in the White Tower was finally once again revealed at the cost of removing the largely unorganised public record office to Chancery Lane. Further threat of insurrection saw a rare example of the Tower's defences being strengthened on the north side with the construction of the North Bastion between the Legge's and Brass Mounts and partly jutting out into the, now dry, moat, which had been drained in 1843 due to the overwhelming stench.

Inside the walls, redevelopment also continued. The fire in the Lanthorn Tower of 1774 had led to its complete destruction two years later, along with what remained of the royal gallery and the charred remnants of the old palace. A new three-storey building had previously been constructed to supersede the Irish Barracks in 1755, followed by a new ordnance office erected to replace the royal apartments, which was expanded after a second fire in July 1788. Rebuilding of the Lanthorn Tower in a medieval style was just one part of the master plan aimed at revamping the Tower to fit the new blueprint, a part of which required the subsequent demolition of the newer constructions. In contrast to the destruction of the Ordnance Office buildings, the task of rebuilding fell on the shoulders of renowned Victorian architect Anthony Salvin whose greatest achievements included restoration of the Cradle and Develin Towers, as well as construction of the 'Salvin Bridge' that now offers tourists a passage from St Thomas's Tower to the Wakefield. Outside the walls, the Tower Bridge at Iron Gate was designed to blend in with the Tower.

An IRA bomb attack on the Tower in January 1885 was part of a not so holy trinity intended to also cause havoc in Westminster Hall and the House of Commons. Despite the widespread security in place, Irish separatists succeeded initially in starting a fire on the first floor of the White Tower, injuring a handful of people but fortunately killing none. Already renowned for its dark connection with Catholic separatists and traitors, not least the imprisonment of the Jesuits and the torturing of Guy Fawkes some 250 years earlier, the attack was somewhat ironically the first successful Catholic-related plot to occur within the Tower's walls and the first to cause any physical harm.

Any worries Wellington and the authorities may have had concerning its reputation as a tourist attraction would prove unfounded, at least up until the commencement of hostilities with an old enemy. Having retained its garrison of several hundred soldiers and been used regularly to train civilian reservists, a fitting dress rehearsal for the problems that would follow came when the Tower soldiers were called out on New Year's Day 1911 to attend what became known as the Siege of Sidney Street. What began as an attempted burglary before leading to the murder of three policemen by Latvian anarchists was only quelled by the valour of the Scots Guard. With the troublemakers largely subdued, the event attracting national attention, it was at least a fitting testimony to the skills of the Tower's loyal soldiers that the ancient fortress was still prepared for combat. And so it would prove, between 1914 and 1918, when the Tower of London, so long having served as the nation's state prison, reopened its cells and closed its gates.

The most memorable of the Tower's German prisoners of war would also be the first. Born Carl Hans Lody in Berlin on 20 January 1877, Lody had grown up in the central region of the country before becoming a naval officer – apparently a reservist – and moving to the USA. A fluent English speaker, Lody had arrived in the UK under false pretences on the breakout of hostilities, his papers reading Charles Inglis. After spending some three weeks around Edinburgh and attempting to ascertain information on the Rosyth Naval Base, a Babington-style exchange with a Swedish contact came to the attention of the newly formed MI5. Realising he was in trouble, Lody managed to flee to Ireland where he was arrested and brought to London for court-martial. Found guilty of being a German spy, the night before his execution, he was transferred from the Wellington Barracks close to Buckingham Palace to the Tower. Ironically, the date was Guy Fawkes' Night.

The story of Lody's final hours are noteworthy for his bravery and conduct, something not missed by Tower personnel. Prior to his being marched from his cell in the guardroom of the casemates to the temporary rifle range located between the Martin and Constable Towers, Lody wrote moving letters to his family and to the officer at the Wellington Barracks, whom he praised for his professionalism. On being met by the assistant provost-marshal to be escorted to his place of execution, Lody is recorded as having greeted him with the words, 'I suppose that you will not care to shake hands with a German spy.'

'No,' the officer is recorded as having replied. 'But I will shake hands with a brave man.'

The doomed Lody was taken to the execution shed, seated in a wooden chair and blindfolded. There, at 6:00am on 6 November 1914, inside the East Casemates Rifle Range, the eight members of the execution squad took aim and fired. So passed the first prisoner to be put to death at the Tower since the Gordon Riots and the first of eleven German spies before Armistice.

Of those destined to join him, less information survives. On 23 June the following year Karl Friedrich Muller was executed in the Tower Rifle Range and just over a month later, Haike Marinus Petrus Jansson and Wilhelm J. Roos joined him at dawn on 30 July 1915 in the Tower Ditch. September saw the end of Ernst Waldemar Melin in the Tower Rifle Range, followed by Augusto Roggin, Fernando Buschman, George Traugott Breekow and Irvin Guy Ries on 17 September, 19 October, 26 October, and 27 October 1915 respectively. The 22-year-old Albert Meyer would be the penultimate German prisoner to be shot at the Tower on 2 December and finally Ludovico Zendery Hurwitz on 11 April 1916, again in the Tower Rifle Range.

After a year that had seen the Tower's haunting past seemingly repeat itself, it seems only fitting it would also witness its first escapee since those of two centuries earlier. In 1916, a young officer was brought to the Tower and accommodated somewhere in the East Casemates. Unlike the spies and POWs before and, possibly, alongside him, the man had been charged with offences related to being unable to honour his cheques due to insufficient funds in his account. The man was clearly attentive to everything around him, as was proved when he nonchalantly passed the distracted guard outside his quarters and marched through the main gate, honoured with the salutes of unsuspecting personnel. Catching the Underground at the original Tower Hill Tube Station – then named Mark Lane Tube Station – the mystery man subsequently dined sumptuously in the West End, paying for his dinner with another fraudulent cheque. Curiously, he decided to return to the Tower, discovering to no great surprise his actions had caused considerable consternation. Of his background, nothing is known. The only reference concerning the man is Subaltern.

Of far greater importance that year was the imprisonment of the controversial Irishman Sir Roger Casement. Born in Dublin and later a diplomat, Casement had been knighted for his bravery in exposing the mistreatment of many UK colonists in Africa and South America, before he ran into trouble in 1916 after attempting to convince Irish POWs in the British Army to fight for Germany in a bid to liberate Ireland from UK rule. Shipped back to Ireland on a German U-boat with a guaranteed small offering of arms following on a separate boat disguised as a Norwegian trawler, the treacherous humanitarian was almost drowned when his dinghy capsized. Questioned by a local policeman, the exhausted and soaked Casement awaited the trawler in heavy rain, when he accidentally dropped a German train ticket. A search of his baggage culminated in his arrest.

Interrogated initially in Ireland and later Scotland Yard, on being brought to the Tower and being harboured in the Casemates, he twice failed with suicide attempts motivated by a combination of his deteriorating circumstances and on learning that the highly ambitious Easter risings had been mercilessly subdued. Tattered and ill from confinement in his cell under the constant watch of at least two guards, he was brought to trial at the Old Bailey. During the trial a police search of his flat in London 'discovered' the so-called 'black diaries'. Inspired by that, notably on learning that the contents indicated that while in Peru and the Congo Casement regularly participated in sexual encounters with young black men for money – at the time homosexuality was a criminal offence even without the monetary issue – the police passed on the discoveries to the prosecution team, who, in an extraordinary show of goodwill, in turn informed the defence counsel. On discussing the diaries with Casement himself, the Irishman's response was bizarre: apparently arguing that 'filthy and disreputable practices and the rhapsodic glorification of them were inseparable from the true genius' and that a given list of truly great men would back up the claim. Torn between making the diaries public, thus losing Casement credibility in the eyes of the people but potentially saving his life on grounds of insanity, the lawyer kept the matter to himself.

Sentenced to death and becoming the first British knight to be deprived of his knighthood since the 1600s, a sentence he gladly received, Casement was returned to the Tower. As his well-wishers both home and abroad endeavoured to secure a reprieve, or at least imprisonment in lieu of death in respect of his earlier humanitarian work, a government smear campaign, centring around the release of the diaries, saw public esteem for the would-be martyr plummet. Whether the claims in the diary of his sexuality and, in particular, his participation in acts of sexual depravity were based on truth or an invention, the world will likely never know. Arrogant in his views that the government feared hanging him in case it should encourage an uprising, Casement was transferred to Pentonville Prison and on 3 August 1916 was led to the prison scaffold. Reciting a speech, in some ways comparable to that of Mary, Queen of Scots, that he had only intended to serve his country, he went to his death. According to his confessor, Father Carey, he 'feared not death' and marched out to the gallows not a dishevelled madman, but 'with the dignity of a prince'. Some forty years later the black diaries were finally revealed to the world in their entirety. To this day debate continues regarding their authenticity.

Successful conclusion of peace talks with the German government and the subsequent Treaty of Versailles ended the Tower's four-year return as a place of captivity, following which the doors were once again opened to the sightseers. This would change briefly in 1937 with an event that, in its own way, helped set the scene for the six-year conflict that would follow. The prisoner on this occasion was a British one, albeit one with Nazi sympathies. His name was Norman Baillie-Stewart.

Dubbed the Officer in the Tower, Scottish-descended Baillie-Stewart had already faced court-martial at Chelsea Barracks in 1933 after being caught selling secrets to foreign powers following a romance with a German woman. Convicted of seven of the ten charges against him, he was imprisoned for five years, at the start of which he was transferred to the Tower. After his eventual release and relocation to Austria, he found fame as a Nazi radio propagandist. It has become widely assumed that it was Baillie-Stewart's over-the-top, highly aristocratic way of speaking that coined the phrase, 'Lord Haw-Haw on the wireless.'

Two years after Baillie-Stewart's release from Maidstone, the Nazi invasion of Poland once again saw the closure of the Tower's gates. With the ancient walls again prepared to harbour political prisoners, the Crown Jewels were moved; new evidence has it to somewhere below Buckingham Palace or Windsor Castle. The drained moat, once regarded as the cesspit of England, had become unsurprisingly fertile over the years and used during the Dig for Victory campaign. Over the course of the next six years, fifteen bombs, three missiles and several incendiaries struck the Tower, destroying the North Bastion and scaring or killing all but one of the resident ravens. With this, the old prophecy was ironically fulfilled.

Unlike the previous conflict with Germany, the Tower's role in the Second World War was somewhat limited. Whereas Nazi POWs are known to have been hanged in London, William the Conqueror's castle was used for just one Nazi-related execution. Taking place on 15 August 1941, the man in question was a former dentist named Josef Jakobs. At the time of writing, Jakobs remains the last man to date to be executed inside the old walls.

Before he followed the doomed Lody and associates to the East Casemates Rifle Range, Corporal Jakobs had been apprehended in January that year after breaking his ankle during a parachute drop into rural Cambridgeshire. So bad was his situation, being injured in a remote field in the middle of winter, Jakobs had been forced to open fire in order to attract attention. In doing so, however, a series of questions inevitably followed. Even now the exact nature of his mission and expertise is unclear. Trained in the arts of espionage and having experience of the German meteorological service, Jakobs argued he was little more than a weatherman, yet being found equipped with a modern, long-range radio transmitter, maps of the local area, false papers and counterfeit money has inevitably drawn this into question. The condition of his injuries, leading to him being brought in for hospital treatment, nevertheless proved insufficient in preventing him from being questioned, during which he maintained that he was part Jewish of Luxembourg birth and had arrived in Britain after making a desperate bid to flee the Nazis. Unconvinced what they heard was the whole truth, Jakobs's examiners handed him over to the military authorities, after which he was held in Brixton prison. As the truth of his background became clear – he had actually renounced his Luxembourg citizenship to serve in the German Army and helped several Jews escape by charging exorbitant fees – he was tried in secret and convicted of a number of crimes that included being a spy and a saboteur. Originally sentenced to be hanged, the situation with his shattered ankle served to complicate proceedings. The sentence was changed to death by firing squad and Jakobs transferred to one of the only places in the city that could accommodate such an execution: the Tower. Carried into the rifle range on a stretcher, he was dispatched by a detachment of the Scots Guards, his bullet-ridden wooden chair passing into Tower history.

Around the time of Jakobs's execution, the Tower hosted one of its final, yet also most famous, prisoners. Deputy Reichsführer to Adolf Hitler, Rudolf Hess had begun his mysterious one-man mission to the UK with a parachute jump over rural Scotland. After being well treated by a local family, Hess was arrested, possibly claiming that he was seeking to negotiate a secret peace treaty. He was taken to London and transferred to the Tower.

In total, Hess spent around four days at the Tower, enjoying the 'charming' hospitality of the Queen's House. Impressed by the drill of the garrison's soldiers, the non-repentant Nazi was ushered away, but not before giving an autograph to a curious beefeater, at which time he apparently learned of his location. He saw out the war at a number of safe houses before being tried on war crimes at Nuremberg where he was sentenced to life in prison.

Victory for the Allied Forces was eventually secured, and with it the liberation of the large number of POWs who had lived a relatively quiet existence in the Tower, the majority of whom appear to have been kept in the relatively modern areas, including the New Armouries block that now serves as a restaurant. Like Jakobs, the majority had been caught after attempting to enter the country by parachute; others had been captured in the English Channel after several weeks aboard a German U-Boat.

With the war over, it could have easily come to pass that the Tower's association with imprisonment and terror would come to an end, but two more stories were yet to be told. After deserting National Service in the Royal Fusiliers, and punching a corporal, the infamous Ronnie and Reggie Kray later assaulted a policeman and were held in the Tower as punishment for their crimes. According to the man responsible for their arrest, one of the brothers asked for permission to remove the handcuffs in order to say goodbye to their mother. Reluctantly agreeing, the twins were soon back in chains, apparently on the orders of their mother not to attempt to escape, undoubtedly much to the man's relief. For a week in 1952, the pair occupied the Waterloo Barracks' sister cells either side of the famous clock after which the Tower's long history as a prison ended.

Since July 1974, when another bombing, again believed to have been the work of the IRA, once again shook the foundations of the White Tower, killing one and injuring over forty, no further harm has come to the Tower. With this, the active history of the great citadel one could argue has at last come full circle. What began with the imprisonment of the slippery Flambard may well have ended with the imprisonment and subsequent release of a different kind of gangster; and what began with the violent conquest of a foreigner also ends with the subduing of one. In truth, the Tower's story leaves us with a bizarre irony. Had the lion-emblazoned Normans never conquered the raven-symbolled Vikings, the Tower would never have been built. Thanks to William's victory, the ravens in turn may just have conquered time itself. Through it all, the Tower continues to represent the heart of the English nation and its proud history. And to this very day, both stand proudly undefeated.

Appendix I

List of Locations Within the Tower

The White Tower – 1078–1100s
The Wardrobe Tower – 1100s (now destroyed)
The Royal Apartments – 1100s–1600s (now destroyed)
The Bell Tower – 1190s–1210s
The Lion Tower and the Royal Menagerie – 1200s–70s (now destroyed)
The Coldharbour Gate Tower – 1238–70s (now destroyed)
The Blundeville (later, the Wakefield) Tower – 1238–70s
The Lanthorn Tower – 1238–70s
The Byward Tower – 1238–70s
The Middle Tower – 1238–70s
The Salt Tower – 1238–70s
The Martin Tower – 1238–70s
Robyn the Devil's (later, the Devereux) Tower – 1238–70s
The Flint Tower – 1238–70s
The Brick Tower – 1238–70s
The Constable Tower – 1238–70s
The Broad Arrow Tower – 1238–70s
The Bowyer Tower – 1238–70s
The Garden (later, the Bloody) Tower – 1238–70s
St Thomas's Tower (and below it, Traitors' Gate) – 1275–79
The Well Tower – 1275–79
The Beauchamp Tower – 1275–81
The Develin Tower – 1282
The Cradle Tower – 1360–77
Legge's Mount – 1275–85
Brass Mount – 1275–85
Chapel Royal of St Peter ad Vincula – original chapel built prior to the Norman Conquest; rebuilt 1519
Lieutenant's Lodgings – 1200s (rebuilt in around 1530 and later renamed Queen's House)
North-Bastion 1848

Appendix II

The Tower's Ghost Stories

Synonymous throughout history as the ultimate penalty for prisoners, incarceration in the Tower is known to have been experienced by no less than 8,000 different people. Many of those who suffered its walls never returned to life beyond them. Those who did, often did so without their head!

It is surely no surprise that the Tower has long been reputed as the most haunted castle in the United Kingdom.

Close to 3,000,000 people pass through the gates each year, the majority of whom leave after a pleasant experience being captivated by tales of the Tower's bloody history. But when night falls and the gates are locked, an eerie silence is said to fall throughout the castle. Portentous mists are reported to appear without warning and the echo of faint ghostly chanting has been heard drifting through the corridors of the Queen's House. Dogs are said to refuse to enter the thirteenth-century Salt Tower, which is one of many to have long been plagued by the sounds of footsteps. One former yeoman warder went as far as to make the claim of nearly being throttled by an invisible presence while on duty in that tower.

E. L. Swifte, keeper of the Crown Jewels in the nineteenth century, recorded his own experience of what must be considered among the most disturbing hauntings ever to have occurred at the Tower. While dining by candlelight one evening in the Martin Tower with his family, his wife was most distressed to gaze upon a strange cylindrical object resembling a glass tube, filled with a bubbling blue fluid and seemingly floating through the air. The mysterious apparition subsequently hovered around his wife, who was frozen with fear at the table. On attempting to rid their lodgings of this strange spectre, Swifte proceeded to hurl a chair at the translucent image, only to see it pass straight through. The cylinder, alas, receded into the wall, never to be seen again. The sighting is of particularly curious note considering the 'Wizard Earl' of Northumberland, Henry Percy, had once used that tower to conduct scientific experiments. Northumberland's ghost is also reputed to haunt that tower as well as the nearby wall walk.

The cylindrical orb would not be the only anomaly Swifte wrote about. A sentry on guard, also in the Martin Tower, is recorded as having witnessed the apparition of a bear emerging from the Jewel Room. Unnerved by the sight, the guard attempted to stab the animal with his bayonet, only to see it pass straight through and become implanted in a door as the bear disappeared in front of him. The sentry sadly died a few days later, possibly from shock, but he had already confided in Swifte and another sentry who verified his story. The sighting has been dated to January 1815 and, surprising as it may sound, is not without validity. As mentioned throughout the book, going back as far as the thirteenth century, a menagerie was established at the Tower with many animals housed in the appropriately named Lion Tower.

The first reported sighting of a human ghost at the Tower was Thomas Becket – once archbishop of Canterbury. Becket, who was famously murdered inside Canterbury Cathedral after four knights acted on the loose words of Henry II, 'who will rid me of this turbulent priest,' allegedly appeared during construction of the water gate around 1240, and, apparently unhappy at its development, reduced it to rubble with a single strike of his crosier. The king at the time was Henry III, grandson of the man ultimately responsible for Becket's death. Fearing any further wrath of the murdered cleric, Henry III wasted no time dedicating the building and a chapel within to Saint Thomas as a mark of respect for the archbishop. This must have pleased Becket's ghost because no further interruptions were reported during the construction of the wall.

One of the most infamous moments in the Tower's dark history, as mentioned prominently in the book, took place in the late summer of 1483. The Wars of the Roses had shed the blood of many of those of the Houses of York and Lancaster as both laid their respective claims on the throne. In order to protect King Edward V, and his brother Richard, Duke of York, their uncle, Richard, Duke of Gloucester, is believed to have housed them in the Bloody Tower.

As discussed in the book, the princes were later declared illegitimate by an act of parliament, *Titlus Regius*, and Richard took over as king, leaving his nephews to live in the Tower. For several weeks the young boys were seen playing together on the battlements; however, shortly after, they vanished from history. Since that time their fate has remained unknown, at least until 1674 when the Tower workmen made their disturbing discovery while carrying out renovations on the White Tower. What they found was a chest containing the skeletons of two children. Charles II assumed them to be the remains of the princes, and the bones were given a royal burial in Westminster Abbey.

Whether the princes were killed on the orders of the man later to be crowned Richard III, history can never be sure, but their youthful spirits have reputedly been seen playing on the battlements, as they did before they disappeared. Similar stories are true concerning the interior of their reputed lodgings. According to one account, guards at the Tower in the late fifteenth century, passing the Bloody Tower, spotted two small figures gliding down the stairs wearing the same white nightshirts the princes often dressed in. They stood silently, hand in hand, before fading back into the stonework. These figures were identified as the ghosts of the two princes and are apparently still seen from time to time, clinging to each other in death as they did in life.

Of all the spirits believed to reside within the castle, the most persistent must be that of Queen Anne Boleyn. Accused of treason after failing with four attempts at giving birth to a boy, Anne was taken to Tower Green and beheaded on 19 May 1536. As with Jane Seymour and Catherine Howard, she was buried, initially in an unmarked grave, before her remains were reinterred beneath the altar of the royal chapel of St Peter ad Vincula – her head tucked underneath her arm.

Visitors to the chapel often describe it as being a sad place, and are overwhelmed by a sense of unbearable despair. The reason for the sombre oppression is possibly due to the circumstances regarding the deceased. Out of the sixty-three who rest there, only nine do so with their heads on. Queen Anne is believed to often return to the chapel and has been seen floating across the floor to her final resting place, as well as leading a ghostly procession of lords and ladies down the aisle of the chapel, before disappearing into thin air. A captain of the guards is also reported to have once seen a lone candle burning inside the locked chapel in the dead of night.

Of all the apparent spirits said to haunt the Tower, there is no doubt Anne's is among the most baffling. Over the years she has appeared headless, with her head and also with her head under her arm. Sometimes, usually around the time of her anniversary, she is reported to have appeared, with her head, near the Queen's House, close to the site where her execution was carried out. Her headless body has also been seen walking the corridors of the Tower. A spectre described as 'a lovely veiled lady that, upon closer look, proves to have a black void where her face should be,' may be the apparition of Anne Boleyn. Though there could be other candidates.

The ill-deserved death of Lady Jane Grey is another tragic story associated with the gloomy history of the Tower. Great-granddaughter of Henry VII, she was queen between 10 and 19 July 1553, her minuscule reign ending in the ultimate penalty. On 12 February 1957 she was reportedly seen by two witnesses, near the site of her execution. The date was also of significance as it was the anniversary of her death. She was described as a 'white shape forming itself on the battlements.'

The Beauchamp Tower at night is reputed to be particularly mournful in ambience. Among its ghosts is Lady Jane's husband, Guildford Dudley, who has been seen with tears flowing down his face, his sighs heard long into the night. A ghostly cavalier has also been seen marching the battlements.

The legendary adventurer, and sometime favourite of Queen Elizabeth I, Sir Walter Raleigh lived a relatively comfortable life within the walls of the Bloody Tower. Modern-day visitors can today see the main room furnished as it likely would have been during his incarceration. He was executed by James I for treason, and has been seen looking exactly as he does in his famous portraits. It is also rumoured that it is the headless spirit of Sir Walter that appears in chains, screaming in agony, near to where he once was housed, though in the view of this author there are probably better candidates. Incidentally, while his body is thought to lie in Westminster, his head has been missing since his execution and may have been kept by his wife.

A similar story involves the infamous gunpowder plotter, Guy Fawkes, whose ghost reportedly appeared in the Council Chamber for many years after his execution. His screams and cries of anguish as he endured the torturers have often been heard.

A memorial on Tower Green offers a trivial reminder of the unfortunate souls executed on the site over the centuries. Anne Boleyn is said to join Lady Jane Grey in haunting the vicinity, and another particularly active spirit said to appear there is Margaret Pole, Countess of Salisbury, who returns to the site in dramatic and alarming fashion. As recorded earlier in the book, hers is surely among the most horrific executions to have taken place at the castle when, at the age of 67, she became an undeserving victim of Henry VIII due to her son, Cardinal Reginald Pole, having criticised the king's right to be head of the Church in England. With the cardinal settled comfortably in France, Henry had Margaret brought to the block on 27 May 1541, thus eliminating one of the last of the direct Plantagenets. When told by the executioner to kneel, to which she sneered, 'So should traitors do and I am none,' she proceeded to duck the executioner's axe and attempted to sprint from the block. After a comical scene in which the brave and screaming countess was pursued around the scaffold, she was eventually hewn to death. The shameful spectacle has apparently been repeated several times on the anniversary of her death, as her screaming phantom continues to be hunted throughout eternity by a ghostly executioner. Similarly, her death is said to have been replayed on the walls of the White Tower with the chilling and ethereal shadow of a great axe seen falling through the darkness.

In 1864 yet another famous haunting was apparently witnessed inside the castle, this time by a soldier guarding the Queen's House. The soldier claimed to have seen an apparition so real that he called out to it. After the soldier's three challenges went without response, he charged at the prowler with his bayonet. To his surprise, like the bear, the bayonet went straight through the figure and the soldier was later found on the concrete, passed out in shock. He was initially court-martialled for neglecting his duty, only to be later cleared by two other witnesses.

Anne is not the only wife of Henry VIII whose spirit is believed to still reside at the Tower. Catherine Howard, beheaded on Henry's orders after being found guilty of infidelity with at least one other man, has apparently been seen frequenting the area where she awaited execution. Incidentally, her spirit is far more famous for haunting Hampton Court Palace, where she has been witnessed reliving the moment of her escape from her room before running down the hallway screaming for Henry's mercy, only to be caught by the guards and taken back.

Built by Henry III for his private apartments, the foreboding Wakefield Tower boasts the thickest walls of all the towers bar the White Tower. Within these walls, the throne room has a reputation for being haunted by Henry VI, who was reportedly murdered around midnight on 21 May 1471. If the words of one of the chroniclers is correct, it was as he knelt at prayer 'the knife with which he was stikk'd full of deadly holes' was wielded by the duke of Gloucester – later the infamous Richard III. On the anniversary of his murder, the apparition of the king is reputed to appear around midnight pacing across the Wakefield Tower until, upon the last stroke of twelve, he fades slowly into the stonework.

Being the oldest and largest of the castle's towers, it is hardly surprising the White Tower is associated with the most hauntings. Within its snaking stone corridors dwells the entity of a lady wearing a long white dress. She has been seen standing by one of the windows, even waving to a group of children in the building opposite. A peculiar smell of perfume resonates around the entrance to St John's Chapel; the scent has been described as being overwhelming and sickly. Whether this really offers evidence for the life of Maud Fitzwalter, one can only speculate. No story of the origin for the mysterious lady has yet been found.

The gallery in the White Tower where Henry VIII's fine but flattering suit of armour is exhibited is a curious area, described by several guards as giving rise to a terrible crushing phenomenon that suddenly descends upon them as they enter, only to lift inexplicably as soon as they leave. A guard patrolling through the armoury one stormy night was unnerved by the sudden sensation that someone had thrown a heavy cloak over him. As he struggled to free himself, the garment was seized from behind and pulled tight around his throat by his phantom attacker. Managing to break free from its sinister grasp, he sprinted to the guardroom. Evidence of the surreal attack was confirmed as marks upon his neck exhibited vivid indication of his wounds.

On another eerie occasion a guard named Arthur Crick decided to rest as he made his rounds. As he sat on a window ledge, he removed his right shoe only to find himself in a state of shock seconds later when a startling voice behind him whispered, 'There's only you and I here.' Alarmed by the voice from the darkness, he made away sharply with the likewise response, 'Just let me get this bloody shoe on and there'll only be you!'

With its sinister silhouette standing tall over the London horizon, the Tower certainly lives up to its reputation as the place of 'ultimate penalty'. Other strange sightings include the ghostly procession of phantom funeral carriages carrying the unfortunate victims of the Tower to their final place of rest. On a dark and misty night in 1941, as the Blitz rained down on London, one unfortunate sentry called out 'Halt! Who goes there?' only to be passed by four guards in fourteenth-century uniform carrying a litter. A blood-red patch was visible under the sheet where a head should have been. Upon clear sight of which, the ghostly procession faded into the darkness.

Appendix III

The Ravens' Conspiracy

Popular among modern-day visitors as an indispensable part of Tower folklore, exactly when the ravens first made their presence known within the walls is unrecorded. That the origin of such tales goes back to William the Conqueror is sadly almost certainly a fallacy; the same may well be true concerning the story of astronomer John Flamsteed. Evidence concerning any conversation between Charles II and Flamsteed mentioned earlier in the book is difficult to verify indisputably. It does, however, fit well with the known facts that the first stone of Greenwich Observatory was laid in August 1675.

Concerning the acquisition of ravens with the intention of being kept permanently in the inner ward, historians are on a far sounder footing. Somewhat disappointingly, accounts show that ravens have only been kept purposely at the Tower since around 1880 and have been loved as pets ever since. Among the members of the yeoman warders, one is specifically assigned the role of ravenmaster, and is assisted in his daily duties by at least one other.

While the relatively modern inclusion of the ravens in the inner ward can perhaps be attributed to the Tower's developing reputation in Victorian melodrama, this partially ignores the fact that wild ravens are known to have appeared in the area well before that time. Dating the beginning of the ravens' time in London or England as a whole is now impossible – more than likely the patterns begin before history itself – yet concerning chronicled history, as far back to the time of the Peasants' Revolt and the Great Fire of London, conspiracies of ravens are known to have flocked together, often feasting on the bodies of the dead.

Throughout history, it has often been remarked how the croaking of a raven has come to be associated with prophecies of doom. For reasons such as this it has always struck this author that the legend of the Tower and the ravens is a strange one. Famed as harbingers of doom, stories dating back to the Roman statesman Cicero tell of a raven entering his chambers shortly prior to his death. Similarly, the executions of Anne Boleyn and Lady Jane Grey are just two events in the Tower's history known to have been watched over by gatherings of the demonic creatures. Why exactly in the Tower's case the reverse is also true, the ravens instead being integral to its survival, is a mystery in itself. Whether the legend is true, of course, remains untested.

Some things are better left that way.

The Ceremony of the Keys

With origins some have claimed go back as far as 1280, the Ceremony of the Keys is famous worldwide not only as one of the world's oldest ceremonies but, even more astonishingly, for being the longest uninterrupted daily military ritual in existence. Unsurprisingly, it is also the most famous formal custom to take place at the Tower.

Whether or not there is any historical evidence for the date mentioned, tradition that some form of locking–up observance has been in existence since the Middle Ages is easily found. It seems likely one of the catalysts for this might well have been the episode during the reign of Edward III when he entered the castle without being questioned, leading to the creation of the Cradle Tower and the punishment of the negligent few. Written instructions for the keys to be left in a safe place can be confidently dated to Tudor times, which may indicate the ceremony evolved around that time. Similarly, the restructuring of the Tower military by the duke of Wellington could also have played a part.

Regardless of its exact point of origin, the ceremony that takes place today is identical on a daily basis. Led by the chief yeoman warder – or alternatively his deputy, the yeoman gaoler, or one of the four yeoman sarjeants – at precisely 21:53 and a certain number of seconds – the exact amount depending on who leads the ceremony that night – the chief leaves the Byward Tower dressed in his Tudor watchcoat and matching bonnet and carrying a lantern. On making his way down Water Lane, he collects his four man military escort from the archway of the Bloody Tower – passing the lantern to the soldier who marches without a rifle as he does so – and, with the company of one other yeoman warder, proceeds to lock the outer and inner gates. As the party marches back along Water Lane, a sentry on duty close to the Wakefield Tower offers the challenge: 'Halt! Who comes here?' to which, the chief will reply, 'The keys.' On being asked, 'Whose keys?' and receiving the answer, 'Queen Elizabeth's Keys,' the challenger will back down, remarking, 'Pass Queen Elizabeth's keys. All is well.'

The march resumed, the party continues through the archway of the Bloody Tower to where at least seven members of the Tower Guard line up on the Broadwalk to await them. On being commanded to a halt, the leader of the escort will cry out, 'God preserve Queen Elizabeth,' to a response of 'Amen,' as the clock strikes ten. There, the duty drummer sounds the 'last post' on his bugle as the chief takes the keys to the Queen's House. Interestingly, only once in its history has the ceremony been noted as finishing late, the night in question being affected by the interference of a German bomb dropped nearby. The ceremony has never been cancelled and occurs every day of the year, including Christmas and Easter when the Tower is closed for visitors.

An interesting side note concerns another ceremony that takes place daily. Known as the Ceremony of the Word, in this, the latest officer of the Tower guard and his escort descend on the Byward Tower at 15:00 to receive the new password. The word is imperative for after hours entry and movement. Attempted re-admittance without it could cause a Tower dweller to be either arrested or face the prospect of spending the night outside the walls.

Select Bibliography

Abbott, G., *A Beefeater's Grisly Guide to the Tower of London*, Hendon Mill, Nelson, Lancashire: Hendon Publishing, 2003

——, *Ghosts of the Tower of London*, London: William Heinemann, 1980

——, *Great Escapes from the Tower of London*, Hendon Mill, Nelson, Lancashire: Hendon Publishing, 1988

——, *Mysteries of the Tower of London*, Hendon Mill, Nelson, Lancashire: Hendon Publishing, 1998

——, *Tortures of the Tower of London*, Newton Abbot & London: David & Charles, 1986

Ackroyd, Peter, *The Life of Thomas More*, London: Vintage, 1999

Anon., *Chronicle of London, from 1089 to 1483*, London: 1827, reprinted Felinfach, Llanerch, 1995

Archer, Rowena E., Walker, Simon (eds), *Rulers and Ruled in Late Medieval England: Essays Presented to Gerald Harriss*, London and Rio Grande, Ohio: The Hambledon Press, 1995

Barker, Juliet, *Agincourt: The King, the Campaign, the Battle*, London: Little, Brown Book Group, 2015

Bartlett, Robert, *England under the Norman and Angevin Kings 1075–1225 (New Oxford History of England)*, Oxford: Clarendon Press, 2000

Barlow, Frank, *William Rufus (The English Monarchs Series)*, New Haven and London: Yale University Press, 2000

Bayley, John Whitcomb, *The History and Antiquities of the Tower of London: With Memoirs of Royal and Distinguished Persons, Deduced from Records, State-papers, and Manuscripts, and from other Original and Authentic Sources*, London: T. Cadell, 1825

Beer, Anna, *Patriot or Traitor: The Life and Death of Sir Walter Raleigh*, London: OneWorld Publications, 2018

Bell, Walter George, *The Tower of London*, London: Bodley Head, 1921

Blackmore, H. L., *The Armouries of the Tower of London: I Ordnance*, London: HMSO, 1976

Botolph, Charles, Joseph Stourton, and Baron Mowbray, *The History of the Noble House of Stourton, of Stourton, in the County of Wilts*, London: Elliot Stock, 1899

Borman, Tracy, *Henry VIII and the Men who Made Him: The Secret History Behind the Tudor Throne*, London: Hodder & Stoughton, 2018

———, *Thomas Cromwell: The Untold Story of Henry VIII's most Faithful Servant*, London: Hodder & Stoughton, 2014

Bradbury, Jim, *Stephen and Matilda: The Civil War of 1139–53*, Stroud, Gloucestershire: The History Press, 2005

Britton, John and Edward Wedlake Brayley, *Memoirs of the Tower of London: Comprising Historical and Descriptive Accounts of that National Fortress and Palace: Anecdotes of State Prisoners, of the Armouries, Jewels, Regalia, Records, Menagerie, &c*, London: Hurst, Chance, and Co., St Paul's Churchyard, 1830

Brooke-Hunt, Violet, *Prisoners of the Tower of London: Being an Account of some who at Divers Times Lay Captive within its Walls*, London: Dent, 1910

Brown, Michael, *James I (The Stewart Dynasty in Scotland)*, East Linton: Tuckwell Press, 2000

Caldwell, Anderson, *The Tower of London*, New Word City Inc, 2017

Camm, Bede, *Forgotten Shrines: an Account of Some Old Catholic Halls and Families in England, and of Relics and Memorials of the English Martyrs*, London: MacDonald & Evans, 1910

Carlton, Charles, *Archbishop William Laud*, London: Routledge, 1987

Carpenter, D. A., *The Minority of Henry III*, Berkeley and Los Angeles: University of California Press, 1990

———, *The Struggle for Mastery: Britain 1066–1284*, Oxford: Oxford University Press, 2003

———, *The Reign of Henry III*, London and Rio Grande, Ohio: The Hambledon Press, 1996

Castor, Helen, *Blood & Roses – The Paston Family and the Wars of the Roses*, London: Faber & Faber, 2005

———, *Elizabeth I (Penguin Monarchs): A Study in Insecurity*, London: Penguin, 2018

———, *She-Wolves: The Women Who Ruled England Before Elizabeth*, London: Faber & Faber, 2011

Chandler, David, *Sedgemoor 1685: From Monmouth's Invasion to the Bloody Assizes (Spellmount Classics)*, Staplehurst: Spellmount, 1999

Charlton, John (editor), *The Tower of London: Its Buildings and Institutions*, London: HMSO, 1978

Cogswell, Thomas, *James I (Penguin Monarchs): The Phoenix King*, London: Phoenix, 2017

Cook, Alan, *Edmond Halley: Charting the Heavens and the Seas*, Oxford: Clarendon Press, 1998

Craig, John, *The Mint: A History of the London Mint from AD 287 to 1948*, Cambridge: Cambridge University Press, 1953

Danziger, Danny, Gillingham, John, *1215: The Year of Magna Carta*, London: Hodder and Stoughton, 2004

Davis, John Paul, *Pity for the Guy: A Biography of Guy Fawkes*, London and Chicago: Peter Owen Publishers, 2010

——, *The Gothic King: A Biography of Henry III*, London and Chicago: Peter Owen Publishers, 2013

Diehl, Daniel, Donnelly, Mark P., *Tales from the Tower of London*, Stroud, Gloucestershire: The History Press, 2006

De Ros, Lord William, *Memorials of the Tower of London*, London: John Murray, 1866

Dixon, William Hepworth, *Her Majesty's Tower*, New York: Harper & Brothers Publishers, 1869

Dockray, Keith, *Henry VI, Margaret of Anjou and the Wars of the Roses: From Contemporary Chronicles, Letters and Records*, Stroud: Fonthill Media Ltd, 2016

Doherty, Paul, *The Great Crown Jewels Robbery of 1303: A Gripping Insight into an Infamous Robbery* London: Headline, 2005

Dudgeon, Jeffrey, *Roger Casement: The Black Diaries: With a Study of his Background, Sexuality, and Irish Political Life*, Belfast: Belfast Press, 2016

Edwards, John, *Mary I: England's Catholic Queen (The English Monarchs Series)*, New Haven and London: Yale University Press, 2011

Ffoulkes, Charles John, *Arms and the Tower*, London: Murray, 1939

Fissel, Mark Charles, *The Bishops' Wars: Charles I's Campaigns against Scotland, 1638–1640*, Cambridge: Cambridge University Press, 1994

Foxe, John, and Charles Augustus Goodrich, *Book of Martyrs: Or, a History of the Lives, Sufferings, and Triumphant Deaths of the Primitive as well as Protestant Martyrs*, Cincinnati: Roff and Young, 1831

Fraser, Antonia, *Cromwell, Our Chief Of Men*, London: Phoenix, 2002

——, *The Gunpowder Plot: Terror and Faith in 1605*, London: Phoenix, 2002

——, *King Charles II*, London: Phoenix, 2002

——, *The Six Wives of Henry VIII*, London: Phoenix, 2002

Fry, Plantagenet Somerset, *The Tower of London: Cauldron of Britain's Past*, London: Quiller Press, 1990

Gerard, John, *John Gerard: The Autobiography of an Elizabethan*, Translated by Philip Caraman, London: Longmans, Green & Co, 1951

Gillingham, John, *Richard I (The English Monarchs Series)*, New Haven and London: Yale University Press, 1999

——, *The Wars of the Roses: Peace & Conflict in 15th Century England*, London: Phoenix, 2001

Gower, Lord Ronald Sutherland, *The Tower of London Vols 1-2*, London: G. Bell and Sons, 1901

Gristwood, Sarah, *Arbella: England's Lost Queen*, London: Bantam Press, 2004

Hahn, Daniel, *The Tower Menagerie: The Amazing 600-Year History of the Royal Collection of Wild and Ferocious Beasts Kept at the Tower of London*, London: Simon and Schuster, 2003

Hallam, Dr Elizabeth (General Editor), *Chronicles of the Age of Chivalry: The Plantagenet Dynasty from 1216 to 1377: Henry III and the Three Edwards, the*

Era of the Black Prince and the Black Death, London: Salamander Books Ltd., 2002

——, *The Plantagenet Chronicles: Medieval Europe's most Tempestuous Family, Henry II and his Wife, Eleanor of Aquitaine, Richard the Lionheart, and his Brother King John, Seen through the Eyes of their Contemporaries*, London: Salamander Books Ltd., 2002

Hancock, Peter A., *Richard III and the Murder in the Tower*, Stroud, Gloucestershire: The History Press, 2011

Hanrahan, David, *Colonel Blood: The Man Who Stole the Crown Jewels*, Stroud: Gloucestershire: Sutton Publishing, 2004

Haynes, Alan, *The Elizabethan Secret Services*, Stroud, Gloucestershire: Sutton Publishing, 2004

——, *The Gunpowder Plot*, Stroud, Gloucestershire: Sutton Publishing, 2005

Hennings, Margaret A., *England Under Henry III: Illustrated from Contemporary Sources*, London: Longmans, Green and Co., 1924

Henry, David, *An Historical Description of the Tower of London and its Curiosities*, London: J Newbery, 1755

Hewitt, John, *The Tower: Its History, Armouries, and Antiquities*, London: 1841

Hibbert, Christopher, *King Mob: The Story of Lord George Gordon and the Riots of 1780*, London: Longman's, Green & Co, 1958

Hicks, Michael, *Richard III*, Stroud, Gloucestershire: Tempus, 2003

Historic Royal Palaces Tower of London, *Prisoners of the Tower*, Hampton Court Palace, Surrey: Historic Royal Palaces, 2004

Hogge, Alice, *God's Secret Agents: Queen Elizabeth's Forbidden Priests and the Hatching of the Gunpowder Plot*, London: Harper Perennial, 2009

Holmes, Richard, *Wellington: the Iron Duke*, London: Harper Perennial, 2007

Holt, J.C., *Magna Carta*, Cambridge: Cambridge University Press, 1965

——, *The Northerners: A Study in the Reign of King John*, Oxford: Oxford University Press, 1961

Horspool, David, *The English Rebel: One Thousand Years of Trouble-making from the Normans to the Nineties*, London: Viking, 2009

Hunt, Tristram, *The English Civil War At First Hand*, London: Phoenix, 2003

Hutchinson, Robert, *House of Treason: The Rise and Fall of a Tudor Dynasty*, London: Phoenix, 2009

——, *Elizabeth's Spy Master: Francis Walsingham and the Secret War that Saved England*, London: Phoenix, 2007

Impey, Edward, *The White Tower*, London and New Haven: Yale University Press, 2008

——, and Geoffrey Parnell, *The Tower of London: The Official Illustrated History*, London: Merrell Publishers Lid, 2000

Inglis, Brian, *Roger Casement (Penguin Classic Biography S.)*, London: Penguin, 2002

Jenkins, Simon, *A Short History of England*, London: Profile Books, 2012

Jones, Dan, *The Hollow Crown – The Wars of the Roses and the Rise of the Tudors*, London: Faber & Faber, 2015

——, *Magna Carta: The Making and Legacy of the Great Charter*, London: Head of Zeus Ltd., 2014

——, *The Plantagenets: The Kings Who Made England*, London: HarperCollins Publishers, 2012

——, *Summer of Blood: The Peasants' Revolt of 1381*, London: HarperCollins Publishers, 2010

Jones, Michael (editor), *Philippe de Commynes, Memoirs: The Reign of Louis XI 1461–83*, Harmondsworth: Penguin, 1972

Jones, Nigel, *Tower: An Epic History of the Tower of London*, London: Windmill Books, 2012

Keay, Anna, *The Last Royal Rebel: The Life and Death of James, Duke of Monmouth*, London: Bloomsbury, 2016

Kenyon, John, *The Popish Plot*, London: Phoenix Press, 2000

Lander, J. R., *The Wars of the Roses*, Stroud, Gloucestershire: Sutton, 2007

Levenson, Thomas, *Newton and the Counterfeiter: The Unknown Detective Career of the World's Greatest Scientist*, London: Faber & Faber, 2009

Lewis, Matthew, *The Wars of the Roses: The Key Players in the Struggle for Supremacy*, Stroud, Gloucestershire: Amberley Publishing, 2016

Loftie, W.J., *Authorised Guide to the Tower of London*, London: Harrison and Sons, 1907

McLynn, Frank, *1066: The Year of Three Battles*, London: Pimlico, 2005

——, *Lionheart & Lackland, King Richard, King John and the Wars of Conquest*, London: Vintage Books, 2007

Macculloch, Diarmaid, *Thomas Cranmer: A Life*, New Haven and London: Yale University Press, 2016

Maddicott, J. R., *Simon de Montfort*, Cambridge: Cambridge University Press, 1994

Marius, Richard, *Thomas More: A Biography*, Cambridge, MA: Harvard University Press, 1984

Mason, Emma, *William II: Rufus, the Red King*, Stroud, Gloucestershire: Tempus, 2005

Maurer, Helen E., *Margaret of Anjou: Queenship and Power in Late Medieval England*, London: Boydell Press, 2005

Miller, John, *James II (The English Monarchs Series)*, New Haven and London: Yale University Press, 2000

Minney, R. J., *The Tower of London*, Englewood Cliffs, NJ: Prentice Hall, 1970

Moorhouse, Geoffrey, *The Pilgrimage of Grace: The Rebellion that Shook King Henry VIII's Throne*, London: Phoenix, 2003

Morley, Charles, Stead Junior, William, *The Tower of London: An Illustrated Guide*, and *Tales of the Tower*, London: Henry Stead,1900

Morris John, *The Condition of Catholics Under James I: Father Gerard's Narrative of the Gunpowder Plot*, London: Longmans, Green, & Co., 1871

Morris, Marc, *A Great and Terrible King: Edward I and the Forging of Britain*, London: Windmill Books, 2009

——, *Castle: A History of the Buildings that Shaped Medieval Britain*, London: Windmill Books, 2012

——, *The Norman Conquest*, London: Windmill Books, 2013

——, *King John: Treachery, Tyranny and the Road to Magna Carta*, London: Windmill Books, 2016

——, *Kings and Castles*, London: Endeavour Press, 2018

Mortimer, Ian, *The Fears of Henry IV: The Life of England's Self-Made King*, London: Vintage, 2008

——, *The Greatest Traitor: The Life of Sir Roger Mortimer, Ruler of England 1327–1330*, London: Vintage, 2010

——, *The Perfect King: The Life of Edward III, Father of the English Nation*, London: Vintage Books, 2008

Morton, Graeme, *William Wallace: Man and Myth*, Stroud, Gloucestershire: The History Press, 2004

Norrington, Ruth, *In the Shadow of the Throne: The Lady Arbella Stuart*, London and Chicago: Peter Owen Publishers, 2002

Parnell, Geoffrey, *The Royal Menagerie at the Tower of London*, London: Royal Armouries, 1999

——, *The Tower of London*, London: Batsford, 1993

——, *The Tower of London Past & Present (revised edition)*, Stroud, Gloucestershire: The History Press, 2009

Penn, Thomas, *Winter King: The Dawn of Tudor England*, London: Penguin Books, 2012

Pepys, Samuel, R. C. Latham, W. Matthews (eds), *The Diary of Samuel Pepys Vols IV-V*, London: Bell & Hyman, 1971

Plowden, Alison, *Lady Jane Grey: Nine Days Queen (Classic Histories Series)*, Stroud, Gloucestershire: The History Press, 2016

Pollard, A. J., *Richard III and the Princes in the Tower*, Stroud, Gloucestershire: Alan Sutton, 1991

——, *The Wars of the Roses (British History in Perspective)*, Basingstoke: Palgrave MacMillan, 2013

Porter, Stephen, *The Great Fire of London*, Stroud, Gloucestershire: The History Press, 2009

——, *The Tower of London – the biography*, Stroud, Gloucestershire: Amberley Publishing, 2015

Powicke, Maurice, *King Henry III and the Lord Edward: The Community of the Realm in the Thirteenth Century (Vols 1 & 2)*, Oxford: Oxford University Press, 1947

——, *The Thirteenth Century 1216–1307*, Oxford: Oxford University Press (second edition), 1962

Prestwich, Michael, *Edward I (Yale English Monarchs)*, New Haven and London: Yale University Press, 1997

Purkiss, Diane, *The English Civil War: A People's History*, London: Harper Perennial, 2007

Reese, Peter, *The Life of General George Monck: For King and Cromwell*, Barnsley: Pen & Sword Military, 2008

Rex, Peter, *1066: A New History of the Norman Conquest*, Stroud, Gloucestershire: Amberley Publishing, 2011

Ross, Charles, *Edward IV (The English Monarchs Series)*, New Haven and London: Yale University Press, 1997

Rowse, A. L., *The Tower of London in the History of the Nation*, London: Weidenfeld & Nicolson, 1972

Royle, Trevor, *Civil War: The War of the Three Kingdoms 1638–1660*, London: Little, Brown, 2004

Saul, Nigel, *Richard II (The English Monarchs Series)*, New Haven and London: Yale University Press, 1999

Sellers, Leonard, *Shot in the Tower: The Story of the Spies Executed in the Tower of London During the First World War*, Barnsley: Pen & Sword Military, 1997

Seward, Desmond, *A Brief History of the Hundred Years War: The English in France, 1337–1453*, London: Robinson, 2003

——, *A Brief History of the Wars of the Roses*, London: Robinson, 2007

——, *The Last White Rose: The Secret Wars of the Tudors*, London: Constable, 2010

——, *Richard III: England's Black Legend*, London: Penguin Publishing, 1997

Skidmore, Chris, *Bosworth: The Birth of the Tudors*, London: Weidenfeld & Nicolson, 2013

——, *Edward VI: The Lost King of England*, London: Phoenix, 2008

Somerset, Anne, *Elizabeth I (Women in History)*, London: Phoenix, 1997

——, *Unnatural Murder: Poison at the Court of James I*, London: Phoenix, 1998

Spencer, Charles, *Killers of the King: The Men Who Dared to Execute Charles I*, London: Bloomsbury, 2014

Spring, Peter, *Sir John Tiptoft, 'Butcher of England': Earl of Worcester, Edward IV's Enforcer and Humanist Scholar*, Barnsley: Pen & Sword Military, 2018

Stanhope, John, *The Cato Street Conspiracy*, London: Jonathan Cape, 1962

Starkey, David, *Reign of Henry VIII: The Personalities and Politics*, London: Vintage, 2002

Stow, John, and Wheatley, H. B. (eds), *The Survey of London*, London: Dent, 1987

Swanton, Michael (ed.), *The Anglo-Saxon Chronicle*, London: Dent, 1996

Szechi, Daniel, *The Jacobites: Britain and Europe 1688–1788 (New Frontiers in History)*, Manchester and New York: Manchester University Press, 1994

Tinniswood, Adrian, *By Permission of Heaven: The Story of the Great Fire of London*, London: Pimlico, 2004

Tomalin, Claire, *Samuel Pepys: The Unequalled Self*, London: Penguin, 2003

Tout, Thomas Frederick, *The History of England: From the Accession of Henry III to the Death of Edward III (1216–1377)*, London: Longmans, Green & Co., 1906

Trevelyan, Raleigh, *Sir Walter Raleigh*, London: Allen Lane, 2002

Trow, M. J., *Enemies of the State: The Cato Street Conspiracy*, Barnsley: Pen & Sword Military, 2010

Warner, Kathryn, *Blood Roses: The Houses of Lancaster and York before the Wars of the Roses*, Stroud, Gloucestershire: The History Press, 2018

Warren, W. L., *King John (The English Monarchs Series)*, London and New Haven: Yale University Press, 1997

Weir, Alison, *Henry VIII: King and Court*, London: Pimlico, 2002

——, *Lancaster and York: The Wars of the Roses*, London: Vintage, 2009

——, *The Princes in the Tower*, London: Pimlico, 1992

Wilson, Derek, *The Tower 1078–1978*, London: Hamish Hamilton, 1978

——, *The Uncrowned Kings of England: The Black Legend of the Dudleys*, London: Constable, 2005

Wolffe, Bertram, *Henry VI (The English Monarchs Series)*, New Haven and London: Yale University Press, 2001

Wriothesley, Charles, and William Douglas Hamilton (eds), *A Chronicle of England: During the Reigns of the Tudors from A. D. 1485 to 1559, Vols 1-2*, London: Kessinger Publishing, 2010

Wroe, Ann, *The Perfect Prince: The Mystery of Perkin Warbeck and His Quest for the Throne of England*, London: Random House, 2003

Younghusband, Sir George, *The Jewel House*, London: Herbert Jenkins Limited, 1921

——, *The Tower of London From Within*, London: Herbert Jenkins, 1919

Websites

http://www.camelotintl.com/tower_site/prisoners/escape.html
http://www.capitalpunishmentuk.org/tower.html

Index